TOTTENHAM MASSIVE

TOTTENHAM MASSIVE

Trevor Tanner

JOHN BLAKE

Published by John Blake Publishing Ltd,
3 Bramber Court, 2 Bramber Road,
London W14 9PB, England

www.johnblakepublishing.co.uk

First published in paperback in 2007

ISBN: 978 1 84454 351 9

British Library Cataloguing-in-Publication Data:

A catalogue record for this book is available from the British Library.

Design by www.envydesign.co.uk

Printed in the UK by CPI Bookmarque, Croydon, CR0 4TD

7 9 10 8 6

Papers used by John Blake Publishing are natural, recyclable products made
from wood grown in sustainable forests. The manufacturing processes
conform to the environmental regulations of the country of origin.

Every attempt has been made to contact the relevant copyright-holders,
but some were unobtainable. We would be grateful if the appropriate
people could contact us.

CONTENTS

INTRODUCTION

MY name is Trevor Tanner, I am 39 years old and I was born and raised in South-East London. I still live there now. It was always my aim to take the Spurs firm to the very top and, from 1990, with a tight-knit unit behind me, that's exactly what I did. But there's more to me than football. After leaving school, I joined the Merchant Navy and I've travelled all over the world. I even lived in the Caribbean for two years. I've got a little daughter, Elena, who I adore and for whom I am currently fighting a custody battle. I'm a passionate supporter of Fathers for Justice.

My firm and I live by a strict code of honour and combat, and to hear us labelled as thugs and hooligans really pisses me off. You cannot compare us, for example, to the street-robbing scum who plague our inner cities.

Apart from the firm, music and fashion are my two

biggest passions. There's no doubt that I'm a frustrated designer. Throughout the 1990s, I also promoted club nights. But the firm always came first. Now that I've been forced into temporary retirement by a banning order, I can see myself getting back into the club scene, running my own place. I love the diversity of people and the buzz you get putting on a successful club night. I've seen pop stars, actors and actresses, gangsters and royalty all under the same roof having the time of their lives.

I have numerous convictions for football-related offences. I got off a few times, too. The sentences ranged from nine months to three years. I served my longest sentence in Wandsworth (the Laugh Factory). This was for my part in a riot with Chelsea outside the Three Kings public house in West Kensington, about which more later. I could cope with prison life. The worst part about it was when my grandmother died. They let me out under escort to pay my last respects, but sealed off the whole street where she had lived. That's something I cannot forgive.

In 1992, I was deported from the European Championships in Sweden. Myself, two Scousers and two Leeds bods were the last English fans to be detained on a serious affray charge. On my return home, I found myself splashed all over the front page of the *Sun*, under the headline: 'England's foulest'. Lovely!

I was also jailed in Australia after I went there on a personal visit. I had my beachfront condo raided by armed police and I was put into a high-security detention centre. I was accused, of all things, of being a national security threat. Over the top, to say the least. Some of the inmates in there were facing possible execution on their return to their various countries, and I'll always remember their humility in the face of adversity.

I was eventually deported back to England, with two Aussie screws to keep me company. I was nearly rearrested at Singapore Airport for stretching my legs when I shouldn't have got off the plane. Thankfully, I made it home in one piece, much to the disgust of Billy Connolly who wasn't too happy that I was taken off the plane before him.

That same year, 1998, I also had to make a hasty exit from France before I could be deported. I'd gone to raise the firm's profile among the England support during the World Cup. I'm happy to say we now have one of the biggest followings within England, so I think that's a case of job done.

I have been given two football banning orders in the past; one for two years after a police dog took a chunk out of me during a fight with Man United on the Seven Sisters High Road (the dog was eventually awarded a medal). The other was a five-year FIFA worldwide ban, which ran with my sentence at Chelsea. I also received a life ban from the club itself. But these are nothing compared with the banning order I recently received for incidents with Chelsea, Man United, Wolves, Millwall and the police. I am not allowed near Tottenham for an eight-hour period during match days. I am not allowed to enter any licensed premises within Central London as defined by the borders of the River Thames and the A406 (North Circular Road). Further, I am not allowed in any town or city where Spurs are playing, except London, for a twenty-four-hour period.

I like to think that I'm well known within the firm for giving people a chance, and I like to think that I command a lot of loyalty and respect because of that. Of course, I can be ruthless and I've handed out a lot of punishment over the years to people who deserved it. It sounds harsh, but that's the way it was and is. I've been stabbed in the back of the neck, broken my hands many times, and have had more cuts than I can remember. I thank God that I'm still here at all.

No one has ever written a book about the Spurs firm before. But, if anyone is going to write that book, it ought to be an insider like me. I'm sick of the absolute crap that's been written about us by complete mugs. And as for make-believe films like *The Football Factory*... don't get me started. Whatever you want to call us – Yid Army, Tottenham Massive, Spurs Firm – this is our story. It's about my time running the most ruthless and organised firm in the country from 1990 to the present day.

For fifteen years, we've taken the country by storm. I like to think we've done it with a bit of style, but one thing's for sure – we take no prisoners. People may not like us, but they definitely respect us. At the heart of this book is the story of our brutal ten-year war with our most hated rivals, Chelsea. Of course, we hate the Gooners too, but the Chelsea game is the one we all want. Speaking for myself, from the early 1990s I've been on a personal crusade to wipe out the Chelsea firm.

This book will put the record straight and put to bed a

lot of myths. It will be a brutal and honest rollercoaster ride, in your face with no punches pulled. I make no apologies for that. It will tell how we forced ourselves into the consciousness of every firm in this country and beyond. You will hear about our alliance with our great friends north of the border, The Mighty Aberdeen. I will obviously be touching on the so-called 'Jewish connection' within the book – what I will say here is that we are a multi-cultural firm and I'm proud of my links with the local community. I will also tell about our battles with Man United, Man City, Leeds, Arsenal, West Ham and, most recently, Middlesbrough. This will be a unique insight into the workings of the most powerful twentieth-century firm, told by the man who started the whole revolution.

Enjoy it. I know you will!

Dedicated, as before, to my beautiful daughter Eleanor (Ellie T).

FOREWORD

YIDS: WHAT IT MEANS TO US

NOW, this is a really delicate subject. I originally wanted to call this book *Yids*, as I firmly believe in our identity. Spurs are a multi-faith, multi-cultural firm, so to pin us down with one particular people or race is bollocks. Yes, of course we have Jewish support, and I have some good Jewish friends, as well as Muslims, Christians and you name it. When you think about Chelsea, who for years hurled the worst anti-Semitic abuse our way, and you think about the man who has put that club on the map, Roman Abramovich, a Jew, the irony is certainly not lost on us. When I was growing up, I used to hate the word 'Yid' being levelled at us. I wanted to stick a glass in anyone's face that mentioned the word.

Pals of mine from other clubs, such as Palace, think it's a great name for a firm and I have to admit it is a fearsome war cry in the right circumstances. But I still wasn't sure and somehow it didn't feel right. Then the Barmies hijacked the whole thing and I despised it even more. But you cannot fight an idea and as time went by I became quite fond and proud of the uniqueness of our firm's name. As our firm grew more powerful, we hijacked the name back from the Barmies and I know for a fact that the rallying cry of 'Yids! Yids!' has struck the fear of God into many a firm over the years. As myself and my people were instrumental in putting that word into the consciousness of every firm in England and abroad, I now embrace and cherish it. Put to people outside the firm it will always be a bit of a mystery and never properly understood, and so it should be. I'm not here to justify anything; I am just trying to clear up people's misconceptions.

I must admit that I was pissed off that I couldn't use the name *Yids* for this book. In a way, it would have said everything – and generated a bit of publicity, too. Although I want this book to do well, it is more important that our story is told properly and that some of the myths around us are put to bed for good.

CHAPTER 1

EARLY DAYS

SHIPPING OUT

It all started for me about fifteen or twenty years ago, this epic journey that's taken me to such highs and lows, from paradise to prison. I've lived in South-East London all my life – when I wasn't in jail or abroad, which was a lot. I'm not going to go into specific areas, school names and so on. It's none of your business. Besides, I like my windows where they are. My family and friends know where I live and that's enough for me. If you can fill in the gaps, good luck to you.

I went to one of the roughest schools in London, so I wasn't too upset when I left at sixteen to join the Merchant Navy. Suddenly, I was mixing with a load of Scousers, Welsh and other assorted Northerners. It was an explosive mix. My first job was on the *QEII* – not a bad little boat, I hear you say. As soon as I walked up the gangplank on to this great hulking ship, I thought, Fuck this. I tried to get off, but got lost instead. By the time I worked out where I was, the ship had sailed. Short of jumping overboard – which I thought about – I was fucked. In the end, I did quite a few voyages on the *QEII*, including four visits to New York, one of my favourite places in the whole world.

Unfortunately, things went pear-shaped one evening in the galley when some Scouser took umbrage at my Cockney accent. I was carrying a pot of boiling water at the time, so I let him have it with both barrels. Next thing I knew, I was up before the Captain. He didn't make an issue of it, but there was no way I could stay on board after that. The Captain realised I'd been provoked, so instead of sacking me he had me transferred to the *Cunard Countess*, a cruise liner working the Caribbean.

It was a dream job, sailing around the Caribbean islands and South America. I even got engaged to a beautiful Puerto Rican law student. They were some of the happiest years of my life so far. But even in paradise I had other things on my mind. I'd be lying on a beach in St Kitts or Grenada plotting to take over the Spurs firm, thinking about what games were coming up, what the boys were up to. Mad, eh?

A TUESDAY NIGHT IN EVERTON

By 1987, I was back in Britain on leave. It was a Tuesday night and I was on my way up to Liverpool for Everton v Spurs. I was straining at the leash to see the boys again, and Spurs (back then I actually liked football). We only had a small mob up there, a real tight-knit crew, just what you need on a cold, wet night away from home. The game was shit and the Scousers were being really mouthy. I was getting really wound up. At the end of the game, we filed out into the cold night air. It was eerily quiet, and I could sense something was going to happen. I was walking in the middle of the road, with my boys to the left of me and Everton to the right. We walked past a bus stop and spotted one of their firm, one of the mouthy fuckers from the ground earlier. I ran towards him... Bang, one punch. He fought back and we went at it. Suddenly, I was grabbed by two Old Bill. Game over. The cuffs went on, then one of them headbutted me in the face. A nice touch. They slung me in the van and took me away. One of the coppers was giving me a load of abuse, calling me a male model and a flash Cockney this and that. You would have thought I'd given his gran a right-hander! I was past caring though. The adrenalin was pumping through me. All I felt was pleasure, probably like junkies feel when they've had their fix. I was charged and bailed to appear in Walton Street Magistrates' Court, the first of quite a few appearances up there. Funny, 'cos I quite like Scousers and I know a lot of their boys, but in the early days I was always getting nicked up there.

REDS AWAY!
Liverpool away. The day they won the title under Kenny Dalgleish. As usual, we were stuck in the fucking corner at Anfield, getting verbals all afternoon, when they scored. I just snapped, literally: I snapped the seat off and launched it like a boomerang towards that mouthy wanker Bruce Grobbelaar. Instead of knocking his head

off, the seat flew past a copper's head, missing by inches. The next thing I knew *I* was flying through the air as four Old Bill lifted me up and carried me out of the stand.

I nearly went down for that one: it was only the quick thinking of a local brief in court that saved my bacon. He told the judge about my good service in the Merchant Navy, which went down well. I was less thrilled when he started his summing-up speech with the words 'I'm a Liverpool season-ticket holder', but to be honest he played a blinder. The judge more or less told me to fuck off out of the country back to the Merchant Navy, and that was that.

Although I was lucky there, my football-related offences were beginning to stack up and I knew it was only a matter of time before the fines and banning orders would be replaced with custodial sentences. But it was a price I was ready to pay. That's what sets you apart from the rest of the firm – the willingness to go that extra ten yards for the cause. I was prepared to gamble my lifestyle, love life, emotions, everything to earn Tottenham's firm the respect and public profile I thought it deserved.

Why did I choose Spurs out of all the London teams? First of all, Spurs chose me, took my heart long ago. Millwall, Chelsea, West Ham... it would have been too easy, too obvious. It's a London thing. We're the fucking Real Madrid of London, except we have a town hall instead of a cathedral. If you can't get your head around that, it's not my problem. Well, that's enough about my past. Let's get this up-to-date. Let me invite you to take an exclusive insight into the best firm in the country. Hold tight.

CHAPTER 2

MERSEYSIDE MAYHEM:
A DATE WITH THE SCOUSERS

I DON'T mind Scousers. I don't know why, considering how many times I've been nicked up there. Maybe it's the humour. It's very dark, very London. As for the old clichés about them all being thieves and handy with Stanley knives, well, that may be true in some cases but London is also full of thieving little slags that wouldn't hesitate to stick you as well. It just depends if you understand the street or swallow the stereotypical propaganda pushed out by the press.

LIVERPOOL AWAY, 1991/92 SEASON
Over the years, our relationship with Liverpool was quite cordial. They didn't bother us, we didn't bother them. Plus, we had a Scouser go with us for years. Things were usually OK between us.

So, when in the 1991/92 season I was invited up to

Liverpool to see Spurs play them away, I accepted their offer. Naturally, I was a bit wary but I trusted my Scouse pal all the way. We went up there alone to avoid the rest of my pals and to show good will. I went up on the red eye and was there in time for breakfast and a quick tour of the city. It was a real novelty to be able to chat to the local talent, or even go for a piss, without looking over my shoulder. We went to the Pump House in Albert Dock, which was right up my street.

That was all good, but then they decided to take me into the lion's den – the main Liverpool pub tucked away handily behind the Kop. I must admit that my instincts didn't fancy this one but there was fuck all I could do. Besides, until then I'd been treated like a king. As I walked into this intimidating stronghold, I could feel every eye in the place burning into me. But once they saw who I was with it settled down and it was drinks all round. However, something told me to keep my wits about me. Sure enough, bang, just as I was walking out with a drink the windows went through. I went outside to find myself confronted by my own firm attacking the pub! Can you fucking believe it? Of all the pubs they could have attacked in Liverpool, they picked the one I was in, being wined and dined by the hosts. As you can imagine, the Scousers weren't pleased. It looked like I'd set them up. A geezer next to me made a move. I had no choice: I smashed him with a bottle and tried to get across to my own people as soon as possible. Easier said than done in what was now a full-scale running battle. You should have seen the look on the boys' faces when they saw me coming towards them. I was pissed off and they were pissing themselves laughing. I can't blame the firm; that's their job.

Reunited with my boys, we charged into the Scousers again before the Old Bill arrived to separate us. Now I would like to put the record straight here. It wasn't planned, it just happened. I would like to apologise to the geezer I clumped because I think he bought me drinks just before it all kicked off. I did learn a valuable lesson, though: don't drink with another firm, no matter how well you get on – especially when your team is playing theirs. Further down the road, Spurs clashed with Liverpool again, right outside the Kop. Not the way I planned my day out, but unfortunately that's the way it goes.

SPURS V LIVERPOOL, CARLING CUP QUARTER-FINAL, DECEMBER 2004

This game was played before my most recent banning order came into effect, so I was able to go up to Spurs to watch the game in one of the pubs up there. My ex had worked out that by only giving me access to my daughter at weekends and on a Wednesday she thought it would stop me going to football. In reality, she did me a big favour – it stopped me getting a banning order earlier, plus it confused the fuck out of the Old Bill who couldn't work out where I was on a lot of match days. Plus, I got to spend a lot more time with my daughter. So, thanks, sweetheart, and the mug that helped you to come up with the plan.

As you can gather, I had to make a late show for this game. After I'd dropped the little one off at the witch's castle and made my way to the manor, it was already

7.45pm. There was a real buzz in the air. I'd arranged to meet a few old pals by the ground, but the buses, tubes and trains were rammed so I had to walk up Tottenham High Road, a right long slog. I can understand how visiting supporters must feel having to take this walk. The only good thing about it is that it forces visiting firms out into the open. You can see them coming and they can't do any smash and grab raids out of the tube – although Chelsea tried in the early 1990s and got battered for their trouble.

That night, Tottenham High Road was especially busy, a never-ending sea of humanity in front of me. Get out the way, you cunts! People singing and dancing. I know they're my people, but when these fucking pricks start singing and jumping up and down, especially in boozers, I just want to punch their fucking heads in. There's a time and a place for all that bollocks – in the ground.

I finally got to the Gilpin. I used to hate the place, but when you keep getting moved on from pub to pub like a firm of gypsies, well, beggars can't be choosers. It's a Wetherspoon's pub and I fucking hate Wetherspoon's pubs. They seem to attract pricks. This one's not too bad in that respect, but it's still a shit-hole.

I arrived at 8.45pm, just as everyone else was going in the other direction. Story of my life. Still, Hans, Snowy and the rest of the boys were there. We spent the night catching up and putting the world to rights. Someone said there was a little firm of Scousers in the pub, plotting away in a corner. I can quite believe it, as the Gilpin's a big boozer, but we didn't see anything.

We settled down to watch the game. As usual, we started brightly followed by the usual collapse. The whole team played shit, especially that ex-West Ham prick Kanoute. We went down to a Liverpool youth team. It was our only chance of getting into Europe that season, plus it meant we missed out on a big Cup final in Cardiff. I hope those pampered pricks in the team remember that. All in all, it was a shit night and at the final whistle we were out on the street, blood boiling and adrenalin flowing. And where were the Scousers? Nowhere. The slippery fuckers were disappearing into the night, happy with their evening's work. You can't blame them really. A few hands were raised in anger that night but nothing to worry about. The Scousers went missing, just like our team.

CHAPTER 3

CHELSEA: THE HISTORY OF HATRED, PART 1

YOU might say there's a bit of history between Spurs and Chelsea. To cut a long story short, there's been a lot of crap written about Chelsea, mainly by gullible, biased journalists and stupid writers. I cannot believe that *The Football Factory*, the biggest load of shit ever written, was actually turned into a film. Never mind all that bollocks. I can tell you that Spurs, not Chelsea, were the top London firm throughout the 1990s. The street doesn't lie. But, before I go into detail about how we beat off Chelsea to establish ourselves as London's finest, I should tell you about a few other teams that gatecrashed the party on the way.

RANGERS AWAY (QPR)
QPR are a funny little firm and they don't travel well, just like a bad wine. But on their manor they can be a different

proposition, especially when they firm up with the mugs down the road – Chelsea – which they like to do, especially against us. On their own, they're nothing.

This game took place back in the late 1980s. We met up in the Bull in Tottenham, our beloved stronghold (which is sadly no more) and took the tube for the poxy journey to Shepherds Bush. We didn't stop at any more pubs en route as we weren't really drinkers at that time. Funnily enough, there are quite a few teetotallers in our firm. They don't need the booze to get them going, as we're all adrenalin junkies. Once at the Bush, we took a stroll around their manor. We approached the ground with no one in sight. Then a few bods popped their heads out of an alley. They were calling it on. It was obviously an ambush, but this was what we'd come for, so fuck it. We took the bait and headed into the alley leading into the estate, and sure enough they were all plotted up. A roar went up and the missiles started to fly. We stood our ground and took it to them. A couple of theirs stood and got severely bashed for their trouble, and one particularly flash wanker who went down in front of me had the humiliation of having his designer shades smashed to pieces in front of him. QPR began to fall back and we spilled out on to Goldhawk Road after them. By the time we got to the top of the road, we'd lost them, so we thought, Fuck the game, and made our way back to the tube. As we passed a pub on the corner, it suddenly unloaded. It was the same firm we'd battled with before, but this time it seemed there were hundreds of them. They really came at us, confident of their superior numbers. I knew we couldn't hold out for long. There were only about fifteen or twenty of us, plus a few youngsters who were looking decidedly nervous about facing such a large firm. I needed to do something and looked around desperately for something to get my hands on. I saw a butcher's shop with a shopping trolley outside it holding a display of meat. Without thinking, I grabbed the trolley and sent the display flying (I do apologise for this). I flung the trolley round, screamed for my firm to get behind me and put my head down and charged towards QPR with all the boys streaming along beside me. The trolley smashed into them like a battering ram. This had the desired effect and we ran them back into the pub. Further down the road, one of their boys got thrown through a shop window. We heard the police sirens at that point and knew the fun was over. Once again, we set off for the tube station, and stopped on the way at an upmarket opticians to pick up some designer sunglasses. I ended up with a pair of Timmy Mallet specials.

We were helped on our way to the tube by the boys in blue. We were all buzzing and pissing ourselves laughing at our newfound headgear. We headed back to our beloved Bull (well, I loved it anyway) and had a top night that ended at 3.00 or 4.00am.

BRADFORD AT HOME, OCTOBER 1991

I have to mention this game because it proves that I'm not scared to tell the truth. It was a night game, no big deal. To be honest, we didn't give them the respect they deserved. I mean, who the fuck are Bradford? Well, me and my pals were about to find out.

We were in the Bull like always, having a giggle, talking

the usual bollocks. I'd recently broken my hand and it was still in plaster, with my arm in a sling. That's how seriously I was taking Bradford. No big deal. A couple of hours before kick-off one of our boys came bounding in saying Bradford were up by the ground. This bloke was a right prick at the best of times, but he really excelled himself on this one. He conveniently forgot to say how many of them there were – a good eighty to a hundred.

You have to understand that a game like this was fuck all to us, but to them it was like a Cup final. And, as our reputation was growing, it seemed like the whole of Bradford had come down for the show. The state I was in I needed this like a fucking hole in the head (which I nearly got). There were only about twenty of us, but it was mostly old soldiers like myself and Terry so I wasn't unduly bothered. We set off up the High Road and about a quarter of a mile from the ground, opposite Gold's Gym, bang, the cunts were all over us, a good hundred strong. They came out of one of our own side alleys. A classic ambush.

We were fucked. I screamed at the boys to stand. I pulled my arm out of the sling and managed to clump a few but it was useless. I was in agony. We were backed up against the gym. They had fireworks, flares, everything. It was like Fireworks Night, and I was Guy Fawkes. I looked to my left and saw four or five of them around Tel. A game little fucker my Terry, but there were too many of them. He went down and they started going at him. I flew into them, putting the boot in, my hands useless.

In the middle of all this, I saw some of our boys – including the prick who called it on – away on their toes.

One of them is now a complete outcast and the others still can't look me in the eye to this day. The Old Bill eventually arrived (thank fuck) and I have to say, hands up, they saved our arses. Bradford can have that as a result, and good luck to them. But they know that if the whole firm had been out they would have been smashed to pieces. My pals and I vowed that this would never happen again. We had games against Sheffield and Chelsea coming up and they were going to feel the backlash. Bradford got lucky... no one else was going to.

SHEFFIELD UNITED AWAY, 1991

I was so up for this one, it was frightening. We went up on a coach and were in Sheffield before kick-off. We marched round the city centre. Nothing. So we headed up to their main drinking street, London Road. We settled in a boozer at the top of the road and it didn't take long for the word to go round that we were there. They plotted up about halfway down the road in another pub. So we left our pub and headed off to theirs, taking it to them. We fired off a flare through the doors. The windows went out; smoke everywhere. They wouldn't come out and the ones who did got smashed and left where they were. A few of the boys had cuts and bruises, nothing major. A result. Job done.

On the journey home, we stopped off at Leicester Forest service station to have a rest. There were only forty-odd of us on the coach, but it was the right forty. I'd put them up against anyone. I noticed a few coaches in the car park and then looked up at the walkway stretching across the motorway and saw it was lined with bods. Leeds. The hairs on the back of my neck stood up. I knew it was going to go. We charged up the stairs, M and Brian with me. One of our boys glassed one of theirs near the door. I charged into the main canteen: 'Yids, Yids, Yids, come on… come on, you Leeds cunts.' Tables, chairs, fire extinguishers, cups, teapots, the lot went flying through the air. It was like a Wild West saloon. We'd taken Leeds totally by surprise. They were jumping over the counters to get away from the onslaught, throwing anything they could get their hands on at us. A few were badly cut, especially the ones in the corridor we came charging through. 'Out,' I screamed. I knew Old Bill would be all over us in no time. We were out and back on the coach as quick as we came in. We had just serviced the Leeds United Service Crew in a fucking service station. It doesn't get much better than that. But the next game was Chelsea away. Perhaps it does get much better after all.

CHELSEA AWAY, 1991 – TEN MAD MINUTES

By now, you'll know there's no love lost between our two firms. In fact, it's pure hatred. This was the big one for our firm. Everything had to be meticulously planned. Two weeks before the game, Richie and me went scouting in Earls Court for a place for the firm to meet. We eventually settled on the Continental in Earls Court High Road. The day of the big game arrived and I was up early at Earls Court by 10.00am. I bumped into M, a welcome sight. There's no one better I could have on my side, except we argue like cat and dog. We found our way to a little pub on the corner at the Kensington end of Earls Court Road. A couple of bods were giving us the eye, so glass in hand

I headed for them. M grabbed my arm to stop me. Thank God, as the geezer I was about to stick pulled up a sleeve to reveal a Spurs cockerel on his arm. Fuck me, that was a close call for him. I still see him to this day and we have a laugh about it now. He's a game bod, so sorry about that, brother.

We made our way back to the original meeting place. All the boys were there and I greeted them individually. What I didn't know was that all the other pubs were rammed with our bods. I put the word out that we would move at 1.30pm. The time came and we emptied out on to the road. It was an unbelievable sight. The whole High Road was full to bursting. We marched on Chelsea, straight past the tube station and on to the ground. I wasn't going to waste this firm by getting trapped on the tube. We approached the Ilfield Road with the Ilfield Tavern at the end of it. Suddenly the bottom of the road was full of Chelsea, at least 150, maybe 200. This is what I dreamed of. Even numbers against these wankers. We tore down the road taking everything we could to hit them with, including an old fridge. Honest. Kieron and me tried getting the door off the fucking thing but it was too solid. We backed them off past the pub twice. It was now going off fucking mental. We turned on the pub and began smashing it to pieces and storming the doors. Terry got hit with a bottle in the doorway and Paul got his neck cut with flying glass. Two fucking game soldiers. They were so happy about what we had done they laughed all the way to the hospital, even though they had about twenty stitches between them.

We went for the pub's main window with a dustbin and

it went straight through the window at full force. A pool ball came flying back out of the window the other way. I went down on one knee. I thought I'd been shot, but the ball had cracked me on the kneecap. I was so pumped up with adrenalin that, with some help from Big C, I got to my feet and shook it off. We were taking such a liberty, on Chelsea's own manor. An Old Bill car reversed into the middle of us, but soon fucked off. What could they do? We didn't even take any notice of the car. We were just going off mental around it. Neither Chelsea nor the police have ever really got over it. The following Monday, the headline of the *Evening Standard* screamed out: 'Ten Mad Minutes – Spurs and Chelsea Go To War... In the name of football we must stop this madness'. We'd really arrived on the scene big time. It brought us to the attention of the NCIS, the police National Criminal Intelligence Service. I knew then that my days were numbered. They were watching us now, and within a year I was serving a three-year sentence following another row with Chelsea. If you still think this is just about football, wake up.

QPR AT HOME, SATURDAY, 23 MARCH – CHELSEA COME CALLING TWICE

You never know what to expect with Rangers: will they turn up or won't they? T and me had a walk around the ground and bumped into the mental midget (anyone from our world knows who I mean). He was skulking by their end and got the shock of his life when he saw us.

'Where's your firm, you little prick?' we asked him.

'What firm?' he said.

I desperately wanted to cane him there and then, so did T, but he knew he was safe. We'd have definitely been nicked. He got out of there quick. See you later, I thought.

The game was a non-event. QPR didn't turn up, so we settled down in the Bull for a beer and a chat. There was just me, Terry, P and a few young kids, seventeen- or eighteen-year-olds. Around seven in the evening, I instinctively looked up at one of the dark mesh windows and saw a fucking herd walk past it. Chelsea and QPR had firmed up together. Suddenly, one of them was in through the door, then another. S and P jumped up and bottled one of them. We've got to hold the door, it's the only way in and out. Even though they were swarming in the doorway, I could see in their eyes that the ones inside didn't fancy it. I ran to the door, grabbing a heavy glass ashtray on the way. I let one of the pricks have it, right in the forehead. Down he went. I could sense the tide was turning. They started to bottle it and we drove them back towards the door. I looked out the door and saw a sea of snarling faces filling the forecourt and out into the street. They were battering the mesh windows and one of the locked doors with a fucking great lump of wood. Our kids were at the windows repelling the borders brilliantly, throwing everything at the fuckers. I was proud of them.

Meanwhile, back at the doorway, things were heating up – literally. I felt something hot at my shoulder. I looked across and saw my old mate the mental midget flicking something at me and it was burning through my clothes and on to my skin. Acid? I suppose so, but I didn't give a fuck now. My adrenalin was pumping and I was lashing out wildly. The other boys were doing the same. It was fucking fantastic. I felt superhuman. I went for the midget and just missed taking off his head by inches. He decided it was time to call it a day and skulked off like the rat that he is. The rest of them were still coming though, ten-deep in the doorway, but we were holding them. I could see that they were starting to lose it, getting mad with each other that so many of them hadn't taken so few of us. We were taking the piss, laughing, laughing manically at them.

I heard sirens and knew that the fun was over. I know Tottenham Old Bill hate our firm but even they couldn't stand by when 150 Chelsea are attacking our pub. They were probably hoping that Chelsea would have taken us out. If the first boys through the door had held their own, instead of getting smashed to pieces, they might have. But the reverse happened. We snatched victory from the jaws of defeat. Tough luck, you cunts. We came away from that battle stronger and tighter, especially the young kids who really came of age that night.

Just to prove that Chelsea knew they had fucked it, they came back the following Saturday night to have another go. You have to admire their consistency, I suppose. It was after Wimbledon at home, another non-event. I guessed that Chelsea would show, so I made sure we had a good thirty or forty in the Bull that night. Sure enough, round about 8.30pm we heard they were on their way. We flew out on to the pub forecourt. There was about the same number of them as the week before, maybe slightly less. I smacked one bod with a pool stick and off it went. They were on the back foot straight away. The boys were steaming them and it was clear Chelsea didn't fancy it.

Before long, they turned and ran for the tube station. We were screaming after them. Mad Ade from Richmond was going bananas. The thought of it still makes me laugh to this day. Big respect to the Richmond and Esher boys. I love you all. I pulled up. Old Bill were everywhere and managed to nick a few boys. Anyway, 2–0. Enough said.

I know QPR are now starting to get it together again. They've got a naughty little firm by all accounts, but back in the early 1990s the fact of the matter is they were having it with Chelsea and we saw that with our own eyes. Sorry, boys, but facts don't lie. One of the things that stayed with me from that day was how they all – Chelsea and QPR – stood outside the Bull chanting: 'West London! West London!' Pathetic. Can you see Spurs and the Gooners teaming up to do that under *any* circumstances? Exactly.

CHELSEA AWAY, 12 JANUARY 2000

We met over in Wandsworth Town a couple of hours before the game. There were 200 of us, filling up two or three pubs. I was really there just to gee the boys up. I couldn't go to the game as the police were watching out for me and I couldn't risk another nicking. The boys were great about it. They urged me to make myself scarce. That's true friendship. I was especially gutted as this was the big one. The police won't admit it, but just look at the numbers they put out for this game. A lot is made of the Celtic–Rangers rivalry, or Reds–Everton, Blues–Villa, the Manc derby and of course Millwall–West Ham, not to mention Spurs–Gooners, but many of these rivalries are still trading on their pasts. In the 1970s and 1980s, these were massive confrontational games, but now a lot of them have been hijacked by the Barmies and not a lot happens any more. For me personally and the majority of our firm Chelsea is the real derby. There's real hate there.

The firm left Wandsworth Town in two waves. The first hundred or so were split up by Old Bill, but the other half managed to get through and hit every pub they could – about three – before being captured. One of my pals described it like this:

'We came straight round the back of Fulham Broadway when we went past the skip. Everything was used as ammunition, then we came right out by Fulham Broadway and steamed into two or three pubs. We ran straight in through one door and out the other looking for their pub. They obviously weren't in the first pub 'cos everyone there just froze, with one geezer dropping his pint on the floor in shock. It was like the Keystone Cops with us going in through one door, running through the boozer having it with anyone who wanted it and away, and the Old Bill running behind. I'm not sure of the pubs we hit, but I think they were the Rose and the White Hart. We eventually got caught and put into Reilly's Irish Bar.'

The second wave, mainly made up of our older firm, bumped into their top boys right outside the ground and by all accounts left a few of them with their teeth missing. I'm not going to say they smashed them to pieces because I wasn't there, but knowing the people that were there I know they would have done some damage. During the game, a little firm of ours was in the Black Bull, about ten- or fifteen-handed. A few Chelsea came to the door wearing black gloves and all that bollocks only to have a chair put over their heads and be chased down the road. A piss-taker whichever way you look at it.

CHELSEA AWAY, 28 OCTOBER 2000 –
A BRIDGE TOO FAR

The next season, we decided to take a chance and head down to Wandsworth Town for the second year on the trot. I called for the meet just across the water from their manor and hopefully just out of reach of Old Bill. It was getting harder and harder to outwit the police and we were running out of meeting places. We found a couple of pubs where we knew Chelsea would know we were there. I was hoping they would come to us, as it would break my heart to waste this firm.

When the time came to move, we spilled out on to the street. I'll never forget the sight that greeted me. The whole road was full of Spurs firm, 350–400-strong. It was another fucking unbelievable turnout. I knew it was too big to get away with but it was an impressive sight. We made our way towards Wandsworth Bridge, trying to be as inconspicuous as possible! I was praying that Chelsea would come flying over the bridge. Instead, all that came hurtling over the bridge were about eighty police carriers, running five abreast, sirens blaring. A load came up behind us as well. I was fucking devastated. We were trapped. We had a go at the riot police but it was no good. They were properly tooled up: dogs, body armour, shields and batons, the lot. They were up for it too.

This was probably the biggest firm we ever took to

Chelsea – in fact, it's probably the biggest firm *anyone*'s taken there and we've constantly taken the biggest firms to Chelsea for the past ten years. Weapons were discarded along the route. Those with tickets were searched, photographed and put in a boozer across the bridge. There were too many of us for Old Bill to even take the risk of escorting us past their boozers. There was no way they could have held us back. I was absolutely gutted. I knew that if we had made it across that bridge we would have fucking smashed the place and everyone in it to pieces. The Old Bill knew this and cleared the streets of any locals or fans silly enough to hang about.

Chelsea were fucking fuming. Once again, we'd firmed up on their manor. A few of their boys made a half-hearted attempt to get at us while we were penned in the boozer. Big mistake. We annihilated the pub inside and we nearly kicked our way out, only being beaten back by waves of attacks from the riot police and horses. The woman who owned the pub was hysterical. I told her to calm down and that no harm would come to her. She soon realised that it was the Old Bill doing most of the damage, with the silly cunts they let through stirring up an already volatile situation to fever pitch. If we had got loose, it doesn't bear thinking about.

It was getting near kick-off by this time and we were eventually escorted to the ground. We passed the Imperial Arms, the boozer I had marked out to smash up. The pricks inside started acting up, but when they saw the size of our firm they fell silent. On the pitch, things didn't go our way. Even though they had a shit team out, we still lost 3–0. It's pathetic how we always seem to fold when we're playing those fuckers. I despised our players for not giving it everything.

After the game, the Old Bill sealed off the streets and marched us to the tube, past some of the most expensive real estate in the country, maybe the world. I bet those rich fuckers must love having that ground right on their doorstep. When we got to the tube, I told the police I wasn't going to North London. I lived in South London and I wanted to get home. I was still with my ex at the time and we'd just had a little girl. Of course, the police thought I was lying and that I wanted to go back and have a go at Chelsea. They forced me on to the tube to King's Cross and I went ballistic, calling them all sorts. By the time I made it back to Victoria, I was fucking fuming. To top it all, there was a moody little firm skulking about the station. Fuck this. Then, from out of nowhere, a little firm of my people came on to the forecourt. They thought it was hilarious the Old Bill had made me ride the magic roundabout. Needless to say, we had a go at the moody little firm. It was over in seconds. Afterwards, I was pissed off, fucked off, tired and hungry. I ripped up my travel card and jumped in a cab home. All in all, it had been an expensive day and I had nothing to show for it. We'd put together a massive firm and it just didn't come off. What a waste.

CHELSEA AWAY, WORTHINGTON CUP SEMI-FINAL, 9 JANUARY 2002

This is what dreams are made of, drawing Chelsea in a two-legged affair. The firm met up at Aldgate on the District Line, far away from prying police eyes. We had a top firm out and looked like we would easily pull in 200. Best of all, there was no Old Bill about, unheard of for a Spurs–Chelsea fixture. I knew that if we made it on to the tube we'd be able to do something – travel down to their manor, bust out of the station and smash the fuckers. I was taking a big risk. Only a few years earlier, I did three years for exactly the same thing. I must be fucking mad. No doubt you've heard all the clichés about how addictive football gang warfare is; well, I'm living proof of that. I probably had more to lose than anyone that day, but there I was, putting myself on offer once again.

We made our way on to the tube at Aldgate East and came out at West Kensington, the same station where I'd been nicked for my three-stretch. This time, though, Chelsea were nowhere to be seen. Someone called and said they were in a pub round the corner. We charged round there but the pub was empty. The next thing, there were sirens everywhere and Old Bill jumping out of vans. It was a fucking set-up. I tried to break away but every exit was covered. We managed to force our way on to the forecourt of a hotel in Chelsea Harbour; a few of the boys actually got into the hotel. I was caught outside. The head honcho even came over to savour the moment. Our day was over. Apart from a few bods choking over their G and Ts in the hotel bar, no one was harmed. We were systematically searched, identified and photographed, then put in a boozer near their shit-hole ground.

A few Chelsea fuckers shadowed the escort, making a pathetic show of trying to get at us. Why the fuck were they not there earlier? As we approached the ground, the Old Bill started to go ballistic. I could hear one prick shouting: 'Nick Tanner, nick Tanner.' The rest of the boys also heard this and tried to protect me. It was a freezing cold night and I was wearing a multi-coloured ski hat. I swapped it for someone else's as we approached the ground. The entrance to the away end is right underneath their main stand. The away section at Chelsea has to be one of the worst in the country. Unless you're sitting right on top of the pitch, it's like watching from inside a bunker. To get to the away end, you have to walk right past the entrance to the old Shed and the Shed Bar to the left. (What bright spark thought that one up?) To the front and to the right is their ridiculous hotel, which runs West Ham's Fawlty Towers close, with its moody cladding and escalators. It should be a shopping centre. (I actually went to a wedding there a few summers back and that was a story in itself. I must admit it does have a pucker view over the pitch through the banqueting suite. It just made me sick being there, that's all.)

As we approached the forecourt, their boys were to our left; it was fucking chaos. The Old Bill were holding up little fluorescent sticks, fuck knows what for: maybe to identify themselves in case you missed them in their fluorescent jackets. So, while we were being directed like planes, total mayhem broke out. I lashed out at a particular individual whom the Old Bill stupidly let in among us. He got a proper clump from someone else as well and ran off towards the Old Bill screaming and shouting. There were vicious little battles going on all around. Chelsea Old Bill are complete cunts and were obviously hoping we would get a hiding. The way it's set up there, the way you have to run the gauntlet, you can easily see how a lot of firms come unstuck there. But this time we left a trail of bodies with holes in them (which made the national news that night). As far as I'm concerned, they only had themselves to blame for getting in our way.

The police that day were an absolute joke. They must take their fair share of the blame. In fact, they were targeting me and blatantly trying to get me hurt. I lost it at one point and had a stand-up verbal row with one little shit who had been on my case all night. It was a muggy thing to do and broke my golden rule: Old Bill love situations like that as they know there is only winner and it's not me. Still, it had to be said. As we were making our way up the stairs in the ground, some fat fucker, separated from us by a little partition, spat across at us. I launched myself towards Fatty only to hear the Old Bill screaming at the bottom of the stairs to stand still. Fuck that. We carried on. I got through the turnstile but the pal I had with me got nicked. What a nightmare finish to a nightmare day. He was a top man as well, someone I think the world of and who I would trust with my life. I can't say any more than that to him apart from good luck with your new life.

After the game, we were put back under escort. We managed to break away from it under the stand, where we had a ten-minute stand-off with the riot police that did get a bit naughty at one point. As we came across the forecourt once again, the Old Bill were standing there with their silly little lights as if directing air traffic. I put my head down, did a sharp left and went to join a few of the boys in the corner. It was off and I went charging across the road. Chelsea were on the opposite side and got a shock when we went into them, especially as there were Old Bill everywhere. Realising they had made a fuck-up, the Old Bill lined up between us and Chelsea. There were riot police, horses and dogs. I had a police spotter watching me, so I got the eye of one of the Chelsea bods and pointed in the direction of the King's Road. He knew what I meant. 'See you down there.' We melted back into the crowd and made our way down the road. I knew we had to stay on the road and out of the pubs, otherwise we'd be trapped. Trouble was, it started to piss it down. One of the boys said we should get into a pub, which admittedly did look warm and inviting. But I was having none of it. I gave him a tirade of abuse which, to be fair, he took. Both Old Bill and Chelsea wanted us locked up in a pub, where they could get at us.

We carried on walking, all the way down to Sloane Square at the end of King's Road. This is where we were going to do it, out on the street. Sometimes it's a good idea to get inside, in a pub, to have some cover, but this wasn't one of those times. But once again the Chelsea cunts were a no-show. Cold and wet, we eventually ducked into a pub in Sloane Square, the Royal Court Hotel, I think. From out of nowhere, the boozer was suddenly blockaded by riot police and vans. What the fuck was this all about? For once, all we wanted was a drink and to get out of the rain. The police were lined up outside and we were inside, trapped with a load of tourists and casual drinkers. One old couple asked me what was going on, and when I told them it was all about football they said how ridiculous it all was and that it made them ashamed to be English. The old fella was probably an old soldier and wondered what had been the point in fighting for freedom if it led to this. A bit melodramatic perhaps, but true.

Anyway, back to the immediate problem. I knew Chelsea Old Bill hated me with a passion and didn't need an excuse to nick me. How the fuck was I going to get out of this one? I noticed a door across the bar and one of the irate punters kindly told me it led into the hotel reception and out to the street. Magic. Follow me, boys. We actually came out on the street *behind* the police barricade. I was pissing myself laughing and I couldn't resist walking up to one of the coppers and asking him what was going on. He told me they had a vicious gang trapped inside and it wasn't safe to go in. I walked away with tears running down my cheeks. It was the only thing I had to laugh about all day, but laugh I did.

CHAPTER 4

CHELSEA: THE HISTORY OF HATRED, PART 2

**CHELSEA AT HOME, FA CUP, 9 MARCH 2002 –
'A FARM IS MY SHELTER'**
This was the fourth encounter between us that season.
Miracle of miracles, we had actually beaten this shower
5–1 to reach the FA Cup Final. Yes, you read it right: 5–1.
A result we could wallow in for a while. There's no point
in writing about what happened in the street for that
game because Chelsea never showed. The riot police were
left standing around looking stupid while our long-
suffering fans celebrated.

For the FA Cup game, we had a couple of Cardiff bods
with us and they were well impressed with the turnout.
What do you expect: it was Chelsea at home and the FA
Cup for fuck's sake. Our firm was at its peak and we were
straining at the leash to get at them. It was obvious they
didn't fancy showing in a firm. To be honest, I couldn't

blame them as I knew the reception that was waiting for them. I'm not just saying that because Spurs is my side: there aren't many firms that would come to White Hart Lane now. Leeds and Boro always show but they also bring massive mobs, which says it all. On this day, I spotted a little firm of Chelsea walking towards the away end. I took a few silly risks and at one stage felt like running into them – but we had our spotter and back-up all over us, and Chelsea just wanted to get in.

They had sold all their allocation and true to form they were being proper mouthy pricks in the ground. A lot of their boys had to be there and I was determined they would get it after the game. Sure enough, the schizo pricks on the pitch let us down – we lost 4–0 – but Chelsea would pay. It was a two-mile walk back to the tube station. We'd get them somewhere along the way. We plotted up halfway down the High Road in a boozer by Bruce Grove. We agreed to hold back until they were nearly on top of us. Someone shouted, 'Oi, oi, they're here.' We smashed out of the pub door and out into the pitch-black night. A little firm approached on our right, then hesitated fatally. One geezer got it bad, which I stopped, and the rest went backwards looking for the Old Bill. I went running up the middle of the road, adrenalin pumping, screaming at the Old Bill and their escort to come forward. Everything stopped for a second then we charged into them, running the Old Bill and Chelsea back towards the ground for a few hundred yards. At one point, I was isolated in the middle of the road, screaming at no one in particular. Then reinforcements came from everywhere and for a couple of minutes it was amazing scenes. The Old Bill were going into our people everywhere. A carrier came hurtling towards me, and I was off and sprinting under the bridge up the road. I threw a left; a helicopter seemed like it was on me personally. I found myself sprinting through a warren of alleys and high-rise blocks. Fuck this, it all looks the same. I was on the notorious Broadwater Farm Estate and I have to admit I was fucking lost. The boys phoned to find out where I was, and when I told them they thought it was hilarious. With the help of a Good Samaritan, I finally made it out of there. I have to say, I found the place quite pleasant, but maybe that's me. Of course, I'd been through there before but not in the pitch dark with a helicopter on my arse, so that night the Farm was truly my shelter.

ATTACK ON THE THREE KINGS PUBLIC HOUSE, 20 MARCH 1993

This attack was part of my personal crusade to put Spurs at the top and to put Chelsea out of action altogether. It was something I'd promised a friend one evening, beer in hand, overlooking the River Thames. He'd been severely beaten about the head with iron bars in a cowardly attack by Chelsea. I swore revenge and I like to think that I upheld my end of the bargain. What do you think? This was the game for me, a game that decided who was who.

But first a little background. I'd had enough of Chelsea at this point. They'd already attacked the Bull twice and I was fucking sick of it. So, one day, even though we had Boro at home, I decided to drop in on a few Chelsea bods that I knew would be up in the West End. I managed to pull about forty boys away from the Boro game and headed off to our destination, the Griffin pub in Villiers Street. I think it's now called the Bell and Compass and it's in the middle of London, just round the corner from Trafalgar Square, where one of my heroes stands on top of his column. We came out of Embankment tube station, me striding ahead, shoppers and office bods all staring at us in silence. Bang, we were in the pub: 'Come on, you cunts.' The governor, who was Chelsea too, took a distress flare to the side of the head. It exploded with such force that a pal of mine who works in Coutts Bank up the road dived under his desk thinking it was a fucking bomb. We burst back out on to Villiers Street, leaving the governor and the fifteen or so Chelsea cowering under their tables not knowing what the fuck had hit them. I ran down the subway laughing like a maniac with a lone copper shouting after me. Can you believe it? A dosser tried to make a citizen arrest. Fucking great, this could only happen to me! 'Fuck off, you smelly prick.' He was as high as a kite. Wallop; end of. I felt dirty afterwards, just hitting him like that, the silly fucker.

So you can see how it was between Chelsea and us at that point. We were seriously kicking arse at that time but still weren't getting the respect we deserved. I was working for British Rail (believe it or not) on the engineering side of things. I actually enjoyed it. On the match day, I called an early morning meet: 8.00am, King's Cross. This was going to be a military operation, run like clockwork. We split into two groups and made our way down to Gloucester Road. As we pulled into the station, every fibre of my being was alert; it had been called on, so I knew they would come. We streamed out of the tube, eyes bulging, ready for war... and they weren't there. So we headed into the nearest pub instead. There weren't that many of us there at the time, not that a small firm won't get you a good result, but sometimes there really is safety in numbers. I was expecting Chelsea to turn up any minute, so we went with what we'd got. I was in the doorway, the boys right behind me. Then, the rest of our boys turned up – followed minutes later by Chelsea. This is it. A flare gun went off and landed in an open-topped Citroën. Whoosh, up in flames it went, the couple inside quickly out and running. There were a good 100–150 Chelsea facing us across the road. I reached inside my CP Balaclava coat and pulled out a sawn-off pickaxe handle. I was bouncing up and down, adrenalin surging through me at such a rate I could hardly breathe. I swung round to my troops: 'Come on, get the fuck out now,' I was screaming. I was off across the road and into them. There was an explosion of people coming out behind me. I smacked one geezer who splintered off and then stepped, turned round and sprinted after the boys, running their main firm back to Barons Court. Thank you God or whoever, this is what I had come for. No excuses, giving it to them at 11.30 in the morning in their own manor. Enough said. Then, as if by magic, Old Bill were everywhere. What the fuck was going on? It was too fucking quick. Something didn't add up. A load of workmen in the station suddenly pulled on police hats and were screaming at us to stop. There were vanloads screaming in from everywhere. This cannot be happening.

One of the boys jumped down on to the railway line, busting his foot in the process, the silly fucker. Mind you, he got away, so good luck. I went into a phone box: for some reason I thought it would make me invisible. Funnily enough, to make it seem real I even phoned my aunt who lives down on the coast. At the same time, I dropped my Perspex goggles on the floor and tried to kick them out of the way. As my aunt and I were discussing the weather, Old Bill were politely knocking on the door, asking me to hang up.

They lined us all up against the wall: names, numbers, the usual bollocks. Somehow, none of us were nicked, but I knew we would pay for it in the end. Sure enough, two months later, on 27 April 1993 at 6.30am to be precise, Fulham CID paid me a visit. 'Guess what, sunshine, we've booked a nice day out in court for you. Turns out that, as well as having cops disguised as tube workers on the day, they were also filming the whole thing from a travel agent's shop. As well as using the footage in court, it was also used in the credits for the ITV *I-Spy* programme for the next couple of years. And there I was, the star of the show, leading from the front. To my mind, the whole thing was entrapment. They deliberately endangered public safety just to get a result. Sadly, the judge in court didn't agree and sent me down for three years for that one.

CHELSEA AT HOME, 3 APRIL 2004

There's no need to start this one off by telling you how much I hate these fucking mugs, is there? OK, I'll carry on. I was really feeling up for this game. I had been really down over the Christmas period with worry and stress over my beautiful little girl, as my ex knows the only way to get to me is through my daughter. But what goes around... Anyway, I picked myself up and decided to take out all my pent-up aggression on Chelsea. I got to our manor and knew straight away it wasn't going to be an ordinary day. There were loads of Tottenham Old Bill around, marching about like the fucking Gestapo. I called for an early meet just in case Chelsea got brave for once and actually came over. This is another myth about those fuckers I want to expose. They tell everyone that the mouthy Yids don't come to them, blah, blah, blah. But what about the Three Kings, where I got my three? What about the Ilfield? Ten minutes of madness, anyone? And did I dream those 400 bods who turned up at Wandsworth Town?

Anyway, back at the game, I saw there were riot police surrounding our pub, the Bank. I could see they were really itching for it. What's going on? It's only 11.00am. For a second, I actually thought that Chelsea were going to make a show, even though I had it on good authority that they weren't. Someone said to me that they were bringing coaches around the back and we were all going to be picked up on Section 60 (held all day without charge). Fuck that for a game of soldiers. I slipped away and went to the British Queen instead. I got a call in the pub with some unbelievable news: the Old Bill had closed down the Bank. Talk about adding petrol to the fire. This was taking the piss and whoever made the decision to shut the Bank for such a sensitive game should hang his head in shame. All it did was stir up a hornets' nest and left the police foot-soldiers to bear the brunt of it. Nice. I was later told by a copper, 'We shut it because we can.' The result was that there were now 200 bods roaming the streets instead of confined in one place. I personally wasn't a big fan of the pub, but it was owned by one of my pals, Gary, so it somehow became the firm's boozer. The fact that I was stabbed in the back of the neck there with a broken bottle didn't make me like it any more, but that was a non-football-related incident and I shall get the little fucker that did it in my own good time.

During the game, me, H and Snowy and all the boys settled down to watch the Grand National. I still wanted a piece of Chelsea, though. Five minutes before the end of the game, I left the pub and headed over to White Hart Lane. The Old Bill spotted me and ended up chasing me round the ground. I bumped into a few Chelsea coming out of the ground but they didn't want to know. Their firm hadn't turned up. With the police still in hot pursuit, I made my way back to the Queen. Game over.

Now I know a lot of their bods are on banning orders, but that's no excuse not to turn up for a game. So far, all the damage has been done by us going to them: Three Kings, Ilfield Road, etc. What have they ever done to us? Fuck all. I got a message later that evening to say they were coming over. Happy days. Sadly, I made one of the biggest mistakes ever by giving out my number. It got into the wrong hands and weeks later I was getting abusive phone calls from a mouthy little prick I'll call the Village Idiot. I swear, if I ever bump into him, I'll rip his head off. Even his own boys say he's a piece of shit. And as for the other mugs that he passed the number around to... Let's just say he'll cop it for the lot of those cowards.

The riot police must have got word that Chelsea were coming over too, as they surrounded our pub. But would the telephone warriors turn up, or were they all talk? To be fair, one of the boys who originally had my number phoned to say that the Old Bill were all over them and they couldn't get over. Then the fucking Village Idiot called me. I reacted like a mug. It was all 'phone calls at dawn'. It taught me something, though: you can't trust them. If one of our firm had been doing that to one of theirs, I'd have come down on him like a ton of bricks. We're better than that. They're just mugs.

So, we were stuck in a boozer, wound up with nowhere to go. We wanted them so bad and... crash, the door flew open and there were a load of them in balaclavas rushing in, waving sticks, lashing out indiscriminately. They were here. Without thinking, I picked up a chair and smashed into one attacker; then I was overpowered by six or eight of them, forced to the ground, hands and arms ripped back from their sockets, face in the carpet, a riot copper on each limb and dragged to my feet. I was taken outside and it was Section 60 time. I was photographed and released. Fair enough, I thought. I'll take a clump any day to the alternative. It turned out some little prick was lobbing bricks at them from a garden and they thought it was us. But that's no excuse for sending the stormtroopers into a pub full of women and normal drinkers. It was bad for the innocent bystanders; for us, it was just another normal day in the Tottenham firm.

WHO THE FUCK
ARE MAN UNITED?

CHAPTER 5

WHO THE FUCK ARE MAN UNITED?

MAN UNITED AT HOME, 1991/92 SEASON

It was a Saturday game. There were Mancs everywhere. They'd really turned up in numbers for this one, which I took as a mark of respect. It was actually one of the biggest firms I'd ever seen at the Lane. They were a pain in the fucking arse though. The manor was full of silly drunken cunts everywhere, so we slapped as many as we could get to. They brought a huge firm up the High Road, but we couldn't really get to them. There was Old Bill everywhere. Don't believe the police when they talk about being undermanned. For big games like this and Chelsea, the number of Old Bill has to be seen to be believed. On top of the regular plods, there are riot police, vans, dogs, horses, carriers and that fucking helicopter. It's like a war zone. There's enough of them to take over a small country. Never mind us, let us get on with it and let the police deal with real crime: the women being mugged or raped, or the street crime that makes people afraid to walk the streets at night.

Right, rant over. Now by this time I was fuming. I knew the Mancs would think they'd got a result, even though they hadn't done anything. Right, let's wait until after the game. I headed down to the Bull to meet the boys. Final whistle: they'd beaten us. No change there. No commitment as usual from the pricks on the playing field. We would have to do better – and we would. We hit the streets in numbers, but we were split up. Not a good scene against anyone, let alone the Mancs. A call went out to me: 'They're here.' I looked across the road in front of the college and there were hundreds of the cunts spilling out on to the streets, giving it large. I wasn't having this. I screamed out the battle cry, and without thinking ran straight in them. A few boys, H and D, were with me. I went straight into a big fucker in the middle of the road. No sooner had I clumped him than the crowd parted like the Red Sea. I soon realised why: I saw a dark shadow in front of me. It had got razor-sharp teeth and was snapping and snarling to be released. Police dog. Its handler slapped its arse and set the four-legged guided missile loose. Next stop, my arse. I turned and sprinted across the road. Even though I was running, I had time to take in the scene of mayhem around me. The boys were running the Mancs back down towards the tube station. Excellent. The Old Bill had also lost the plot and were going in very heavy. I saw my old friend Luds on the ground with a load of coppers wading into him. Bastards. There was nothing I could do. As well as the dog, I now had a horse after me too. I swung a sharp left into Tescos. The horse reared up and the copper fell off into a hail of boots. I just made it through the electronic doors. I thought I was OK but the dog was still after me. It must have just squeezed through the doors. It was nearly on me so I looked around for something to throw at the fucker. Unfortunately, I was in the women's underwear section. I grabbed a handful of nighties to throw in its face. Too late. His teeth tore into my calf and I went crashing down. The fucking animal was out of control. I tried to kick it off and it went for my face. I threw up my arm instinctively and it tore into my elbow, crunching right down to the bone. I was screaming at the Old Bill to get the thing off me. Instead, they picked me up off the floor by my ponytail – I had very long hair then – with the dog still attached to my arm. 'You fucking pricks, I need a doctor,' I snarled.

'Fuck off, Tanner, you're nicked.'

The cells were full, with all our boys together. I was given a dirty old cloth to stop the bleeding. The boys were going mad, saying I needed a doctor. I knew it wasn't life-threatening and couldn't give a fuck, even though I would be scarred for life. I knew I'd also lose my job as a postman, seeing as I'd need treatment on my arm for at least six weeks. I know now I should have sued the police. It really bugs me that I didn't. Maybe I still will. To cut a long story short, I was found guilty of violence and received a six-month banning order. To rub salt into the wound, the dog was given an award for bravery. The press even turned up for the award ceremony. I couldn't believe it when I saw the fucker in the newspaper under the headline: 'Hero police dog Newton tackles thug in Tesco'. As you can imagine, I'd love to get at his food.

The section below is a witness statement of the incident submitted by the dog handler. As you'll see, it differs from my version is quite a few ways.

WITNESS STATEMENT – INSPECTOR DENNIS DOLLERY

I am currently employed as a police inspector at Haringey Borough, but during the 1990s I was a dog handler based at Claygate House. During this time I was regularly posted to football matches to assist with crowd control, both at THFC and AFC. I've been asked to provide a statement in my relation with Trevor Tanner, whom I arrested after THFC v Manchester United football match during the above period. Mr Tanner refers to this incident in the book *Terrace Legends*, on page 126, and this time I was handling police dog Bob, a German Shepherd, about three years of age. My recollection was that the game had finished and sporadic problems were occurring up and down Tottenham High Road amongst rival groups of supporters. I was walking along the High Road towards Seven Sisters underground, escorting a group of supporters. As I neared the Bull public house I became aware of a group of approximately twenty to thirty THFC fans rushing from the direction of the public house into the crowd. As they ran they were punching and kicking at people indiscriminately. I could hear nothing coming from the Manchester United supporters that could have incited this. I noticed that a male at the front of this group was a man I now know to be Trevor Tanner. He was shouting obscenities and appeared to be leading the group. I saw Tanner knock a Man United fan to the floor by punching him around the head. He then began to kick at the man's head and body as he lay on the floor and was joined by other hooligans. I shouted at them and the group broke up leaving Tanner standing alone over the man. He kicked him again and then looked up at me. I shouted for him to stand still or I will release the dog. Tanner turned and ran south down the High Road towards Seven Sisters Road. I sent police dog Bob to chase Tanner, who was weaving through the crowd knocking people aside as he ran. Both the dog and I continued to pursue Tanner as he turned into the front door of the Tesco store. He vaulted over the entrance barriers and ran down the aisle as Bob crawled under the barriers and pursued him. As Tanner passed the section containing frozen sausages, Bob detained him by biting him on the right forearm. I joined the dog and arrested Tanner for assault and public order act offences.

MAN UNITED AT HOME: THE BATTLE OF SOMERS TOWN (ON BAIL AND MAD FOR IT)

As the title suggests, a few of us were on bail when this fixture reared its ugly head and a low profile was definitely the order of the day. But, as you've probably gathered from reading so far, things just don't work out like that for me. I was hoping the Mancs wouldn't turn up for once. So would you if you were on bail charged with rioting, something that can carry a life sentence – especially if you get one of those ancient, loopy judges.

We met up at a quiet little pub called the Beehive down Tottenham High Road. Someone told me United were on the manor so, fuck it. If they want it, they can have it, big time. With that, the boozer doors flew open and there was a tall, hairy fucker in the doorway. 'Come on, you cunts,' he said. So we did, bottles in hand ready to ram in his face. We got to the door and saw that there were Old Bill everywhere, and they were filming the whole thing. I could see what they were thinking, Go on then, boys, this'll send you away for a bit. I didn't want to give them the satisfaction, but I couldn't let the Mancs get away with it either. I'll never forget one of the Old Bill on a horse, laughing at me, saying, 'Go on, Trevor.' Fuck it. I bowled out the door and set off down the road towards the Mancs, my boys and half the police force after me.

We followed the Mancs to the ground. There were a lot of them; well, they are London's most popular team, aren't they? Because of the police, we decided to break away and sort something out for later. You can imagine how wound up we were as we headed for the pub. We hadn't been there long before one of our boys came in with some good news: the Cockney Reds had been locked out and were being escorted to Euston. It was on. I knew exactly where they were going: Somers Town Estate, to a shitty little boozer called the Vic. Even though me and the other boys on bail were taking an enormous risk, we knew they had to get it. There were forty-nine of us exactly, all wound up like springs. We arrived on the estate and headed straight for the pub. I'll never forget the look on their faces as we walked through the door. They were fucking stunned. One of their main boys, who has a bit of history with us, ran up to the flat upstairs and kicked the door off to escape, screaming for his life. I told the rest of them to tell their proper firm that we'd be in the pub up the road and to come when they're ready. I wasn't interested in just thirty or forty Cockney Reds; I wanted the full firm. They were completely stunned. Stunned that we didn't completely annihilate them; stunned that we'd sniffed them out in some shitty back-street pub in Euston; and stunned that we wanted more later, with their whole firm.

I looked across at the boys with me. Or should I say men. We all agreed no one was going anywhere, whatever happened. It's something that creates a really powerful bond. A very old pal of mine, a Scouser, was with us that day and you can imagine his elation at just being involved. It was great from our point of view too, as we had someone with us who could verify everything that happened.

Time passed, then my Scouse pal, who'd been keeping watch, ran into the pub: 'T, they're coming,' he said.

'How many?' I asked.

'About 200.'

Fuck, but who gives a fuck? This was what we wanted and I was blind with rage. We armed ourselves to the teeth with every fucking chair, pool stick, glass and bottle. Let's do these cunts once and for all. We came out as one on to the road. It was dark. They stopped at a crossroads about 200 yards from us. The crowd seemed to stretch back as far as I could see. One of their boys was doing a little jig in the road – come on, you fucking

Yids, we're not going anywhere. I focused on him and charged, stick in hand, not breaking stride and screaming like a wild man. The boys followed. We were nearly on them when their main man started to turn away. A kind of ripple effect kicked in and they started to shift. One went down in front of me and got fucking battered. They were falling like nine pins. The rest were being driven out of the estate and on to Euston Road itself. My Scouse pal ran up and hugged me: 'You're making history, la,' he said with a manic smile. He was right, we were. Don't get me wrong, the Mancs have a formidable firm and I've even recently rated them in a friend's book as one of the top five firms in the country, but I don't respect reputations alone. This was our day not theirs. This was a new era. I remember chasing them into Euston station itself when just outside a copper on horseback shouted out to me, 'Give it a rest, Tanner. You've had a good night.' He was right. We'd smashed the mighty Reds with numbers that we had no right to. It just goes to show that bigger is not always best. We went back to a boozer next to Green Park station where we spent the night dancing on the tables, literally a magical evening. One for the history books.

MAN UNITED AWAY, 20 MARCH 2004

We've had a lot of little battles with Man United over the years, so here's one from more recent history. Make no mistake, Old Trafford can be a naughty place to visit. But if you consider yourself the top firm in the country then you've got to go there. Not that they're particularly special, it's just that there are so many of the fuckers.

There's no doubt that Old Trafford is a nice ground but it's a big old soulless place.

We went up on two trains and met in a pub called the Moon Under Water in Deansgate. I wasn't feeling too clever that day and had a high temperature, but we had called it on and were hundreds of miles from home so I just had to get on with it. We left the pub nice and early, around 1.30pm, just to confuse the Old Bill. To fuck them up even more, instead of heading for the ground we marched on the city centre instead. We fronted up a few pubs with no joy. Oh well, let's hit the ground. Trouble was, we were miles away and I was getting seriously tired. Considerately, the Old Bill herded us on to a tram that took us to the ground.

Most of the boys headed straight for the ground, but I spotted a pub by the car park and headed towards it with just a few boys. I called out the Mancs and they couldn't believe what they were seeing. A few Spurs fronting their boozer! By now the rest of the firm could see what we were up to and started to catch up. Unfortunately, so were the Old Bill. The Mancs, realising we were taking the piss, started to put on a bit of a show to save face, but I just looked and laughed. I had an Old Bill video camera trained straight on me, so I knew it was game over – until after the game at least. Or was it? As you go into Old Trafford, you get frisked by their own security. A couple of our firm took exception to some bully-boy tactics, and Nash, my little pal (I know he would love a mention so here it is), took exception and was going radio. To my left, Johnny M was ready to start throwing right-handers. I was in the middle with the Old Bill running around like headless chickens. Then, JM came through with an entourage of security hot on his heels. What the fuck was going on? I moved after him instinctively. T was with me and said it was going to go. We stopped under the stands. Security were to my right, M to my left. J, H and a few other boys arrived and I wound up to throw a right hand. Just then, the bloke in front of me said, 'All right, Trev!' I clocked him and realised him and his mates are security for the city-centre clubs that we had taken over once when we played the Gooners in the FA Cup semi-finals. I'd really admired the way they handled that night, effectively letting us police ourselves. Because I also put on club nights in London, we had a lot in common and stayed in touch. The result was that everyone was confused as Marlon (the security guy) gave me a big bear hug. My boys and the security heavy mob were looking at each other: 'What the fuck's this?' I told them he was my pal and suddenly we were all friends again. The only problem was that Old Trafford is CCTVed to the max and now the Old Bill were watching. Lose your pal in the ground, said Marlon. Nice one, brother. I got J to swap jackets with Josh and in we went.

Spurs lost the game, which was the only bad result of the day. With the help of Man United's own security, we avoided a bang-on nicking. Outside the ground, the police escorted us away from the Mancs, but it wasn't long before it went off. The two firms went into each other and we quickly got them on the back foot. This is what it's all about. In the shadow of Old Trafford, we were forcing them back and back. They regrouped and there were fucking hundreds of the bastards now. I ran into the middle of the road with the intention of having a toe-to-toe with a bod in black bouncing up and down. We locked eyes and I headed straight towards him. But Tottenham Old Bill and their trusty video camera were there too and had other ideas. I lashed out a hopeful right hand at the grinning prick before the Old Bill closed in. By this time, we were starting to get a bit straggly so I screamed for everyone to stand: the only form of defence when you're outnumbered is attack. Suddenly, we were back in control, spilling out over the major dual carriageway heading back towards the station. Old Bill were now arriving in numbers. They had been well and truly caught out but Tottenham plod were having a field day with the camera. The Mancs were on the right, with us on the left and the Old Bill in the middle. We fought a running battle for a good ten to fifteen minutes and now and then a few of the boys would break through, get right in amongst the Mancs and absolutely terrorise them. They were fucking fuming and we were taking the piss big style. The Old Bill were now on the scene in numbers: horses, dogs, helicopters – you name it. They marched us back to Piccadilly station, which was fucking miles away. I was feeling like shit with a raging temperature. We were eventually put on a train back to London, or so we thought. We were told to change at Birmingham for our train home. What a fucking nightmare journey this was going to be. The Old Bill didn't give a fuck; they just wanted us out of Manchester. We were packed in like sardines. Thankfully, I managed to bag a seat. We arrived at New Street station in Birmingham after what seemed a day to be told by a big, fat grinning copper that there were no trains back to London and we would have to go to Coventry by coach and then by bus back to London. 'What?' I screamed. 'Fuck off.' With that, I marched out to the taxi rank to ask a minibus driver, 'How much to London?' His eyes lit up: '£200.' I bargained him down to £120, which I thought was a touch for six of us. The poor bastard was already asking where Victoria was when we were only halfway down the M1. After making a detour into North London to drop off H and J, we finally got to Victoria. The driver was a gibbering wreck. He didn't know where the fuck he was. I felt sorry for him so I tipped him an extra score.

MAN UNITED AT HOME, 29 SEPTEMBER 2001 – TO MEET OR NOT TO MEET, THAT IS THE QUESTION

Everyone knows about the Mancs' rivalry with Liverpool and even West Ham, but they'd be surprised at the history of naughtiness between Spurs and them. We met at Wood Green for this one, a couple of miles from Tottenham. The Mancs were up the road in a Wetherspoon's pub. We asked them to come to us because we'd shaken off the Old Bill, so we had a free hand. We were 200-handed. A proper naughty firm with all the right people there. This one was going to sort the men from the boys. But to my surprise the Mancs wouldn't come to us. They wouldn't even leave their boozer. Fuck it, we'll go and get them. That's the sort of firm we were. As we approached their pub, up pops the Old Bill. The sneaky fuckers had been keeping tabs on the Mancs, so now they had to come out of their hidey-holes to protect them. We had a good go at the Old Bill and tried to get through to the Mancs, but it wasn't happening. What a waste of time. I know one of the Manc faces who is a pal of a pal tried everything to get them out of the boozer. He even ended up having a proper row with one of his own people. Respect for that. You know who you are. As for the rest of you – you know the score. I don't really have to say it, do I?

I walked all the way back to Tottenham and went straight to my favourite watering hole, the Cool Bory Club. Outside, about fifteen to twenty Mancs were giving it the big one, so we stepped outside to say hello. They dived on to a double-decker bus for safety, so we ripped the doors off. I tried to get to them but they were literally fighting for their lives and no one was getting up those stairs. Fuck it, we had to let them go. Still, it was half-time and my schizo team were leading 3–0. Unfortunately, we didn't know the Mancs would come out in the second half and score five. They were taking the piss and that just rubbed salt into the wounds. It's a shame their fans didn't know how to fight back too.

CHAPTER 6

GOONERS ARE GONERS

ARSENAL AWAY, 1993

We firmed up at our beloved Bull and a proper little firm
it was too. Well, not so little – 100–150-strong. We were
not gonna take any prisoners on this one; we were a
young, hungry firm, striving for the stars. There was a nice
mix of old and new as we filed into Seven Sisters tube
station. I could taste the adrenalin in my mouth. We were
going straight to Finsbury Park – two stops, job done, no
fucking about. We had no Old Bill with us (those were the
days). As we came out of the dark tunnel and into
daylight, here we go. They were fucking here on the left.
It's off, and two firms go to war. We went straight into
them and the Old Bill went straight into us. I looked to my
right and one of my pals had a German Shepherd hanging
off him. It actually took a chunk out of his arse. I kicked
the mad dog in the head. It was going off all around us.

We had a bit of a stand-off, and then, as if heaven sent, a fucking milk float trundled up: crates, bottles, then the milk float itself got thrown at the Gooners – and came flying straight back at us. It was fucking mayhem. We had a running battle with them all the way up to the North Bank. It was going off right up to the away turnstiles and I have to say the Gooners were game that afternoon. One particularly brave individual was trying to pull Terry back from the turnstiles. He got a nasty headbutt for his trouble. As usual, we were taking it to the Gooners and because we'd been direct we'd done what we wanted to do.

This was the time when our firm was beginning its rise to dominance and when the Gooners were getting past their peak. Still, we did manage a good few rows with them, plus I managed to squeeze in a few individual bust-ups of my own.

SOHO – LUCKY TO GET OUT ALIVE

A hazy one this one, from the early- or mid-1990s. The Gooners were playing Man United at Wembley in the FA Cup final that day. Bravely or stupidly, me and two pals, Little K and Andy (God bless him, as he's tragically not with us any more), decided to have a look round Soho to see what was happening. Naturally, the place was crawling with pissed-up Gooners and Mancs. We walked into a little old pub round the back streets of Soho with a long, narrow bar. We went straight to the top of the bar, away from the door, probably not the wisest thing to do in hindsight. At first, everything was cool, but that didn't last. The place was full of Gooners. In situations like this, all fear seems to evaporate from me. I heard the usual stuff – 'Fucking Yids, fucking Jews' – and my blood started to boil. In situations like this, I honestly believe attack is the best form of defence. There was no way we were going to get out of here in one piece otherwise. I felt responsible as I'd dragged the other two into this. I made sure K got to the end of the bar and nearly out of the door. Andy was in a shop across the road, oblivious to everything, so that just left me. I had a bottle of Beck's in my hand, so that was smashed straight over the closest Gooner's head. I then threw a table into the baying mob. Nothing, except being brought down, was going to stop me making the door. You cannot underestimate how powerful the human survival instinct is. I steamed through the pub, knocking people over as I went. I was like a hurricane, with tables, chairs, bottles and glasses all raining down behind me being sucked up in my wake. I remember a table falling straight across the door between me and my pals and survival. I vaulted it with all the superhuman strength that an adrenalin charge gives you. Once out on the street, I turned and threw some wild punches before retreating into the Soho night air. We ended up in a boozer not too far away when I said to K, 'Where the fuck is Andy?' He strolled into the boozer right then. He had a bit of a shiner, but apart from that was fine. The little lunatic (bless him) had walked straight back into the pub without a care in the world. I don't think the Gooners could believe it. Fair play to them, they didn't hurt him too much. I think he just got shoved out the door as they were trying to get out of there.

50/50 IN THE GOONER STANDS, EARLY 1990S

One of the boys managed to get a block booking in the Gooners' main stand. I had to hand-pick fifty bods for this job – something I'm not a fan of – but it had to be the right fifty. There were some old faces there, great pals of mine, who have left the scene now: Peckham, Al, all the other old crew. We didn't have a bad team then. Chris Waddle was at his peak, a dodgy Barnet but fuck me could that boy play football (just no penalties). We got into the ground without too much drama, apart from a little stand-off further up the hill. We really wanted to get into the ground and show the Gooners just how powerful we now were. There were some proper mouthy cunts sitting a few rows in front of us, so we knew who the targets would be. Chris Waddle was brought down right on the edge of the box, right in front of us. The referee waved play on and the Gooners started pissing themselves laughing. Well, we went ballistic and started raining coins down on them. The atmosphere changed completely. The Gooners, the stewards and the police all knew we were there now. The stewards and police got to us first and surrounded us. The Gooners, silly fuckers, didn't know it was us though. One of them even came up to me and said, 'There's fucking Yids everywhere.'

'Yeah', I said, 'right fucking next to you. Come on, you cunt.'

Luckily for him, the Old Bill and stewards moved in again.

It had been a brilliant idea to get into their end, but it hadn't really come off. It was still a result for us – the

Gooners were frothing at such a piss-take – but apart from a few digs at the exits it didn't really go off. Shame.

FA CUP SEMI-FINAL, WEMBLEY, 2 APRIL 1993

No explanations for this one, a monster game whichever way you look at it. They reckon they could have sold Wembley twice over. I find that hard to believe with the Gooners: did you see the number of empty seats at their end for the 2003 semi at Old Trafford against Sheffield United? Fucking embarrassing. More on that later. Anyway, I'll give them the benefit of the doubt this time. Now I'm writing about the night before because I wasn't really with it for the day of the game. You'll see why as you read on.

There had been a bit of a piss-up organised in a dingy back-street pub outside Tottenham. It was supposed to be a private do: just us, a few birds and some tunes. Of course, it didn't go to plan. The boozer was a shit-hole and I sensed a bad atmosphere straight away. Out of the corner of my eye, I saw this little mug start to play up. Why is it always the little ones? Anyway, who was the little prick? We didn't have that many in the place at the time, but they were good boys. He was really giving it now and he'd fronted one of my pals. Fuck this. I marched over and clumped him one. Somehow, we both managed to go down, probably because he was so fucking short. I managed to get a grip of him, turn him over and give it to him good style. Then, I got a whack from behind to the head. My head was spinning; I couldn't make out what it was but there was blood running down through my hair and into my eyes. I'd been cut right across the top of my head. Meanwhile, the little fucker had broken free and was out the door. Sean went after him, and I followed on. I nearly had him in the middle of the dual carriageway. I kicked his legs away and he staggered, almost going down. But he was like a fucking rabbit and kept going. He was out of his head, that much was apparent. Sean got in a few proper digs, but by this time I'd lost a lot of blood; my hair was matted with it and I was pretty spaced out. The thing that pissed me off most was the thought of having my hair cut off. I wore it long in those days and I didn't want to lose it.

I went to a girlfriend's place to be cleaned up. I made a mate pour TCP and hot water on to the open wound and I nearly passed out. This was literally a blood bath. Although my hair was matted, it did help to stop the bleeding. My pal nearly fell into the bath when he saw the amount of claret in there. I was really pissed off about the whole incident. It should never have happened but unfortunately these things do. I'm still pissed off with certain people over that night and they know it, but that's in-house. Suffice to say, I wasn't in good shape for the next day. It was a non-event anyway. The Gooners were a no-show *and* we lost the semi. Not a great weekend, but they can't all be good ones. I know it left me with a headache in more ways than one.

FA CUP SEMI-FINAL, OLD TRAFFORD, APRIL 2001

This game was one of the big ones. They could have sold it out three times over. People were flying in from all over the world for the match. As it was a Sunday game, we drove up on Saturday for a night out in Manchester. We checked into our hotel and everything seemed hunky dory. The hotel had a spa, indoor pool, its own boozer and a lovely sort on reception. The only problem was the room. It didn't have any windows, just a mural of the New York skyline. Now, I love New York but this was taking the piss. It's not too much to ask for a window, is it? I even had a window in fucking Wandsworth nick! Turns out there was no window in order to stop the local toerags from breaking into the rooms. Welcome to Manchester. To get out of the poxy room, we decided to have a look around. I love that moment when you first come out and start to explore your new environment. It's like being a caged lion let loose for the first time, surveying your kingdom and waiting for the local predators to have a go.

Although we were up in Manchester, it was as if London had been transferred up north for the day. We decided to meet up in the Wetherspoon's right smack bang in the town centre at 6.00pm. The message was also conveyed to Gooners. It was only midday, so they'd been given fair warning. We'd called it on; would they show? In the meantime, we explored the city and met up with a few more of our boys. We plotted up across the road from the hotel, and I have to say the landlord was good as gold. He even laid on some food to make us feel welcome, which was a really nice touch and most appreciated. You see, it comes down to respect: he respected us and in turn we respected him and his establishment. It's not rocket science and if a lot more landlords had that approach with football bods you would have a lot less aggravation in pubs on match days. Trust me on this. I'm an expert.

So, a good time was had by all. To be honest, I could have quite happily stayed there, but we had the slight matter of the Gooners to deal with before we could party and I wanted these mouthy cunts once and for all. In London, for one reason or another, apart from a recent nasty little incident of hand-to-hand fighting on a moving tube train, I couldn't really say I'd had much with them lately. They'd kind of gone off the radar. It was now all about Chelsea and West Ham, at least for me. But this was now and we were playing our so-called deadly rivals in the semi-final of the FA Cup. Surely the Gooners would have a herd out for this one, wouldn't they? They're a funny little firm, the Gooners. Fifteen or twenty years back, they loved a row, but these days their star has definitely waned, as we've grown more powerful.

Soon it was time to head down to the Wetherspoon's pub. As usual, it was huge, even by the ridiculous size of these places. The boys were gathered by the doors in expectation of Arsenal arriving. The 6.00 pm deadline came and went without Arsenal showing. I wasn't surprised in the slightest. That was me finished with them, but the night was still young. There were about forty or fifty of us in there, so we knew we'd be OK if anything happened. Sure enough, what with all the locals and assorted riff-raff knocking about someone soon set it off. Some little mug came up to my pal as bold as brass and started asking questions. I got hold of the wrong end of the stick because I was in one of those moods and demanded to know why he hadn't clumped him. We had a stand-up shouting match in front of the entire pub, which to neutrals must have been very amusing. It was only our second row in twenty years of friendship and we soon kissed and made up. No sooner had the dust settled than a little firm of about twenty to thirty appeared from the back of the huge gaff. They started giving it, 'We're Wednesday till we die' and I was only too happy to oblige – as soon as I got over their sheer fucking audacity and stupidity. 'Come on then, cunt,' I screamed and launched a bottle over the nearest head. It smashed completely in half and nearly knocked the mouthy fucker clean out. I picked up a bar stool and waved it around like a light sabre. This is fucking brilliant; nothing can beat this, smashing into whoever was in front. The boys had the rest of them backed up against the doors, taking a battering. There was claret everywhere. They had no choice but to stand and have a go in the doorway as it took a good few minutes for the Old Bill, sitting right outside, to figure out what was going on. When the panic button was finally pressed, the Old Bill stormed the doors just as Wednesday were trying to get out. The result: a complete slaughter. The Old Bill made a beeline straight for me. I thought I was fucked, but it was Manc Old Bill, not ours. The sniffer dogs came in and had a field day, just another inflammatory tactic the Old Bill like to use. Surely everyone knows there are no drugs in football, don't they?

As the Sheffield bods had started the whole thing and didn't want to press charges, there wasn't a lot the Old Bill could do. We were lucky. We were all IDed, photographed and searched one by one until we were finally released into the night air. The Wetherspoon's was shut down, the first time ever apparently, not that it's anything to be proud of – it's just a fact. We made our way across the square until we came to a couple of bars that looked decent. We ended up in a club called Edwards, I think. It was early evening, so we had no trouble getting in. By the time the doormen arrived for their shift, there was a good hundred Spurs in there. Accepting the situation, the doormen decided not to make an issue of it and treated us with the utmost respect. I'm still pals with the doormen to this day. In turn, I made sure that they were treated the same and that everyone behaved, which I'm glad to say they did. It was a win-win situation for everyone. We were already in the place, we were behaving ourselves and it was one of the best clubs in Manchester, full of gorgeous birds, having a great time with all your pals around you. It doesn't get much better than that. The best thing was the look on the faces of the Tottenham Old Bill watching us through the massive glass windows as we had a good old boogie. At one stage, I sat on top of the stairway wearing an earpiece and telling the boys on the door who to let in. I felt like Marlon Brando in *Apocalypse Now*, directing operations. Some of our boys who had earlier been turned away couldn't believe it when I got them in. I must admit it was a real buzz but I think I let it go to my head a little bit, especially when I started telling Jimmy to bring me JDs and cokes, and he politely told me where to shove 'em. Lovely. Anyway, respect to Gary, Marlon and all the boys on the door. It was a great night.

Back at the hotel, there were more fun and games. One of the guests was loudly proclaiming his allegiance to Arsenal, so he got a bit of a clump for that. Nothing major. We partied through the night, so I never saw the New York skyline again that evening. It was a great idea going up the night before the game, but it wasn't much fun the next morning. The word hungover doesn't even begin to describe how I felt. At one point, standing under the shower, I really did think I was on the way out. Even though we had a 9.00am meet, I just had to lie down. I was knackered, my hand was cut and I was covered in bruises. If I was going to be any use to anyone, I needed a lie-down first. I had to have a bit of R and R. I stretched out on the bed, but it was no good; the room was spinning. I got out of there and hailed a cab to catch up with the boys at Salford Quays. On the way I'm sure I saw Arsene Wenger out jogging. It was him or his double.

I needed to get my head straight sharpish. All the boys were there and a lot of them were suffering too, although Swainy made me feel like shit again when he bounced up to me, fresh as a daisy. He's teetotal with little sympathy. There's always one. He's as game as they come, though, and my pain was self-inflicted so you have to take it on the chin. A few of the boys wandered off on their own and bumped into the Gooners' main firm, nearly coming unstuck. Suddenly it was on and it was time to stop feeling sorry for myself. Off we went round the corner after the Gooners' scalps. A roar went up as it does when two massive firms are about to clash. The Gooners retreated and the Old Bill arrived on the scene. About time, too. I hadn't seen them all weekend. I'll never forget one of the Gooners who jumped up on a wall and ran along it to escape getting battered, then when he was safe and at a distance stood there with his arms open as if he was the governor. Stupid prick. It was going off mental between the Old Bill and us as we desperately tried to get to the Gooners. I'd been clumped and filmed too many times by our Old Bill in the past to be doing this, but fuck it. I knew I was risking a nicking, and probably jail time, and my ex had just given birth to our little girl and I didn't want to be separated from her. But I wouldn't expect any of the boys to do anything I wouldn't do. I got the shout: 'Oi, oi, they're here.' They were down a side street, but there were Old Bill everywhere. I just don't understand the Gooners. They had their chance on Saturday night, with no police, and didn't show. Now here they were with Old Bill everywhere. If it had been Millwall or even Chelsea, it would have been going off all night. The Gooners remind me of the Geordies in a way – although the Gooners are a bit more ethnically diverse. They're not like us – one firm and fans separate – they all mix together, and in situations like that the actual supporters become more of a nuisance than the firm. There was one little prick with a flag really winding me up. I managed to get through to him and give him a couple of digs, but the Old Bill were swarming all over us and he didn't get the battering he deserved.

Going into the ground, I did manage to unload a couple of punches – and got hit with a telescopic truncheon for my troubles. As for the game, well, the scum scored and our pathetic team rolled over once again. 'Fuck this, I'm off,' I said to Jimmy.

'You can't go out there on your own,' he said.

'I don't give a fuck who's out there,' I said. 'I'm not watching these cunts celebrate.'

GOONERS ARE GONERS

I made my way back to town. And even though the cunts won you wouldn't have known it. We had a small altercation with a little firm celebrating outside the hotel and sent them packing, but all in all the Gooners were very disappointing once again.

One thing did happen that weekend that still winds me up to this day. It was totally outside the rules and marks out the fuckers who did it as total cowards. Fifteen of our boys were staying in a hotel called Jury's Inn. But the hotel, and the pub attached to it, was where a lot of the Gooners were staying too. We didn't know this, otherwise we would have been around there lively and smashed the gaff up. Jimmy and the boys were enjoying a drink in the hotel bar, which was packed with around forty Gooners. One of them came up to one of our bods and told him to shut the fuck up and that this was a Gooner hotel. Obviously, the reply was a smack in the face and it went off mental. By all accounts – and this comes from a Gooner who was there – the little firm of Spurs from Reading and Oxford more than stood their own, with one of them, J, I think, knocking out all out before him. It was already forty on to fifteen and the Gooners, realising they were getting nowhere and incredibly that they could even get done, summoned another forty from the boozer next door. It doesn't take Einstein to figure out that it was now game over, big time. J was cut up bad and needed emergency hospital treatment. The most sickening thing of all was that as J lay on the floor bleeding, drifting in and out of consciousness, having gone down fighting fifteen against eighty, the brave slags took pictures of him and turned them into T-shirts. Enquiries have been made and, if the cunts that took those pictures are found, they'll be torn limb from limb. You live by the sword, you die by it.

The journey home was a fucking nightmare. We got lost and ended up pissed off and starving, especially as every service-station restaurant seemed to be closed. It dawned on us then that we hadn't eaten anything all weekend. We managed to pick up some crisps and manky ready-wrapped sandwiches, but the food was so disgusting that we ended up shoving a load of it under the car seats. Paul, who was driving his wife's brand-new Ford Focus, was clearly proud of his little car but didn't realise we were turning it into a four-wheeled fridge. A few lagers even got spilled when we fell asleep. Apparently, his missus went ballistic when she got in the car the next morning and had to wade through a ton of shit. Paul's still getting it in the ear now, bless him, so I guess I'm not the only one who remembers that weekend well.

CHAPTER 7

SPURS AND THE ENGLAND SCENE

ENGLAND V SWEDEN, STOCKHOLM, SUMMER 1992

After this game, I was, according to the *Sun* newspaper, 'England's Foulest'. Let's see. I decided to go on the spur of the moment. It was to be Graham Taylor's penultimate game in charge, thank fuck. I needed to get out there and mix it up for Spurs before we got knocked out of the European Championship qualifiers. We didn't have many bods out there but I didn't give a fuck. I was determined to put us on the international map and turn us into one of the biggest firms that go with England. In that respect, I think I have achieved my aim. You have to understand there was a big mistrust of us on the England scene going back years. The Spurs firm is a multi-cultural one, something I'm proud of. It's not all white like a lot of firms and some people don't like that.

Me and a pal flew over to Stockholm the day before the game. There were a few Chelsea bods on the plane and my pal said they wanted to say hello – we're all England and all that. Bollocks, I thought. Fuck them and fuck you for even suggesting it. I nearly gave my pal a right-hander for even putting me in that position. We landed and went to the campsite. What a fucking cesspit. It was like a refugee camp. I wasn't going to spend any more time there than necessary, so I made my way out and on to the streets. I bumped into a Chelsea bod, D from St Neots near Cambridge. By the way, a big hello to the St Neots Spurs massive, especially Mark and Rich: we go back a long time. I have had some great nights down there; the people are great and I spent a lot of time there when I came out of the nick. Spurs have always had a strong little firm from that neck of the woods. So have Chelsea, unfortunately. I said hello to D and we exchanged civilities. He was on his own so everything was cool. He persuaded me to come for a beer. No sign of my boys anywhere, so why not? We walked up a back street and what appeared to be another firm was walking towards us, holding a fucking great big flag. I thought it was mardi gras time at first, but then I noticed the flag had a swastika on it. So this must be Sweden's famous Black Army that the English media had told us about, who were waiting to kill the English invaders. I know the English press (the cunts) and government (bigger pricks) were hoping we'd get a battering, so let's see. I flew out into the road. 'Come on, you Swedish mugs, let's have it.' The geezer with the flag just stared at me as if I was from another planet. I smashed a right hand into his temple and down he went. D and a few other England boys flew into the rest and the Swedes were fucking rubbish. Jack boots and black flak jackets running everywhere just like I knew they would. Another load of anti-English propaganda dreamed up by our own people. The trouble was these silly Swedish fuckers actually believed it and got a hiding for their trouble. I'd only been there a few hours and this little shindig had got me right in the mood.

I ended up going to another bar and it was full of mouthy (you guessed it) Chelsea. Why did I go in, I hear you ask? I know. It had to end in tears. Sure enough, a young kid in a Spurs shirt walked past with his dad and some big, brave Chelsea bod spits at the kid. I'm not fucking having that. He might as well have spat at me. Without thinking of the numbers with him, I smashed my fist into the side of his nut. He staggered badly but didn't quite go down. The whole fucking place turned on me. I started to back-pedal as tables and chairs and bottles came flying at me. The next thing: bang, a night-stick slammed into me, then another. Swedish riot police. Fuck it, I was nicked. They asked me what the fuck I'm doing 'you crazy English bastard, fighting your own people'. 'They're not English,' I said with a completely straight face. 'They're Chelsea.' I walked off and they didn't come after me. Too bemused, I suppose.

I was on a fucking roll now and thought I should get a ticket for the game. Of course, I wasn't going to pay for it – I was going to liberate one from one of the greedy bastard touts. I headed for the ground and by an underpass I spotted a big, blond fucker, obviously a Swede, waving a load of tickets around. This shouldn't be too hard. I grabbed the tickets, but the fucker wouldn't let go. In the struggle, the tickets tore to pieces. Ruined. Oh well, at least I'd probably done the FA a favour by stopping him selling tickets for the Sweden end to a load of rampaging England fans. One thing was for sure, though: I was not going to the game any more. I headed down the road to find a bar to watch the game and ended up in a McDonalds, of all places. The atmosphere was bad. England were losing 1–0 and heading out of the European Championships. Just like Spurs, they don't deserve the support they have. Overpaid pricks the lot of them. If they were out on the streets, I would fucking lynch 'em.

It started to go with the locals. They were giving it large, silly fuckers. One got clumped, then another. Soon the whole place was getting it. Fuck this, I'm out of here. I saw a big wheel in a mini-fairground and I headed towards the bright lights. I saw one of the fairground stalls go over and the locals started to arm themselves with pieces of it. It was seriously kicking off. The Swedes had called it on and were getting spanked big style. There is not a firm in the world that can touch an England firm together, and that's a fact. Out of the corner of my eye, I could see a van reverse towards me. The doors swung open and four plain-clothes police bods leaped out. They grabbed a limb each and bundled me into the van. Inside, they trussed me up like a turkey. Soon another punter joined me, a squaddie on leave from Germany. We were both in a lot of shit and heading for a Swedish prison. By the time we arrived at the nick, we'd been joined by three other bods. We were to be the final five, and infamous, fans to be deported from Sweden. The *Sun* newspaper picked up on it, and dubbed us 'England's Foulest'. The prison we were taken to had had an entire wing emptied in anticipation of trouble. It was a grim place, as prisons tend to be, but very Swedish: a bit too clinical. It must be what Ikea is like in hell.

We were put on to the top floor reached by elevator, stripped, hosed down and numbered. Not a word was said the whole time. I know the Swedes speak very good English, better than a lot of us, so this was all part of the mind game.

To make matters worse, the only thing on the TV they let us watch was *Poldark*, surely one of the most depressing TV series ever made. They say Sweden has one of the highest suicide rates in the world, and I can see why. What with the crap TV and lager at £6 a pint that forces you to drink cheap, dodgy spirits. Exercise was an equally depressing affair in the nick. We were taken on to the roof separately and put in a kind of rooftop cage. I refused exercise after that. They weren't going to have the satisfaction of seeing me walk around a fucking cage, not for the time being anyway. The British Consul came and saw us the next day. He looked younger than me. Innocent until proven guilty? Not if you're an England fan abroad. The little prick from the embassy allowed me one call home. I found out that a Swede had been badly hurt in the rioting that night and they were trying to put it on us. When I phoned home, my mum told me it was all over the papers and news in England. We were the only ones not to know. After a while, we were taken to court by an underground corridor. I had a blanket over my head to avoid the press, which turned out to be fucking useless. The Swedes were going mad outside. The local media had stirred them up to a frenzy.

Now I just have to right a wrong here. This might sound like macho bullshit but it's important to me. The *Sun* said that I cried in court. Well, so what if I did? But I didn't. We all know the *Sun*'s reputation. I was too fucking shocked to speak, let alone fucking cry. I just sat there with my long hair hanging down and my head in my hands. Of course, I didn't look happy, but neither would you if you were facing a possible ten-stretch in a foreign prison. My hopes rested on an American interpreter who could have been saying anything. The evidence against me rested on a white baseball cap. Suffice to say they didn't have enough evidence to hold me, so I was bailed for further enquiries. This meant I could have been dragged back over there any time. Thankfully, time has now lapsed on that, but it wasn't good I can tell you. I was fucking elated to be going home. I was taken under police escort back to the campsite to get my belongings, which had already been taken home by friends. All I had to wear were the clothes I stood in. My shirt was ripped, so while we were waiting for the plane the tasty blonde police officer who had been part of my escort – and who I'd been chatting to in English – bought me a T-shirt. Fair play to her, but it was an official Euro '92 top, with a great big fucking bunny rabbit logo on it. Fuck it. I still wore it home. Before I left, I jokingly told the police bird that I'd like to come back and see her under better circumstances, and that maybe she could show me around without the handcuffs! She said she would love to, so I told her to send me a postcard. Two weeks later, I nearly fell over when she did send me one. Sadly, it would be a long time before I could ever think about going back there for a holiday and I never got to meet her again.

When I arrived at Gatwick, I saw that *Sun* headline for the first time. So much for a quiet return. And, just to end this story on a high, a little while later I was having a drink in Brixton in a pub called The Hope with an old pal of mine. He'd been taking a lot of stick from the local Chelsea and Gooners for associating with yours truly, so I decided it was only right I went down there and had a drink with him. Sure enough, someone in the bar started to take the piss with little comments about the *Sun* headline. I let it go for five minutes then got up as if to go to the bar. Then, I turned and sprinted towards this geezer and hit him on the run. Full on. I swear I lifted him off his feet. He hit the back wall and slid down the banister like something you see in a movie. I'd never connected like that before and I don't think I ever will as long as I live. It turns out the bod was a Kiwi who was just a mouthy local. What the fuck I did to him I don't know, apart from knock him out of course. The whole place was in stunned silence, so I just carried on walking out of the door. I walked up the street with a smile on my face, and when I was a good distance away I turned round and saw the whole pub standing out on the pavement. The only person who got really excited about it was my mate's brother, believe it or not. Get the fucking irony of that. Stupid prick. I was going to go back but I didn't want to spoil a nice afternoon. Like I said, it's nice to be wanted.

ITALIA 90 – WORLD CUP 1990

This was my first venture on the England scene. At the time, Spurs weren't really that prevalent on the English scene. We weren't even that welcome to be honest. I was determined to change that. I love my country and its flag and that's that. It's only in this country that you get slagged off for supporting the flag, like you're some sort of racist. What a load of bollocks. Thankfully, the last European Championships allowed us to reclaim the flag. It was great to see so many cars on the road sporting it, or to see it hanging from house windows. But once upon a time it was a different story. All I know is that I've always loved my country and I've never been ashamed to show it. For Italia '90 a pal and me really only decided to go at the last minute, to watch the semi-final against Germany – the one where Gazza, God bless him, turned on the waterworks. We arrived in Milan and then we made the two-hour train journey down to Turin for the game. There were quite a few Tottenham out there in different little pockets and, I later found out, a few Aberdeen with them. Nothing much happened trouble-wise, apart from the fact I didn't get into the game. We had a little row with some Germans outside the ground, but they were not really in our class. Of course, we lost that game on penalties, for a change, and I made the long journey back to Milan. Things got a bit better after that – apart from the fact that some local pulled a blade on me in a back alley. We scared him off, but it wasn't nice. Still, we had some good food and beer there and the people were great. I love Italy – the food, the culture. On the flight home, I met a couple of Italian students. One of them was absolutely gorgeous and we ended up going out for a little while in England. She was an exchange student living in Brighton and I went down to stay with her a few times. I was a bit of a rascal then and no one was going to tie me down. But it had given me a taste of what it was like to go abroad with England. I wanted more, which was just as well with Euro '92 coming up – but I've already told you how that went.

1998 WORLD CUP – THE BATTLE OF LILLE

This was my third foray into a major championship with England. After Sweden, it's fair to say that I wasn't even confident about getting into the country. We were heading for Lille, just outside Paris. We were playing Romania in the last group-stage game. Beat them and we might get Argentina in the quarter-finals. What a prospect. Luckily, with France being so close, there's always a way to sneak in so long as you've got your passport. England were lucky to have qualified at all. After that useless tosser Graham Taylor had us fail to qualify for the USA World Cup in 1994 (what a trip that would have been!), we were rescued by the Messiah – Glenn Hoddle. We scraped through the qualifiers, culminating in a battling draw in Italy. And battling is the word. While the players were giving their all on the pitch (for once), the England fans were being smashed to pieces by Italian riot police.

So, it was on to France. I hadn't long finished my three-stretch and was under a five-year worldwide banning order, but rules are made to be broken, aren't they? I have to say I was amazed my passport was not pulled. Not that I'm complaining. The night before we went, a few of us met up at my local, including my mental Aussie girlfriend. It was a great night; life was good then. A beautiful girl, great mates, going to the World Cup in the morning. Enough said. We had a massive flag with THFC through the middle so we trooped outside for the obligatory photo-call. I still smile at that photo today, apart from the Aussie witch in it, for whom I ended up doing time in an Aussie detention centre. The next morning, we were off. I had my leather satchel bag, Armani shorts, plain shirt, leather sandals. I didn't want to look like a typical England fan. And it's how I dress anyway. We made the train with minutes to spare – Waterloo to Lille in under two hours. Fucking amazing. Three of my Palace pals were waiting for me on the train, Eamon, Frank and Tony. It was great to see them and so far so good. Head down; no fuss. We settled down to the usual banter. I've known Eamon and Co. for years and, as the majority of my people are north of the river, it's important to have such good friends close by. I was quite subdued on the journey. I was having a bit of trouble with my love life, to be honest. My relationship with the Aussie girl was a disaster waiting to happen. We'd both walked out on long-term relationships, mine of ten years, hers of five, so the karma was bad from the start and it was starting to take its toll on me. If I'm honest the whole thing was based on lust on both parts. Nothing wrong with that, of course, but that sort of relationship does tend to end in tears.

All in all, it was not a good time to be going away but I tried to stay focused on the job in hand. The train pulled into Lille on time and there we were. No sign of Old Bill yet. As we got on to the station concourse I broke away from the boys, heading for a passport-control queue made up of families and holidaymakers. The policeman there was smiling, so I took a chance. 'Hello,' I said. He took a quick look at my passport. 'Bonjour, monsieur. Welcome to France.' I'm in! I knew there were police everywhere, English and French, so I had to get out of the station before I was recognised. Keep cool. Luckily, there was a commotion going on in the corner causing a distraction. I kept walking and I was out. I met my Spurs boys down the road as arranged. 'Where's Phil?' I asked. Blank expressions. The commotion in the station was him being carted off. Can you fucking believe it? Of all people. I felt really bad as before we left we both agreed that if one of us was sent back the other would go with him. But it was too late now; I was through.

We made our way down to Lille town centre. Stormtroopers everywhere. There was a big shopping centre to my left with riot police ten deep. They were obviously expecting World War III to break out and they were not far wrong. When we entered the main square, it was full of bods, proper people. It looked like all the firms in England were concentrated in the square. Birmingham had a massive firm there, so did Leeds. I knew that when it started to get dark things would liven up big time. Birmingham started to kick off with Wolves – just what the stormtroopers wanted. They love it with England, the Northerners. While all this mayhem was going on, our little band of desperados, about thirty-strong, was tucked away in a little back-street bar. All top boys, though. I walked into the bar and saw some of my old co-defendants and the rest of my pals sitting in there. I couldn't believe it. We all fell about laughing. We couldn't believe that we'd made it out there and had all found each other. That's one of life's great mysteries. Wherever you go in the world, you always find your own people if they are near by. As we sat there chatting, tear gas canisters were flying all around outside. Occasionally, one would fly into the bar and someone would kick it back outside and carry on talking. I swear, none of the boys even spilled their beer. We were not going to get involved in what was going on outside. It was all Brummie nonsense. If it had been Chelsea outside, it would have been a different story. We'd just landed and the last thing we wanted was to get involved in a domestic, get spotted and get fucked off out of it before the real fun started. We left the bar and made our way to our digs, not a bad little place, and then went off to explore our new neighbourhood. We were fired up and ready for anything. We nearly had a little altercation with some French youths, but it was all a case of lost in translation more than anything else.

By the time we got back to the main square, it was starting to boil up nicely, but it was going to be a muggy turnout fighting the riot police. There's not much mileage in it. They're too well armed, plus, believe it or not, I can't stand senseless violence! Give me Chelsea or Dutch or German fans any day. We decided to fuck off lively and get into Lille town centre and see who was in town. The bars were heaving with English, the locals looking on nervously and the bar owners grinning at all the money they were making. I just hope they had decent insurance, that's all. We headed towards the Arab quarter where I bumped into Tim and a couple of his pals. At the time, he was just starting to get involved with me. I always liked him, and now he's game so I was proved right. We were walking along this quiet street when out of nowhere a scooter came screaming by with a passenger on pillion, shouting something which obviously wasn't friendly. Also, the cunt had something in his hand. He turned and came back. The bike and its passengers were brought down in a rain of boots and fists. The locals weren't going to like this. We headed to a bar down the street to gather our thoughts. There were about twenty Wolves in there and we told them it was probably going to go off with the locals. We had no real bad blood with Wolves at the time so we went outside and set out some tables and chairs. Soon after, I saw a bunch of people heading down the road towards us, all armed and ready to go. We were well outnumbered so I went back into the bar to get some back-up, but the Wolves bods didn't want to know. Slags. I ran back outside. One of them was standing in the middle of the road waving a pair of nunchucks around himself like Bruce Lee. Enough of that. I picked up a table, ran across the road and smashed it over his head. He went down like a lead balloon. I could see that the rest of his little firm didn't fancy it now but I knew we had to keep going. Tim and the others came screaming up behind me and the locals started to back-pedal. A few objects were thrown, a few optimistic fists lashed out and they were on their toes. What a fucking result. Brilliant stuff. The adrenalin was pumping and I was now on that delicious post-fight buzz. To anyone who hasn't experienced the feeling, it's just impossible to explain. If you could bottle that feeling of victory after a little battle, you'd make millions. We went back to the bar where the Wolves boys were standing with red faces. They couldn't even keep eye contact with me. I didn't have to say anything to them. They had to live with their shame.

It was getting close to kick-off and the priority now was to try and find somewhere half-sensible to watch the match. All the strange little bars and cafes were full to bursting. We dived into what looked like a half-decent bar on the corner. It looked like it was into football. Inside, it was a fucking madhouse, with people literally dancing on the bar. No sooner had we stepped through the door than some little bod came up to me and announced that he was Carlisle. 'You're not very big for Carlisle,' I said, taking the piss. This took him back. I knew exactly what he meant and he knew exactly what I meant. I was still buzzing from our previous encounter. 'Tottenham's here,' I screamed in his face. 'Go get your boys and we'll have it whenever you fucking like.' He walked away a little confused. I didn't realise that half the fucking boozer was his boys, but he didn't realise that there was only a handful of us. The rest of the boys looked at me as if I'd taken leave of my senses and I can't blame them because I was thinking the same. I knew we had to get tooled up, so we went outside and found a skip, which was pretty lucky. Skips are armouries, pure and simple. We grabbed everything we could and, when the first fucker put his head out of the door, we let them have it big time: bottles, bricks, bars, the lot. They had no choice but to retreat into the bar. They obviously thought we had loads outside. If you have enough front, you can sometimes get away with it – but only sometimes. We heard sirens and knew that that was that. Unfortunately, a few of the windows had gone through, which isn't our game. I leave that to Chelsea and West Ham. There's no surer way to give the Old Bill the hump anywhere. You should know that they place a higher priority on property than on people's lives. At football, especially. So we're on the move again. The place was boiling over; there were English everywhere. All football bods swimming in different directions, all going against the tide. The robocops had now got the manor well under control, so there was nothing left for us. To add insult to injury, England lost the fucking game, so it was back home on the Eurostar for me. Well done, England, the fucking con-men of world football. The amount of money they have taken off the man in the street under false pretences is criminal. Would I do it again? What do you think? Also, I would just like to say respect to the boys from Cambridgeshire and Bedfordshire who stayed with me throughout that night. It was fun while it lasted. We always knew deep down that we weren't going to make it to the Argentina game.

CHAPTER 8

FEYENOORD, AMSTERDAM'S MONSTER FIRM

THE history of Spurs and Feyenoord is a brutal one to say the least. It goes back to the 1970s and 1980s when Spurs were the first English club side to be banned from European competition after a savage night in Rotterdam that resulted in near-fatal stabbings on both sides. I have friends who still bear the scars from that night, and there really were some horrific injuries. The catalyst for all this mayhem was that Spurs were in Feyenoord's end in numbers. They started at the top of the stand and ran down, cutting through Feyenoord like butter, only to end up at the bottom in a pitched battle played out on TV to millions back home. This was all before my time, but in the 1990s I was involved in two big battles with Feyenoord that helped to continue the rivalry.

For the first one, we were playing Nottingham Forest on the Tuesday in a League Cup game so we decided to go to that first, then on to Harwich, then the Hook of Holland. The ferry we travelled on was one where I used to work. I wanted to squeeze in the Forest game as we'd had quite a few naughty rows with them up there in the past. One funny incident that always springs to mind happened when I went up there on a ban. In those days, you were just banned from the ground, not the whole city like I am now. As I was crossing the Trent, I got separated from the others as I couldn't go into the ground. I was spotted by a few of their boys so I nutted the geezer in front of me and fucked off lively to the astonishment of his two pals. I jumped into a passing taxi. I asked the driver what was on in town that day and he told me horseracing. I'll have some of that. So off we went. The Old Bill had spotted me, so a police carrier began to follow us. The taxi driver saw the carrier and decided to drive nice and slow as he thought they were after him for some driving offence! So there we were, motoring along at all of 5mph. The Old Bill obviously thought I was heading off to a pre-arranged meet, so you can imagine their faces when I was dropped off at the racetrack. I gave them a wave and went in. I put a fiver on a horse ridden by a new jockey called Frankie Dettori. Love a duck, it came in. It's the only luck I've ever had on the horses.

But for this Forest game I wasn't so lucky. There was a bomb scare that delayed kick-off and we had to leave at half-time to catch the ferry. All the usual hi-jinks were going on at sea. It got so bad that people were actually afraid to go to sleep in case you woke up with your head shaved or your eyebrows missing. With my long hair, I knew I was a prime target – though, if any fucker had tried, it would definitely be a case of man overboard. In the main bar, my old mate Chinner was teaching a group of bewildered tourists how to swear in a London accent, which the silly fuckers seemed to be enjoying. Eventually, we arrived in the Hook and then made our way to Amsterdam. We were young, not so dumb and full of come, and this was three nights before the game. We ended up in a little place just off the main square, right in the middle of the red-light district. What could you do? There was a lot of fun and games going on, I can tell you. I remember going down to breakfast in the morning and, as all the other guests tucked into their ham and cheese and muesli, we ordered red wine and Stellas. Those were the days. I look back now and wonder how I survived it. I have to say in my defence that I've eaten food from all over the world, and while Holland is a beautiful country the food is fucking shit. As you can imagine, the hi-jinks from the boat carried on in the hotel. I remember pushing a pal of mine down the stairs. At the time, I thought it was hilarious, but I could have killed him, poor sod. Sorry about that. Amazingly, he was fine. Another night, pissed up and God knows what else, I woke up to go for a piss. For some reason, Tel had emptied a load of Dutch coins over my hair as I slept, so when I stood up they all fell out. In my freaked-out state, I thought they were actually falling from my head. Tel still thinks it's hilarious to this day.

The night before the game, we headed for the Bulldog Bar, where every Brit goes on a visit to Amsterdam. Places like this are usually hard work and worth a swerve, but when in Rome... As expected, it went off a bit and a few silly cunts got proper slapped for their trouble. It was time to hit the streets again and we ended up in the side roads and alleys where the Moluccans control everything. That is until a naughty firm like ours comes along and upsets the equilibrium. If they went for us, we would go back harder. And so we did when one of them was dragged off a pushbike and battered because he had tried to cut one of ours earlier. My pal Kenny and me had another set-to with a bunch of them later as well. This was fuck all to do with football and fuck all to do with Ajax or Feyenoord. It was just inner-city shit. We were all used to it from London, so they can bring it on all night. The Old Bill were going mental, literally driving into people. Time to fuck off lively. We mobbed into a bar in the more touristy bit of the red-light district where we settled down to talk things over for the big event. Then there was a big commotion at the door. I went outside to see what all the fuss was about. Standing there in a moody tracksuit, with his name on the back in case he forgot who he was, was Herbie Hide. He was fighting some other bum in the Hilton Hotel, I think. Anyway, all the boys were slapping him on the back, wishing him luck and all that. He was loving it. Then he said to me, 'Thanks for coming to Amsterdam to support me.'

I replied, 'Fuck no, mate, we haven't come to support you; we're here to support Spurs.'

With that, he spun round with his entourage and walked off, shaking his head.

By now, it was time to get some rest, which meant playing table football at the hotel bar until 5.00am and trying to chat up the hotel cleaner who pretended she couldn't understand us. The morning of the game came round and the weight of history was heavy on my shoulders. We started mobbing up from early afternoon at the Grasshopper pub. I have to say we had one of the naughtiest firms on records in that boozer. People had flown in from around the world. When we left the boozer, we must have had between 400 and 500, an amazing turnout on foreign soil. I knew straight away though that this was too big a firm and that the Dutch Old Bill were shitting themselves. There was no way they were going to let us loose. I think we stayed too long in Amsterdam and should have gone into Rotterdam straight away, but there you are. We were herded on to the train and made our way to Rotterdam.

When we arrived at the station, I was on fire with anger and passion. 'Come on, come on, let's fuck these Dutch cunts right up.' All the boys were in the same state. The doors clicked open and we stormed out on to the platform. We could actually see the Dutch down by the stadium staring up at us. Come on, you pricks. We stormed the fence, but were beaten back by riot police. We tried again and a few got over. They reckon there was over 1,000 Dutch Old Bill backed up with our Old Bill for the game. Everyone was trying to break out, and amazingly we fucking did. Come on, come on. I was jumping up and down like a complete maniac. Fuck, we could actually get away with this. The Dutch were getting braver and closer. Come on, you fucking pricks. With that, a massive roar went up and we went into them *and* the riot police. The mugs had it on their toes straight away, but stranger still so did the Old Bill. This was unbelievable. What the fuck was going on? With that, the Old Bill ranks parted and there in front of us was a massive cage. The cunts. It was a set-up – apart from Feyenoord running, which was real and expected. Riot police with guns, horses, vans and dogs had now joined in. They were seriously nasty individuals who had obviously been brought in to do a specific job. We had a running battle with them that lasted a good ten minutes. The Dutch pricks were now behind the cage and taunting us big style. We had to get at them and in my desperation I sprinted towards the cage, which was blocked at both sides by an army of robocops. I actually took off and nearly jumped straight out of the fucking thing. I knew I had one shot at it, no more. My foot just missed its mark and I fell backwards, landing heavily on my left foot. A few of the boys had come with me and did exactly the same thing, although one of my pals actually got on top of it before he was beaten back. It was worth it though to see the Dutch run back fifty yards when they thought we'd got over the fence. This just about summed them up.

This was a fuck-up. We were corralled like cattle for nearly four hours before the fucking game had even started. We thought that by arriving early we could catch the Dutch Old Bill out, but with help from their mouthpieces from the Met it was never going to happen. It was heart-breaking, what with the firm we had. The majority of us never even had tickets, which proved we came for business. I didn't care about the game. I wanted their mouthy firm: the same firm that turned out thousands for Ajax and terrorised most of Holland; the same firm who have it regularly with the Germans. A few of the boys who had tickets were allowed into the game. By now, there was a whole media circus around us, taking pictures like we were animals at the zoo. When the local Old Bill realised that about 90 per cent of us didn't have tickets, the writing was on the wall. They brought in a load of coaches to bus us out of town, and for a while it went radio rentals again. Next stop: back to Amsterdam to drown our sorrows. All we could hope for was that the Dutch would show at our place the following week for the return leg. As we sat in our little bar dissecting everything, the local news came on: 'Spurs hooligans caught by riot police' and all that bollocks. There was one funny aspect to it, though, when my old pal Chinner got nicked for allegedly thumping a police horse. I could sort of believe it. Even though he could practically walk under the fucking thing if he wanted to, he had the heart of a lion. I haven't seen him in a while but I'll always have a soft spot for him, as a few years later he was to be my co-defendant in the Chelsea trial, for which he received two years to my three. I said I'd give you a mention, so there it is. You deserve it, pal.

So, game over and back to London. I couldn't wait. I know it's a shit-hole at times and full of scumbags but, as the saying goes, a man who's tired of London is tired of living.

FEYENOORD AT HOME, 1991 UEFA CUP, SECOND LEG

This was our time. The firm was at its peak. If Feyenoord showed their heads in London, then Feyenoord would go. The streets and pubs of the West End were ours. If they were foolish enough to actually set foot as a firm in Tottenham itself, it didn't bear thinking about. We firmed up in the West End early in the afternoon as word had got around that they were in town. They had sold all their ticket allocation – something foreigners normally never do on English soil – so it was happy days. We split into two groups on Carnaby Street. I walked about thirty/forty bods out of the alleys of Carnaby Street and on to Regent Street and my eyes locked on to a little firm, roughly the same size as ours, walking past the Aquascutum window as if out for a Sunday-afternoon stroll. I knew straight away it was Feyenoord. All that lay between us and the team we despised most after Chelsea and the Gooners was the traffic and a road gang. Fuck the traffic. It would have to stop for us. We quietly strolled out on to the road, hands up, traffic-cop style. The road gang saw us and just stopped and stared. The cry went up: 'Yids, Yids, Yids, Yids.' I usually get pissed off with that being used, especially by cunts in pubs who have no right or bottle to use it. But this wasn't one of those times; we were going into battle and all is fair in love and war. The words struck the fear of God into them and for a few seconds they just stood there like rabbits caught in the headlights. We went straight for the throat, straight through the roadworks and into them. Half of them ran away. The ones that stood had their fate sealed. Bone hit bone as a vicious little row took place. The roadworks near by became a ready-made armoury, not that much of it was needed. The Aquascutum window bowed three times before finally crashing in. Some were left where they were; others literally ran in front of cars and buses to get away. Job done. I know it sounds callous, and I'm not trying to justify anything and two wrongs do not make a right, but you have to remember the brutal past between our two clubs, and a lot of our people were badly cut over there in the 1970s and 1980s.

Back in Carnaby Street, another little firm of theirs was giving it the big one in a back-street boozer, thinking they were safe. They were wrong. The other half of our firm walked in and made sure of it. I still wasn't satisfied. I knew they were bringing thousands, so where was their main firm? Surely this couldn't be it. I give them credit, though. At least they had the bollocks to actually drink in the West End. I think they were somehow expecting not to find us there.

We made our way back up to the Lane. It was getting dark and Tottenham was buzzing with the anticipation of another historic European Cup night. I still had faith in the team then and was certain we could have turned around a narrow 1–0 defeat from Holland. We only needed two goals. Two poxy goals, not much to ask, is it? Well, yes actually. As usual, the mugs on the field let us down badly, going out 0–0. I fucking hate 0–0 draws. What's the point? I'd rather lose 10–0. Maybe that's a bit extreme, but you get my drift.

We waited and waited and waited for Feyenoord to show. We had plotted up all over the High Street and then the strangest escort I had ever seen up the Lane started to snake up the High Street as far as the eye could see. It was an impressive sight, except that it was all coaches. I couldn't believe it. Feyenoord's firm had come by fucking coach, knowing full well they would get an escort straight from the ferry. What complete and utter tossers. To make matters worse, the fucking idiots were actually giving it large out of the skylights in the coach's roofs. It was a silly thing to do and any little bit of respect I had for this Dutch Chelsea-style firm went out of the window. Obviously, the coaches were getting bombarded with missiles from every side, but that's a muggy game as nine times out of ten you end up hitting some poor fucker who doesn't deserve it. It's also a silly nicking. But these pricks deserved everything they got, although as usual they were protected like gold dust by our Old Bill, who showed a ferocity and hatred for us I have not witnessed since. Was this getting political? I think so.

The coaches parked up round the back of the Lane, lined up as far as the eye could see. This was going to be our one and only chance. I was going to get at them if it was the last thing I did – which it nearly was. We had plotted up in the Park Lane estate when from nowhere riot police with dogs and on horseback sealed every entrance and exit to the little estate. They then unleashed an unprecedented attack on us, wading in with riot shields and fists and boots on anyone that moved. There were fucking hundreds of them and it was well on top. I admit it was a scary situation as we were totally trapped. They weren't bothered about nicking. It was like an assassination squad sent to take out certain individuals, and I was one of them. I remember being surrounded by dog handlers who goaded me into having a go. I lashed out at one dog. 'Put the fucker away and we'll go,' I said.

They just laughed and laughed. 'Come on, hard man,' said one copper. 'Where are your pals now?'

'You call this fucking brave?' I spat back. I lost it for a second and told one of them to take a walk.

Thankfully, I was pulled back by one of my pals. All around was mayhem. Those bastards went into us with relish, something they'd obviously wanted to do for a long time. People received head wounds and other assorted injuries, with one of my close pals losing two of his front teeth. But out of sheer bloody-mindedness I still made three or four attempts to get to the Feyenoord escort as it was brought through. It was impossible though as there was an army protecting them. And we're supposed to be the thugs. Don't make me laugh. The Old Bill in London love a good row at football as much as we do. It never ceases to amaze me the way they protect the opposition supporters with a passion, but wherever we go, abroad or in this country, we have to take on their firm and their Old Bill together.

FEYENOORD V SPURS, 1983

For once, these aren't my words. This is one man's account of what went on that dark and crazy night. Take it away, mate:

Some games are just meant to end up in violence. One such was Feyenoord v Spurs in the UEFA Cup in 1983. We had heard from some of the older faces about the battles out there in 1974, with Feyenoord and the Dutch police. Now it was time for us to go out there and find out how good this Dutch firm was. Rather than go out with the main firm, I decided to go out with a few Northern Spurs mates, Rich and

Cheg from Chester, Tony from Northwich and a couple of Midland Spurs as we wanted to go a couple of days early. Our first move after arriving in Rotterdam and getting somewhere to stay was to go up to the ground and buy tickets for the Feyenoord end. We had to better the boys of 1974 and they had done the business out there. After buying our tickets, we sneaked into the ground for a look and noticed that the Feyenoord end was like nothing I had seen before, with a couple of flights of stairs, and the stand then being set back a good bit. This was never going to be easy to take, but I knew Spurs were going to have a go. That night we were drinking in a disco pub in the town centre, and a mob of Feyenoord walked in. I thought it would go off but they were quite friendly and spoke better English than my two mates from Chester, and started telling us stories of how they battered Ajax and we replied by telling them how we battered Arsenal and Chelsea and anyone else that gets in our way. At the end of the night, we went our separate ways, but agreed if we met again on the day of the game it was fucking war and the truce was over. The morning of the game came around and there was Spurs everywhere in every bar. The sounds of 'Glory Glory Halleluiah' and 'When the Spurs Go Marching In' rang out. The word went out to meet at a massive English pub called the Double Diamond, and leave together at 5.00pm. Like prats, we went for one last look around the red-light area and got to the Double Diamond at 5.10pm and found it empty. It was a sick feeling to know we had missed the main firm. We walked around and then found a coachload of Spurs in a pub with a couple of our top older boys with them. We had a couple of beers with them but couldn't get on their coach as the driver was a jobsworth who didn't want to overload. We were now on our own, so we marched down to the train station. To a team like Feyenoord, five drunk teenage Spurs was an easy target and within a minute a little firm of them fronted us. We went straight into them, backing them off. Another bod came down the stairs at us. We stood there and said, 'We're Spurs, who wants it?' Unfortunately, they did, and pulled out blades to prove it. Good old Dutch police turned up and saved us getting cut to pieces. They put us on a cattle truck that stopped near the stadium for our own safety, as by now every platform was full of Feyenoord looking for Spurs stragglers. We got off near the ground and it was going off all over the place. I found out that one of the top older boys I knew off the coach had been done in the back with an axe. Spurs had cut a few Feyenoord up already. We lost the two Midland Spurs and Cheg during one of the rows, which left me, Rich and Tony on our own. We decided to go into Feyenoord's end and keep quiet until our main firm came in. As we got in there the whole end was singing 'Argentina, Argentina', a reference to the Falklands war (which had finished the year before). I would probably describe it as the most fanatical end I have ever seen. The hatred for Spurs could be seen in everyone's faces. To be honest, we lasted about a minute before they sussed us, and we had to get out quickly. Some stewards took us round to the Tottenham end and said we were lucky not to be killed. I can't explain the relief I felt when we got into the Spurs end, with 4,000 other Spurs around us. We were standing there for about ten minutes when we spotted a firm of about a hundred Spurs marching up the stairs into Feyenoord's end with our two lost mates with them. Then they gave a massive charge and every single one of the hundred went flying, fists first, into the Feyenoord mob, who tried to fight back but were getting battered. The end started to open up as Spurs kept moving forward. The roar came up from our end of 'Hello, hello, Tottenham aggro... Tottenham aggro', the battle cry whenever the Spurs firm went into action. Then, within two minutes, they had fought their way into the top of the end. It was then that they made the worst decision they could have made. If they had stayed where they were, Feyenoord would not have got near them. But they decided to move to the centre, which gave Feyenoord a chance to get together again and come from behind, pulling out knives and stabbing the people at the back of the firm that were separated from the rest. The police had by now arrived and started to take Spurs out of the area. For the first time ever, a mob had infiltrated Feyenoord's Kuip end and battered the fans big time. But the truth is that we also suffered the biggest amount of casualties in any one single row, and I felt sick when I saw the mob escorted round the pitch with a few stab wounds and cuts.

One fan lifted his shirt up to reveal his stomach ripped open. A picture of this was used on the front page of the *Daily Mirror* the next day. As the firm climbed back into our end, the riot police started to batter them, so we turned the tables and battered the riot police. The violence continued throughout the game as a mob of Spurs had a top row of seats at the side of the ground and we climbed into them and had a two-minute toe-to-toe with some more of their boys before getting caned by the riot police. We finally saw our two mates who'd been at Feyenoord's end. They'd lost their shoes and were covered in other people's blood, but they said it was their best row ever, and in true Scouser style they had nicked some shoes off some Dutch fans. After the game, the violence continued, with Spurs getting revenge for the stabbings by throwing two Feyenoord off a bridge and cutting some more. By the time we met up with everyone back in town, everyone agreed that no one would have done the business out here like we had done. Not Millwall, not West Ham, no one. This night, in 1983, we proved to the whole of Europe that we are the governors.

There you have it, straight from the horse's mouth. I can only imagine what it must have been like that night.

CHAPTER 9

DEVOURING THE WOLVES

WOLVES AWAY, 15 MAY 2004

This one had been a long time coming. The game was right at the end of the season, plus, before that, Wolves had been in another – lower – division. Say what you like, but I'm convinced our fixtures are set by the police, not the FA and its computer. Big Brother? You bet. We'd played Wolves earlier in the season and they were pathetic. They came as far as King's Cross, plotted up in a boozer and stayed there. What the fuck was that? I'd expected much more as they had been giving it plenty of mouth that they were turning up in force. They even made a call to a friend of mine and said where they were and how many they had. He told them not to bother because they'd get annihilated, which they most certainly would. I had all the troops – 200-strong – in the pub by 11am, so they made a wise choice fucking off back to the Black

Country sharpish. But this was different. We were now going to their manor. They had just been relegated so they had fuck all to lose. I knew this one would go. They would have no choice in the matter as we were most definitely coming for them. The 8.30am train from Euston would get us into Birmingham International at 10.30am. Lovely. That's the time you need to get somewhere, and I had it on good information that Everton, who had played Wolves a week before, had all been put in the ground at 11.00am and there was no way I wanted that to happen to me. We were a good 100-plus at Euston at 8.00am with more on the way and more already there. I really did not want to waste this firm. I wasn't going to go straight into Wolves and give it to them, show them what a proper firm looks like, because you have to think about these things rationally. Big word, I know. I still hadn't worked out how to approach it by the time we got near Birmingham International, but after discussions with the Northern Spurs boys, who said the Old Bill would definitely be waiting for us, I made my mind up to get off at Tipton, one or two stops before. We ended up in a fucking pie factory, believe it or not, which was too far from the station for my liking. The geezer in the pie factory was chuffed though, as he probably sold up on the takings. In fairness, he treated us really well, so thanks for that. And, yes, I did have a top pie in case you're wondering.

The local plod tracked us down to Tipton and decided to keep us company. We were a bit of a freak show for the locals who'd obviously never seen anything like it before. Fuck this, I now knew nothing would be happening before the game. Had I made the right decision to get off at Tipton? I'm not sure. I know one thing for sure, with 200 of us on the train, they'd have never allowed us to get off at Wolves. So, the twenty or so of us that had got off at Tipton made our way to Wolves on the local train, escorted by the cops, of course. By now, it was nearly 3.00pm. We'd had a bit of nonsense with the local plod on the way. They were totally outclassed and totally clueless about what they faced. We drove them back three or four times and dictated the pace. Wolves made a half-hearted attempt to get over the flyover, but that's all it was, half-hearted. As we approached the ground, the adrenalin kicked in big style. I was ready for anything. A little too hyped. Plod were all over me and I had to calm down. One particular nasty piece of work took a dislike to me so I needed to get into the ground before I was nicked. One of the Northern Spurs bods lost it outside the ground and took a terrible beating from Old Bill, which obviously provoked a reaction. To top it all, I had this lunatic copper trying to force me into the ground, but I didn't have a fucking ticket. One of the boys had got me a ticket on his season ticket, but with the Royal Mail being full of thieving parasites the ticket went west. In fairness to the stewards up there, they could see the hard time I was getting off the plod and more or less told them to fuck off, as there was nothing I could do if the ticket had to be collected from the box office. Even a local tout said he'd give me a ticket if mine didn't turn up. He must have bought a job lot, poor fucker, going by the fistful he was brandishing. Still, it was a nice gesture. Eventually, Marcus turned up with my ticket. Happy days. I spread the word around to meet five minutes before the end. Everyone was there so it wasn't hard to do. It was good to see Paul, Ed and the Park Lane boys there. So were Mark, Keith, Sammy, Neil – all legends from the past who have my total respect, even if they don't think so personally. I salute you. And to the back-stabbers: bollocks to you.

We came out as one. It looked a bit chaotic as they were let out as well. I knew it would go off. I could smell it in the air big time. We walked back up the hill towards the station and town centre, where the Old Bill were flapping big time. They tried too hard to herd us in at the top of the road. I was having none of it. I spotted a fucking great big gap that wasn't policed. It was crazy. It was only a thigh-high wall that led out on to the front of an estate with a little green that led straight to where we wanted to go. It's quite funny when I look back now. It was like trying to stop a dam bursting by putting your finger in it. Once one went over the wall, the rest followed like lemmings. There was a cascade of bodies pouring over, unstoppable, even for the riot police. We were out free and running. Let the game begin. Through a garage forecourt and into a car park, exactly the place they'd had it with Everton the week before. Where were the fuckers? Here we go. They were on our right across the road, trying to get across. Old Bill were having kittens, trying in vain to keep the two warring factions apart. I leaped over the railings and into the road, running to the front to signal my intent. Fuck me, who's this? Fifty bods were right in front of me. Somehow, they'd shaken off plod. There was lots of jumping up and down on their part but nothing more. They wouldn't come any further. It gave the Old Bill time to steam in, which if they are honest is what they wanted. It was gone now. I tried in vain to get at them again, but it was too late even though they were long gone. At least where I was it was too late: the boys at the back were having it with them. I didn't know this until a few minutes later. Someone asked me why I wasn't there. I can't be in two places at once, can I? Normally, I would take great offence to that sort of question and would answer it with a smack in the mouth, but as it was in the heat of battle and emotions were running high I rose above it. Cheeky cunt, though, and lucky.

'Get to the left,' I screamed. Plod were trying to put us back in the station but I had other ideas. I wanted another go at these mugs. We broke away again, about forty of us, down past the station, a big wasteland to our right. We were in the middle of nowhere. What a shit-hole. The road widened and headed towards the subways. That will do. Five or six Old Bill, including our spotter, broke away to shadow us. At the bottom of the hill, there was a boozer, back street, middle of nowhere, right round the back of the station. It was like a scene from *The Long Good Friday*. Shall we or shan't we? that is the question. I am not one for smashing up boozers for the sake of it, but it does feel fucking good, I've got to admit. It's also a sure way to get your efforts recognised – although it's not always the recognition you want. If plod get you on film, you're nicked. Now it just happens that Tottenham Old Bill were pointing a camera straight at me. This cooled my heels considerably. One of the boys put his head in the doorway. No response. It was packed inside, which was strange to say the least. But they didn't want to know and we're not Leeds, Chelsea or West Ham who are into smashing up empty pubs or ones that are full of Joe Public.

So we moved on, followed by our little fan club. We had come full circle and because of the geography of the place there was nowhere else to go except back to the station. It meant going under the subway. Now these were supposed to be the famous subways of legend, of the subway army and all that bollocks, surely it would go there.

We walked on deeper into the lion's den. We came out into daylight and the welcoming sight of the train station. I was knackered and we must have run miles chasing Wolves, leaping back and forth over metal barriers and fighting plod all the way back to the station.

We were met with the surreal sight of seeing our own firm being escorted into the station. This was mad! There was lines of plod with all the locals lined up behind them, mostly shirts.

The Old Bill panicked as fucking usual when they saw us and one heavy-handed prick pushed me in the neck from behind. I went back at him, but it would have been stupid to have been nicked then (although I came very close). I had been stabbed in the neck before so I did not take kindly to being touched there. This provoked angry scenes on the station concourse.

What with everything, I went down to the end of the platform and collapsed down on an empty bench. That was me. I was exhausted. There was a funny train guard keeping me amused though while I was waiting. He seemed to hate the Wolves firm, the local Old Bill and every fucker in Wolverhampton itself. He got a sympathetic ear from me and, when the train pulled in, I plonked myself down in first class, while he ran around telling the other guards to fuck off and let me sit where I wanted. Nice one, mate.

Back at Euston we were met with a battalion of riot police, fully kitted out in Darth Vader mode. It seemed as if Leeds had been going mental, up to their old tricks, smashing up boozers in Euston and Kings Cross. Chelsea and Arsenal (the scum) were also firmed up and shouting in the background.

WOLVES AWAY

So happy days and we had just arrived to enter the mix. Why though, with the firm Leeds brought down, they were not smashing up the Kings Road, was beyond me.

Later in the evening, they did smash Chelsea, though at Camden Town! They released us onto Euston concourse in groups of ten or twenty at a time. Fucking great: you have all these young mugs in London firmed up, and we were being released in dribs and drabs. I could sense it, something was going to happen. I was proved correct.

ARSENAL ON THE TUBE

The Old Bill really did a number on us. The train pulled in screaming and it was battle time as it entered the last stages of the journey in darkness, bursting out of the tunnel with lights blazing. It just about summed up London, kicking up a hundred years of filth into the already rancid air. Welcome to the London Underground system on a Saturday night; where angels fear to tread.

The doors rang and swung open menacingly, daring us

to get on. We took the bait. The carriage was mobbed with geezers. My senses were on red alert. I scanned the carriage. Red and white fucking everywhere. Gooners scum, fuck it! There were four of us: me, Tony, Yos and Paul. They had just finished celebrating the title and were now tanked up and on their way home. Two young kids sat down were the target of their abuse.

'Fucking Jews, fucking Yids'. I nodded at one of the boys. No choice, it had to go. The train pulled away into the darkness once again. The cliche 'Nowhere to run, nowhere to run to' came to mind, except this time it was true as it comes. Imagine fighting in a lift and you come close to what I'm describing. I nodded at one of the boys who was sitting down and without saying a word I slowly walked into the middle of the beast. My eyes werelocked on my target like a guided missile, as was the rest of my body which was then on automatic pilot. I was listening for the snarling, baiting, mouthy Gooner who was having the time of his life.

I dipped my shoulders and unleashed a right hand straight into the instigator's head. He's out on his feet, his mind asking his body why the fuck he was still standing. He slumped against the doors. The proverbial had well and truly hit the fan.

In a surreal moment, two or three bods ran straight past me heading for the other three. I dived back into the melee. The two boys were throwing right handers, once of the Gooners was cut, people were screaming and were running in all directions.

The train pulled into a station after what seemed an age. The carriage spewed out its cargo. Rather than disappear up the escalators I went back for another go. I was consumed with rage and hatred and was after the mug who threw a rabbit punch at one of the boys.

'Get the fuck off now' I screamed. They all cowered by the doors nearest the tunnel. Every time I went into them with fists and kicks. At one point I nearly lost my balance and almost ended up getting dragged into the carriage, which didn't bear thinking about.

'You fucking mugs, you fucking scum' I scream. They won't come off. 'Do you know who I am?' I'd totally lost it. The doors shut vice-like with a bang and it was all over. As simple as that.

I watched the train disappear down the tunnel. One of the boys grabbed me and told me to get the fuck out of there. Which I did. We were fucking elated and grabbed a drink in the West End to calm down. The governor of the pub told us how mad it's been 'round there all afternoon with Leeds running riot'.

'Really!' I said, 'That's terrible.' Back to the Escape bar in Herne Hill for some tunes and pretty girls. What more could you ask for?

CHAPTER 10

NICKED

THROUGHOUT my time on the Spurs firm, I've had one or two run-ins with the law, so I want to talk about my time inside. After our attack on Chelsea, I eventually found myself up in court. I'd been on bail for almost a year, before being handed a nice little three-year sentence at Knightsbridge Crown Court on 29 March 1994. I know that football violence isn't everyone's number-one hobby, but the word scapegoat does spring to mind. If you could see the number of police out on the street on a match day, you'd weep. Where the fuck are they when you need them? When crack dealers are shooting up neighbourhoods and each other? When old woman are being mugged and young women raped on their doorsteps? Fuck off, Old Bill, and do your job and leave what we do to us. To make matters worse, I was dropped in it by a dirty, grassing co-defendant of mine who couldn't handle the bird. Keep looking over your shoulder, Brian Humphries. I hope it was worth it.

My co-defendants' sentences ranged from nine months to two years. Altogether, the fucking old lunatic of a judge handed out 108 months' worth of time. Thanks for that, mate. I knew that I was in trouble when my barrister started summing up with the words: 'Of course, Mr Tanner must go to jail.' Fucking hell, even my own barrister had given up on me!

I remember going to a little boozer at lunchtime with the boys when we were suddenly called back to court. I had just ordered a Bud and I asked the barmaid to look after it for me. Little did I know that was to be my last drink for a few years as I was remanded straight away. That's when it clicked that I'd been grassed. On my way to Wandsworth, sitting in a tiny sweat box (prison van), I looked out at Westminster Bridge and all the other familiar landscapes: the Castle on the river, where we had all spent so many great times; people going to work; to the pub; in their own little world on the outside, while we were trapped on the inside, looking out. I touched the Perspex glass; everything was so near but so very far away. Despair, sadness; I think numbness described it best. We started off in Wandsworth, which has a bad reputation as one of the toughest nicks in the country. I was in there for a few months and I have to say I settled down fine there because it's a time killer. Then I was sent to Down View.

I thought long and hard about going into detail about my time inside. Believe me, it's a book in itself. The other boys with me had their own experiences and they're for them to tell. This is how mine went.

We all suffered personal losses. Three of us lost close relatives while we were away. It's something that will be with us forever, but we came through it even stronger. When my nan died, they let me out to pay my last respects, but sealed off my road. I'll never forgive that, never, never. God bless you, Nana.

Selina fucking Scott. I'd just done a three, trying to get my life back in order, when one evening I turned on the television and there was a programme about people caught on CCTV on. *I-Spy* it was called. And who's that starring in the credits at the start of the show? That's right – yours truly. Cheeky bitch. No royalties or anything. I actually went to see a media lawyer to ask if I could sue Carlton Television as I'd served my time and didn't need to see myself on TV every week. Not very clever for jobs, relationships, that sort of thing. The lawyer was about as much use as a chocolate teapot.

To reflect back on it all, the hardest thing for me personally, apart from the obvious like missing family, girlfriends, losing my job and missing out on life in general, was having to watch each of my co-defendants going home before me. That was hard. I cannot explain the feeling. You have to understand these were not just co-defendants in the literal sense of the word; these were and still are my close friends. It was like watching a member of your family walk out on you. Of course, I was over the moon for them on the days of their release, and I hope I never showed any different. I was quite hard on some of them inside, but that was my safety mechanism kicking in.

I think the world of them all and it means a lot to be able to put this in. I hope they realise that.

Days out here and there cannot compensate for being inside. It must have taken its toll on my mind, I'm convinced of that. If I was an Irish terrorist or, pardon me, a freedom fighter, I'm sure I'd be holding a big fat compensation cheque by now. What do you think?

TOWN VISIT MAYHEM

Towards the end of my sentence, the jail I was in used to reward a drug-free wing with town visits every other weekend for a few hours on a Saturday afternoon. These were good and bad, as anyone who has been on one will tell you. It's fantastic to go out to see your family or friends, but at the same time an absolute killer to go back; and many people simply didn't, and amazingly this seemed to happen when they had done nearly all their sentence – a phenomenon which is hard to explain.

Ninety per cent of my visits were with my then girlfriend and which we spent doing what comes naturally. Thankfully, at the time I didn't have children, which would have thrown a whole different perspective on the matter; but as I only had myself to look after, now and again you need a run-out with your pals. As I was at the end of my sentence, now was as good a time as any.

Anyone who says jail is easy is either a scumbag or a fucking liar. It's mentally, more than physically, that it takes its toll. For me, this was the case anyway and these visits were a great release mechanism. You cannot be locked up with your own thoughts, away from your loved ones and children for a certain length of time without it having an effect on your mental health.

Don't get me wrong, a lot of people belong in jail:

nonces, street muggers, filth like that. But there are also a lot of people who don't. Although there were obviously people in there doing a lot longer sentences than my three years, everyone's sentence weighed on them in its own way. I remember one young black geezer who was in the cell next to me in Wandsworth. I think he was doing three months or something like that. I'd only been weighed off a couple of weeks and he came up to me and said, 'If I'd got three years, I'd have killed myself.' I thought at the time, 'Thanks a fucking lot,' as I still had a year and a half to do, but I could see he was suffering and tried to calm him down. I told him that before I even got allocated to another nick he would be back on the streets in no time. It didn't help that he had been put in with a nutter who should have been put in a mental asylum instead of a jail.

During the night, my worst fears came to light as my new mate lost the plot completely and caved the other bod's head in with a broken table leg. All I could do was lie there helpless in the dark and listen to the screaming of alarm bells and the screaming of human beings crying out in pain. It only ended with the thud of the Kangas – the screws – as they stormed the cell next to me to pick up the pieces.

In the morning, the peter (cell) was being washed out as I passed by with my bucket of piss to slop out. I glanced in to see the remnants of blood being washed away. 'Move along, Tanner,' growled the screw. The nutter did survive, as nutters always fucking do. As for my new pal, I guess he's doing a lot more than three months now.

That's the brutal truth of prison: inhumane conditions, human degradation and every now and then animal instincts rising to the surface in devastating fashion. It's not like that shit programme *Bad Girls* or Ray Winstone strutting about, giving it 'I'm the daddy'. In today's jails, all that bollocks wouldn't last two minutes.

Croydon town centre became my little haven during my sentence, as that was as far as I could possibly go and make it back to jail in time on my days out. We met in the centre of town and a lot of the boys had come out to meet me, which was a fantastic boost. I knew even then it was going to be hard going back. Anyone that hasn't been in that situation will never understand that feeling of putting yourself back in jail. It goes against every basic human instinct you possess. People are not meant to be locked up, it's as simple as that.

We ended up in a new bar just beside the market. Everything was good with the world for a couple of hours, but I was constantly watching the clock and asking the time. Terrified that you will be late puts everyone with you on edge and makes you out to be a lunatic with some sort of time phobia. But everyone knows: five minutes late, no point in going back as you are now officially on the run.

I felt fantastic. I was fit, coming towards the end of my sentence and the alcohol felt great, as my body had not had any crap in it for months. None of the excessive junk we all gorge ourselves on in the free world. I was surrounded by close friends and soon I would be free to join my loved ones again. One of the boys with me on the visit had two months left on a ten-year armed robbery sentence. Terry was a Millwall bod, but also well known to the local bods I knew in Croydon. He was good to have around and we all liked him.

As I was leaving the bar, followed by a few of the boys, there was a high-pitched scream just to the right of the bar. As usual, everyone was just walking by, doing fuck all. There was this big black geezer who had a bird round the throat and was also tugging at her bag. Well, it didn't take a genius to work out what was going on. I broke my golden rule not to get involved in domestics, as we have all been out with an hysterical woman and then some nosey cunt sticks his oar in and makes everything ten times worse. This was a straightforward street mugging though. I ran into the bod and smacked him straight on the side of the head. He released his grip and then turned his attention to me and we had a proper toe-to-toe for a couple of minutes. Chaos was going on around me now, as other people joined in, thinking I was attacking this geezer for no reason.

Eventually, I knocked him to the floor and he got what he deserved, a good kicking. The Old Bill sirens started up and the mugger disappeared. The bird disappeared too, so I made myself scarce as well, not wanting to endanger my freedom. I couldn't believe this was happening. As I ran off, a couple of market workers decided to make themselves busy and got their barrow of fruit and veg turned over for their trouble. The Old Bill were falling all over the potatoes as they chased me. It was like something out of a film. As I turned a corner up a steep hill, I literally ran into the Old Bill. I was fucked, I couldn't take another step. I was just about to say something when I noticed a puzzled look on the Old Bill's face, which gave me a little bit of hope so I kept quiet.

When we got back to the station, they asked for my

name and address. 'Down View Prison,' I said. Classic. I was put in a police cell and for the next thirty minutes I thought my world had come to an end. But it quickly came to light that I was only running as I'd stopped a bird being mugged. They asked for a description of the attacker, but that's not my style. Mind you, even if I wanted to, I couldn't remember what the ugly cunt looked like.

They took me back to prison where I was given a hero's welcome by the boys. Even some of the screws were pissing themselves. I learned a hard lesson though and from that time on I never took another town visit. Back inside, I asked the boys where Terry was and they told me he'd gone AWOL. I couldn't believe it. I felt half-responsible, but he was a big boy and knew what he was doing. It turned out he had a bit of personal shit on the outside to sort out and handed himself in a couple of weeks later to finish off his sentence. They added a few weeks on, which is fuck all to someone who has been away for over five years. I said to him, 'That was a long town visit,' and we had a good laugh about it. I think he even got out before me.

The rest of my sentence passed without much incident. Most of the screws were cool with me but there was one who was a horrible little prick, who obviously hated the fact that I was doing time for Spurs in a South London jail and that I was obviously from South London. What pissed him off the most was that I was respected and well liked by the majority of the wing. There was one particular time when I was coming out of my cell and I heard him talking to a few of the boys on association. All

I heard was, 'How can you let him bowl about like he owns the place?' I carried on walking and copped an imaginary pump-action shotgun above his head when he wasn't looking. The bods he was talking to pissed themselves laughing, so his little game backfired big time.

The late Roy James, who was the getaway driver for the infamous Great Train Robbery, was on my wing and I bent his ear a few times for pearls of wisdom on prison life. I found him to be a true gentleman. I knew he was unwell and I urged him to keep on at the screws for proper medical attention as he was always getting chest pains. Tragically, a few years back, I heard on the grapevine and read in the papers that he had died of a massive heart attack. If he'd had proper treatment earlier, I'm sure he would still be alive.

I was eventually released from Down View on 12 September 1996. I can still remember the feeling when I heard the screws' footsteps approach my door to unlock it. Then the heart-stopping moment when they actually stop outside your door and you see the lock turn. 'Tanner, get a shower, get your kit: you're out of here.' The best words I've ever heard – after being told I was a father. It's an indescribable sensation. Feeling brand new is as close as I can get for you.

I partied long into the night that weekend. I got the whole firm together down at the Buzz bar in Central London, a place we used all the time – until the boys had a few serious situations in there and battered a few Chelsea faces one afternoon and it became too hot. It was a great night. No grief at all, just young, free and my whole life in front of me and a stunning blonde on my arm. Actually, she once thought the world of me but I fucked that relationship up – something I'm not proud of.

A mate of mine, Dave, was over from America at the time and we had a few good nights together after I got out. He's a top bloke. He's someone who has seen it all before. In fact, he'd had his throat cut years earlier in an East End pub. Some say it was West Ham, some say locals. Anyway, it's irrelevant. They left him with a twelve-inch scar across his throat. After that, he got fucked off with the gang warfare in London and moved to Las Vegas. He's got some fantastic tales, like the night the boxer Lloyd Honeyghan slept on his settee. This is the same Lloyd Honeyghan that ripped the world Welterweight title from the seemingly unbeatable Don Curry in 1986.

And, while I'm on the subject of boxing and Dave, here's a little tale worth telling. Dave was over again from the States and we met up. We were both massive fight fans and Tyson was fighting Bruno that weekend. The fight was on in the States and was being shown live on UK TV at something like 3.00am, so we set off to find an all-night boozer on Wapping that was used by all the newspaper workers based down there. We started off in my then local, the Vic in Bermondsey. We stayed until midnight, then pub-crawled our way to Wapping. Bruno lost as usual but at least he went out on his shoes. The atmosphere in the boozer was fantastic. Everyone was in a party mood, regardless of the result.

Dave and me got chatting to a couple of birds, one of whom was stunning (it's always just one, isn't it?). They were high-flying City girls and had a flat looking over St

Catherine's Dock, right next door to Tower Bridge. Dave and me both steamed into the stunner, but for some reason she took a shine to my irresistible charm. Dave took it like a gent and settled for the other one. The blonde and me were all over each other within minutes. Even though she had a fantastic job, she was a Northern girl and really down-to-earth. We moved on to a restaurant called Babe Ruth, which was done out in an American baseball theme. Funds were getting seriously low by now as we had been out for nearly two days, but the girls weren't bothered and a gold card was swiftly dispatched over the counter. As Dave lived in the States, he was in his element with all the Yank cocktails and insisted I had a Long Island Ice Tea. I'm not really a spirit drinker, but I had one for the road and it nearly blew my fucking head off. Then I had another. I dived into the khazi, threw it up, washed myself down and went back for another. This happened about four times. We eventually got a table and sat down before we fell down. We tried to eat but were just too mangled.

I was having a fantastic time with my new girlfriend and all we needed was a room. The next thing, I just came out with it: 'I love you. Will you marry me?' She launched herself at me.

'Yes,' she cried.

Dave and the other bird are sitting there, stunned, so we order Champagne. Somehow, the waiter found out and the next thing it flashed up on a giant screen above the whole restaurant: 'Congratulations T and your stunning bird on your engagement'. With that, the whole place applauded and cheered and another bottle of bubbly was sent over, with Dave cheering and laughing like a lunatic. There you are, engaged within forty-eight hours. I actually did go out with her for a few weeks. She was serious about it all, but as I got to know the people around her I knew it wouldn't work out. It was only a matter of time before I knocked out one of the City pricks.

CHAPTER 11

THE RICHMOND BOYS

NO Spurs book in my opinion would be complete without some input for this little firm. They have the respect of everyone at Spurs, especially the older generation. At their peak, in the late 1980s, there were fifty-plus of them. Not bad for a little firm from the suburbs. I've known the Richmond boys for many years and have a lot of time and respect for them. They're good people, and not just because they can have a row. It's the way they go about their business that I like, and I like to think that it is reciprocated. Make no mistake, though, they're a naughty little firm. I for one was eager to hear of their exploits, as I'm sure are a lot of other little firms that have crossed them in their time.

I wanted to use their words as much as possible, so I decided to go along and interview them. Names have been changed to protect the innocent (and the not-so-innocent).

How did your firm come about?

Paul: We all met at school and were all Spurs fans. We came from different areas around Surrey and we met up at Richmond because it was the nearest tube stop into London. We were made up mostly of bods from the Twickenham area and none of us actually lived in Richmond itself. There were little pockets of us from all around, a good hardcore of forty to fifty of us. We used to congregate and drink in Twickenham and Richmond on a Friday night and we were the hardcore of this little area.

We just grew and grew. We were like a little pilot firm. We didn't particularly want it with the bigger firms, we just wanted to go out and do as much damage as we could.

Stuart: At first, it took us a while to get to know each other, but after that it was plainly us. There could be nothing worse than going into battle and getting turned over because you didn't know who you were having it with.

You have a big rep at Spurs. What game or row would you say cemented your reputation? Like myself, I know you have an intense hatred of Chelsea, maybe you could tell me about that.

Paul: When it comes to Chelsea, with us it was personal. When we went up North, for instance, to be honest they were not in our league. We used to go up there and cause mayhem. We used to just steamroll any little firm that got in the way and come home. With Chelsea, one particular row that sticks out was at New Malden in the early 1980s. A few from North London came over as well, but it was basically the Richmond Spurs. What you have to remember is that us forty-odd Richmond Spurs were on the frontline at most of the away games and we wouldn't budge for anyone. We were fucking solid. We all knew each other and we knew each other's strengths. We wouldn't bottle under pressure. Double the numbers against us and we'd still come out on top. No bullshit.

We met Chelsea at a wine bar in New Malden.

When they arrived, we were already plotted up; there was about seventy or eighty of them. We weren't even playing them that day. It was a Sunday night and had nothing to do with football. It was personal. It was the Chelsea firm from our area, so it was a local thing.

When they came off the train they were already tooled up and came steaming out of there with bits of wood, rocks, tooled up to the fucking teeth. We were on a bit of wasteland and had the higher ground and they just let go with everything. This went on for about five minutes, then suddenly they ran out of things to throw at us. That's when we attacked them. We went through them like a dose of salts. I was chasing this geezer and I heard a bang like someone had let a shotgun off.

Simon: It wasn't a shotgun though. The geezer ran straight into the bus shelter and cracked his head against it.

Paul: We were tooled up as well as them. We absolutely

mullered them. Chased them up to the train station and they ran down the tracks. We mugged them right off, and remember that was their firm and our firm. That sticks in my mind the most: we grouped for our two firms to meet head-on. We both stuck to the agreement. They turned up and we fucking mullered them, simple as that.

What's the naughtiest firm you've come across over the years?

Stuart and Simon: West Ham, without a doubt.

Dave: Yeah, West Ham and Everton.

Paul: West Ham and Stoke City. Stoke were like proper fucking geezers. We had a row at Stoke where we ran into their end and they came out like you wouldn't believe. They were geezers. They smashed us for twenty minutes without a shadow of a doubt. Put us right on the back foot.

Simon: Remember, though, we were young then. It was like geezers fighting grown men.

Stuart: What about when we went up there and fought toe-to-toe with them for twenty minutes all the way down the road, non-stop.

Paul: They were backing us off because we were thirty-to forty-handed against a fucking end full of geezers. They were just coming at us from everywhere. We didn't really have any choice but to fight them.

Personally, I think that West Ham are overrated. Do you agree?

Paul: I think they had the psyche over us really. They were no way near as good a firm as us, but they had the psyche over us. Back then, they were better organised, that's the difference.

Simon: West Ham were like a tight-knit community then.

Stuart: That's right. Back then, they all knew each other. Spurs fans come from all walks of life, from all over the place, and it's taken years for everyone to get to know each other and trust each other. That's why I think Tottenham are stronger than West Ham now.

Apart from Stoke and Chelsea, would you say the West Ham encounters were the naughtiest rows you ever had?

Stuart: No, I would say the naughtiest row the Richmond firm had was when we were playing Everton at Tottenham and all the Richmond went back to Euston station. We were all sitting on a wall outside Euston, about thirty of us. All of a sudden, you could hear them singing 'E.V.E.R.T.O.N.' at the top of their voices as they came out of the tube. Then their fans came up the stairs, a good hundred of them. They spotted us straight away and started giving it. We end up having it right outside the station. Out of about thirty of us, there was about five or six who never got cut that day. As we were fighting, one of my pals stood back and said, 'They fucking got me with something.' We looked at him and there was claret shooting everywhere. They fucking had blades. There was such a little mob of us that we had to have it on our toes. As we ran down the road, I looked at my mate's back and it was opened up from top to bottom. Another geezer was cut right across the head. Thank God, there was a hospital across the road. I carried my pal into the hospital and the Scousers followed us in. All of us were covered in claret and they were still trying to get through the doors and have it with us in Casualty. I picked up a fire extinguisher, stuck it through the door and let them have it. Then the Old Bill came storming in. At first, they were going to nick me but soon calmed down when they saw how badly we were all cut.

Paul: They slaughtered us because we were trapped. Outside Euston, you've got that horseshoe shape and unfortunately we had to move because they had blades and the only way to get away was to climb over an eight-foot fence. If you did that, you got it from behind.

Stuart: Looking back, it really does affect you. I was only young then and you think, Fucking hell, that's not going to happen to me again. So, the next time they came down to London, I made sure I was armed. I thought that if they've got blades then I'll go one better and I got myself a little axe. When I told everyone, they were pissing themselves. Everyone was going, 'What have you got? What have you got? He's got a fucking axe.' Everton were playing at West Ham, so we got to the station early to wait for them to come in. There were about seventy of us waiting for a train of 200-plus. They came out and it went off. We chased this little firm of about twenty Scousers, about six or seven of us. We cornered them and they all pulled out blades. I went, 'Fucking blades,' and pulled out my axe. The whole fucking lot of them ran off as one. We chased them as far as we could but they got away. As we came into the station, I saw one of my pals rolling around on the floor with a Scouser who had pulled a blade and was just about to cut him. Instead, the geezer got an axe across his boat. They got run absolutely everywhere that day and it was all over the football scene. The mad axeman, all that sort of thing.

What do you think of all the other football books out there? I don't read them much, and I think a lot of them are bollocks.

Paul: I got hold of this Bristol Rovers book and I read about three chapters and thought, What an absolute load of bollocks. I got to the fourth chapter and the geezer goes, 'I just thought I'd let you know that my second team is Chelsea.' That summed him up for me. I just shut the book as I knew then he was telling porky pies.

Tell me about the Pompey row you had when they were playing Wimbledon. I have family down there and get on well with all their boys. I know they respect us, as I do them.

Paul: Pompey was a one-off. It came at a time when we had drifted away a little bit from going up to Spurs, week in, week out. There were a lot of nickings at the time and the Old Bill were on us. A lot of the boys turned to other things as it was getting harder and harder over there. At one time, the whole day was a freebie: the trains, getting in the ground, but as things tightened up people had no choice but to do other things. How it came about with Pompey was they were playing Wimbledon, which was a local team to us. A group of us got together, mainly Spurs, but also a few close mates from other London clubs. We met at Wimbledon train station to have it with Pompey because we knew they were an up-and-coming firm. We walked around Wimbledon looking for them for about an hour and a half and not a sausage. A few people were carrying bits and pieces so we plotted up in this boozer. About half an hour later we were sitting having a drink outside by a bridge when up walks this enormous firm. The road outside was literally full of bodies. Some geezer looked at us and said to his mates, 'This firm looks like they want to have it.' Well, with that we just steamed them everywhere. They couldn't believe it. We smashed them from pillar to post. They thought we were Chelsea but we soon put them right. If you ask any true Pompey supporter, he will tell you about that day, because we ran them everywhere.

I missed the Richmond firm at its peak by roughly half a generation. That saddens me as we could have had so much fun.

H, myself and Snowy. Two of my best pals in the world out striking a pose. Outside the Cockerel Bar (now shut); the scene of many a drama over the years.

Above: 1990 World Cup, Turin, Italy. From left to right: me (with the long hair), Mark, Luds, Kieron and John. All of us a lot younger, fresh-faced and on the march for Spurs with England and still pals 16 years later! This picture is pure gold.

Below: Me and H in the garden at Roothies.

Above: Scottish League Cup Final 26 November, 1995. Aberdeen (with backs to the camera) kicking it with Dundee.

Below: The Pittodrie Bar. With the ASC (Aberdeen Soccer Casuals) after watching Celtic vs Aberdeen. It was just like watching Spurs as AFC lost.

Above: Feyenoord vs Spurs.

Below: Tottenham vs Arnheim (pre-season 1999). The boys enjoying the cafe culture.

Above: Bobby, me and Nev who runs the security on my beloved boat (the Tattershall Castle). We had some great times when we weren't arguing. Taken on the Embankment gangway to the boat.

Below: Spurs waiting at White Hart Lane for the Gooners.

Above: Spurs trying to get at the Gooners, when Arsenal were at White Hart Lane.

Below: Me and Terry (centre), my oldest friend in the world. Surrounded by some of the boys. And yes, you've guessed it, another night at the Gilpin. Unfortunately, we haven't got much choice where to drink as the Old Bill have shut down every decent boozer we had in Tottenham.

Top: A few of the boys striking a pose outside the Gilpin.

Below: Tottenham Yoof. The gamest and oldest youth firm in the country; just ask West Ham!

Paul: We always tended to keep ourselves to ourselves. If you're in with about 200 it's really easy to get nicked, so we never really mixed in too much. We'd always go up to away games on the earliest trains, turn up at different times. I swear, we went in every away end at every ground.

What were your most active years?
Paul: Probably 1979 to 1986.

Tell me about Cardiff City last year. What's your take on it?
Paul: Cardiff was fantastic. They had a bit of a rep, but I can't remember seeing a Spurs firm like it in memory, ever. Every man and his dog turned up that night, it was awesome.
Dave: We must have had about a thousand out.
Paul: The High Road and outside the ground was like a *Who's Who* of football hooligans at Spurs. They just did not know which way we were coming from. We were coming out of every alleyway, every corner, every house, kebab shop, chip shop, you name it.
Simon: The Cardiff fellas we knew were convinced it was another Luton turnout, with Chelsea, West Ham and every other fucker there.
Paul: The only time we have ever had a couple of bods from another firm was when Pompey had Wimbledon, because that was a local thing.

What happened to the poor geezer that was killed on the escalator crush against the Mancs? That was your era, wasn't it?

Stuart: Yeah, that was when we all first met years ago; we knew him well. He was a right nice geezer. We were above the Mancs and they were at the bottom of the escalator throwing everything up at us. Then they pressed the emergency button and everyone fell forwards. At first, he was just sitting there, and then he was taken upstairs as we were all being led away. We learned later from the newspapers that he had tragically died in hospital. He used to work on the railways and we'd go down to Waterloo, to the railway club with him.

Paul: Going back to that era, we had a big downturn then and the Gooners were coming into their own with the Denton–Miller era. Before that, 200 or 300 of us would go into the North Bank and just charge and they would run away. But by this time they had a few more bods in there. There was one time when Stuart and me were quietly standing there and Miller and his pal with the Mars bar fronted us, giving it, 'What are you doing in here, Yid cunts?' We looked at each other and just went bang, knocked them both out. With that, the whole fucking end went forward.

As you said, Spurs had a dip in the 1980s. What would you put that down to?

Paul: Like I said earlier, loads of nickings. I was nicked five times in one season. Plus, when you have 200 and it's the same thirty at the front every time they're bound to become too well known.

Did you rate the Gooners back then?

Simon: Yeah, I did.

Stuart: No, because they've never ever done what we have, ever. [Paul and Dave agree.]

Simon: But we haven't always had it all our own way. I remember being chased from White Hart Lane with two of our faces back towards Stamford Hill. Then they came back in the evening to attack the Bull.

What year was this?

Paul: It's hard to remember, mate. Early to mid-1980s, I think. It was an early kick-off, about 11.00am. There were only about forty of us, so we decided to go to the Bull and regroup because we knew they would come over. We got to the Bull and it was embarrassing. There were thirty people in there, tops. The governor Tony said we had to defend the pub. We heard they were coming so we tooled up as best we could. We came outside and they filled both sides of the road. It was unbelievable. A good 300 of them. Well, they came up the road and we fucking held them.

Did you ever get a result against West Ham?

Stuart: At King's Cross once.

Paul: Everyone was there as well. When we got in the ground, everyone was up the other end so we decided to walk along. They came at us and, to be honest, at first we went. Then suddenly everyone got together and went into them. After the game, it was all-out. They were on one side of the road and we were on the other with Old Bill in between. We were on top that night, we just kept coming across the road, attacking, attacking. We just didn't let it go. They knew they had been in a row that night.

Dave: All you could hear was coins pinging against the windows. Bottles as well, you name it. Even a big old dustbin got launched across. It was just a constant battle.

Tell me about your trips abroad in the 1980s. You've got plenty to choose from, not like now, which is just my luck.

Paul: Anderlecht away, 1984. Spurs abroad was a different level. Two levels up from the league games.

Simon: It was like going to a country with no law.

Paul: And we were lawless people. We stole, thieved, fought and blagged everything. We made our way out there on the ferries with all the usual lawlessness. A few geezers had gone out there a couple of days early on the piss, including a geezer called Brian Flanagan, a great friend of ours. A fearless, strong geezer. Just eighteen years old. His old man ran the Finsbury Tavern in Finsbury Park. He phoned and told us to come over early, but we couldn't get over because of work commitments. He was drinking in a bar and there was a dispute over the bill. As Brian left the place, he was shot in the back and killed instantly.

Did anything happen against Anderlecht that day?

Paul: Not really. They were not in our league, but the Old Bill copped it that night. As you can imagine, feelings were running high. We went back to the district where Brian had been shot and smashed the place to pieces, and anyone that got in the way.

You had some battles with Bayern Munich, didn't you?

Paul: Bayern Munich was a completely different kettle of fish. We went out there a week before. We stayed in a pension and told the woman who ran it that we were English students.

Stuart: We had a fight every night.

Simon: The old girl in the pension would show us the paper and say, 'See what the English fans are doing.'

Paul: There was a team there called Schalke 04 and they hated Bayern. They were all skinheads and they came in our end with us, about forty of them.

Simon: On the night of the game, the pitch was covered in fog and you couldn't see the game, so someone said, 'Oh well, let's do the Germans.' We smashed them to pieces.

Paul: We had it out there every single night. We were fighting with the Germans, fighting with each other sometimes, fighting over prostitutes; it was the night of a thousand knives. Someone nicked a till out of a boozer and a gun was fired off into the ceiling. It all went off.

Dave: We never went to a ground and didn't have a row, either in our end or theirs. Man United at home; thirty of us went in with them.

Simon: Watford away. I mean, who the fuck fights them?

Paul: We made it our business to find out as many people as we could. Even if there was a firm going home in different directions at Waterloo, we would be there to meet Millwall or Pompey or someone. Sometimes we would lose, and sometimes we would win. We used to drink in a boozer by Waterloo Bridge, so we'd have it with anyone going through the station. It was our manor. One Saturday night, there was a mod party going on, about 500 of them, so we had it with them. It was like our birthdays and Christmas all rolled together. There were scooters in the river, the lot. We bashed them silly. Welsh rugby fans were a pain in the arse too, and sometimes we would still be fighting with them at 2.00am in Twickenham High Street.

Finally, would it be fair to say the team that Richmond Spurs hate the most is Chelsea?

Paul: Without a shadow of a doubt. As I've said earlier, it was personal and we made it our business to hound them whenever we could. I got fifteen stitches at the Ilfield Tavern. But our boys stood firm. Even though I walked out of there covered in blood, we did them.

CHAPTER 12

HAMMERED

WEST Ham hold no fear for me whatsoever. I know that before my time the boys had a few harrowing experiences against them, but times change and the pendulum of fate has swung back well and truly to our side. Only recently, they threw their toys out of the pram when 200 of their bods couldn't do thirty of ours. Instead, they smashed the boozer up (from the outside) and then whinged about it when they all got nicked. Come on, if you want to pull strokes like that, you've got to take it on the chin. You know the rules.

WEST HAM AWAY, FA CUP QUARTER-FINAL, MARCH 2001

We met up at Brick Lane for this one. Cosmopolitan, trendy: just my sort of place. It would also provide great cover, as I was sure it was the last place the Old Bill would expect to find us. The problem was getting there in the first place. We had to duck and dive a bit to avoid the local plod, but come meet-up time the boys were there.

The turnout was less than expected if I'm honest. I tried not to let it show but deep down I was really pissed off with certain people. Whenever we played West Ham, it was always the case that certain people went missing or were suddenly on holiday. I was determined to show that there was fuck all to worry about, and that it was no different to playing Millwall or Boro or Birmingham away. Being brought up with a South-London take on things helped. It had always been drummed into me that they were fuck all. Make no mistake, though, in the late 1970s and early 1980s, when an old pal of mine was running with them, they did have a lot of fun and had a naughty little firm.

Anyway, so far so good. There were a few stroppy cunts knocking about as you would expect in East London, but I was determined not to get dragged into some silly little local scuffle and fuck up the main objective. By the time we go to Plaistow, where West Ham had called it on, we were a good seventy- or eighty-strong. I was happy with this. Not too big and not too small, because whatever you think of West Ham there's no point going there twenty- or thirty-handed. That's just silly and you'll get all you deserve.

On the train there, it was made quite clear that no one was to take a backward step (and no one did). The train pulled into Plaistow and this was it. Time to lay some ghosts to rest. This was our time and we had to take it with both hands. I was so fucking pumped it was unbelievable. We poured out on to the platform and I really wanted to smash the gaff up big time. We sprinted up the stairs, not a sound except for the collective beating of adrenalin-pumped hearts. Would they be there, just beyond the barriers? Please be there. We staggered out of the darkness of the ticket hall into the bright sunlight of Plaistow High Street. Fuck, fuck, fuck, they're here. Fucking go straight through them. A few of the boys did just that but the majority of us were well and truly captured. And it's not West Ham: it's Old Bill, fucking hundreds of them. Tottenham Old Bill as well, with a full camera unit.

We tried to break free but it was no use. We were fucked. I could see their fucking boozers just down the road. We were only yards away. I was devastated. Some grassing cunt had once again wrecked what I'm sure would have been one of our finest hours. Still, the day wasn't over and if I'm anything it's optimistic. At least West Ham knew we were on their manor, that much at least I could guarantee. We tried a few more times to shake off the police but it was a no-go. But, even so, for a change we all had tickets – or so they thought – and up to now we hadn't done anything wrong.

As soon as they had us where they wanted us, the Old Bill turned all nice and polite and put us in a boozer until kick-off. They searched us all and took mug shots, which was a nice memento of a day out in East London. I felt a bit sorry for the poor punters enjoying a quiet Saturday drink in a back-street pub when the police suddenly led us lot into their boozer. You should have seen their faces. They all had that 'this could only happen to me' expression. Can't say I blame them. But the boys were good as gold though.

As it got closer to kick-off, the Old Bill were getting nervous. They knew they had to split us up. Those without tickets were told to stay where they were. I admit that I was enjoying myself in the pub, having a giggle with the barmaid, but I really wanted to show for this one. Normally, I wouldn't give a fuck about the game, but this time I wanted to march right through their manor and into the ground, loud and proud.

When we came outside into the escort, I saw how many of us actually had tickets, and it wasn't that many. In a strange way, this just got me pumped up even more. I knew because of the numbers we had the Old Bill would ease off a little at some stage and I would get a chance to break away. I stood right on the edge of the escort as we came close to their boozers, right in the firing line. We were surrounded on either side. I could hear the baying mob and my adrenalin was up. The Old Bill were panicking and I took the chance to side-step between two of them. I was out on the white line in the middle of the road, facing the boozer, hands apart. I stood out like a sore thumb, wearing a beige three-quarter-length Stone Island coat, blue jeans, white trainers and a white woollen hat with a fucking big bobble on the top (don't ask).

I had a manic grin on my face. Come on then, you fucking mouthy cunts, I'm here, we're here, come on, for fuck's sake. I was urging them to break through the thin blue line as they more than had the numbers. One of them was screaming someone's name. 'Fuck him, I'm here,' I screeched back. Fuck this, I'm going for it. Then all of a sudden my body was slammed unceremoniously back into the escort, which by now was all over the place, as all the boys had followed my lead. We were now playing up big style even though it hadn't gone off properly. I could see West Ham were fucking mad as I would be if a firm came marching through my manor like this.

They were shadowing the escort now, so the fun would soon begin. 'Watch my back,' I said to Paul. 'They want me bad.' We tried to go into one particularly mouthy cunt and my pal ended up whacked with a metal stick. The Old Bill were starting to lose it so I took a chance and threw a hopeful right-hander at some horrible cunt who was getting too close for comfort. I missed, much to his amusement, and nearly got trampled under a giant police horse. As we approached that fucking monstrosity of a ground (what the fuck is that castle thing about?), the Old Bill got back round us in proper numbers. As we crossed the road to go into the away end, it was like the parting of the Red Sea, with thousands of them either side baying for blood. The funny thing was that about ten of our boys were standing right there with them. I was going to say hello but I don't think they would have appreciated that.

I really didn't want to go in. In fact, I was fuming that I had a ticket now that I had done the walk. The adrenalin was nearly overpowering me, plus I had an uneasy feeling about leaving the boys behind in the pub – and I was to be proved right. I didn't even bother going up into the stands. I knew even we would beat this lot and I think Rebrov scored one of his very rare goals. Sure enough, my instincts were right. I had a phone call to say a mob of West Ham had attacked the boozer during the game. By all accounts, the boys did really well, considering their numbers, and backed West Ham off before the Old Bill turned up in force. Apart from a few broken windows, courtesy of West Ham, and a few terrified locals, everything was cool. Oh, apart from one copper who got cut. Needless to say, a few nickings were made, and a few naughty charges were handed out, more in spite than anything else.

I was like a caged tiger after hearing the boys' news. I just wanted to get back out there. I tried a few times but it was no-go. By now, the Old Bill knew that we knew. Just before the end of the game, I saw one of the most surreal sights I've ever seen at football. Four guys came running past me at speed with the smaller one in the middle holding his head down with a hat and scarf on. I just managed to get a glance at his face. No, it can't be! 'Ian Wright, you cheeky cunt,' I shouted after him. He turned his head while still running for the exit and flashed me a grin and then was gone. I couldn't fucking believe it. This was the prick that had scored countless goals against us in the last fucking minute. I had literally dreamed of strangling him with my bare hands and he'd run straight past me underneath a stand at West Ham in our fucking end! You couldn't make it up. They must have brought him through from another part of the ground. He can't be a closet Spurs fan. Can he?

Final whistle. We did them, 3–2. But that was the last thing on my mind now. I said to the boys, 'Stay together. Let's finish this.' We got outside, headed down the road a bit and it was off. I smacked one and kept going, bearing in mind I was like a moving target in my white bobble hat (why I didn't just take it off I don't know). We went through the depressing streets of this part of London. It always seemed to be dark there, whatever time of the day it was. The Old Bill were going loopy as we were on one side of the road and West Ham on the other, and all the way to the tube there was sporadic fighting. We were more than holding our own but a lot of people let the Old Bill split us up, which was fucking stupid. I said to my pal Paul, 'Whatever you do keep with me.' So what does the greedy fucker do? He stops for a kebab. He ended up getting booted up the arse by a little firm. When he told me about it later that night, the thought of him sitting on his arse covered in a kebab nearly made me wet my trousers. The worrying thing is that he thought it was hilarious himself. He's a good boy, though, as game as they come. I think the world of him even though I give him a hard time.

Nothing much happened after this. We did try to get it on with them later but some people had had enough. It did go off at Liverpool Street later and the boys did OK there. A few people fucked off a little bit too early, and J and me had an argument about it, but it's more to do with the Old Bill splitting us than anything else. We couldn't have done any more. It would have been fantastic if the Old Bill hadn't been waiting for us, but that's life. The fact of the matter is we were on West Ham's manor at 11.00am at the point where they wanted it. I think that all in all we could claim to have done OK and came out with a lot of credit on this one.

I got a taste for West Ham around 1990, when we came over with our emerging firm, fearless and ready to prove a point. We met in our beloved Bull and went straight to Upton Park. A lot of the boys that I was to go away with years later were with me. We got pumped up on the tube and came charging out to their famous wine bar. I clapped my hands outside: 'Come on, you cunts, the Yids are here.' One of my co-defendants went for it and we tried to steam the bar. But the Old Bill set the dogs on us and you really can't argue with those things. Still, West Ham knew we were there. I was fucking elated; no one does that there. They were shadowing us on the opposite side of the road but the Old Bill were well on top. We tried charging across the road but got beaten back. One of the bods who was with me that day, and I have to say who stuck by my side and was giving it out, would grass me up years later at the Chelsea trial. Fucking dog. You know who you are.

WEST HAM AT HOME, 29 OCTOBER 2003 – THE BANK

I've deliberated about whether to go into this or not because I didn't get over to Spurs until after the main event. It's something that still fucking grates on me. But it happened and if this book is to be true to itself then it's got to get a mention. I'm not going to go into too much detail as people have lost their liberty over it and there's all sorts of legal complications going on, and that's something I wouldn't wish on anyone – apart from nonces and terrorists. I think the general public would be surprised at this strong moral code among the so-called hooligan community. I've been locked up in some of the toughest jails in this country and abroad. I've known some truly nasty, violent individuals. And I know what sort of people I would rather have around me, that I would have round for dinner.

As the saying goes, I will always remember where I was when West Ham attacked the Bank. I was at home, arranging my daughter's Christening with a local priest and my ex, who was sitting there with a face like thunder because she didn't believe in it (and it turned out to be a fantastic day, despite her and her family's pathetic attempts to derail it).

Anyway, there I am talking to the Pie and Liquor when my phone rang. I don't know why but I had a funny feeling it was not going to be good news. As soon as I answered, I could hear sirens going off in the background and my heart sank. I knew it had gone off before my pal had even told me. I'd arranged to get there for 5.00pm, which I thought that would be fine. I was wrong. The sneaky cunts had come over at 2.30pm, up to 200 of them. Fair play to them, though. They came over and gave it to us. I'm really bugged that they didn't call it on properly, instead of coming over five hours early when no one was going to be around. The good news was that thirty-odd Spurs bods split and backed West Ham's huge firm into the station twice, which was a fantastic achievement in itself. Because they couldn't do the thirty-odd Spurs, West Ham took it out on the boozer's windows.

I was in a rage by the time I arrived on the manor, ready to vent my anger on anyone. The usual inquest was in full flow but I didn't want to hear it. Feelings were running high, which was understandable, and I remember one of my so-called pals giving me a 'where were you?' look.

That cunt doesn't know how close he came to having a pint glass wedged between his eyes. The look was enough and the friendship was over. I had more important things to do, like get to West Ham, which wasn't going to be easy now that the manor was like a war zone with horses, dogs, helicopters and foot soldiers running everywhere. It was not a good place to be if you were of the claret-and-blue persuasion. Little mobs of West Ham were getting smashed and their main firm had only themselves to blame. I got put up against a wall by a vanload of Old Bill as I was trying to get to the away end. They released the other boys and dragged me into the van for a Section 60. My heart sank as it was my little one's Christening that Sunday and for one horrible moment I thought that they were actually going to nick me. But because it was kicking off everywhere the driver just forgot I was aboard. They gave me a severe bollocking and fucked me off, which for once for me was very lucky. I must admit I was tempted to carry on, but I'm not a fool and I had to take their advice.

After the game, Spurs went ballistic. I spoke to one of West Ham's bods in a boozer in South London some months after and he told me that he and a firm of West Ham had been run down to Bruce Grove station and that he got a dustbin on his head for his trouble. He said it was the naughtiest place he had ever been to and unlike a lot of West Ham he actually said that he thought we had a top firm and knew that we terrorised Chelsea (which pleased me). All joking apart, I really respected his honest opinion on things.

CHAPTER 13

YORKSHIRE TERRIERS

LEEDS AT HOME, 20 NOVEMBER 1993

This is always a fixture to excite the taste buds. Make no mistake, Leeds have always had a decent firm and as you read this book you will see how many clashes we have had with them. It is impossible to put them all down on paper. All I can say is that I have a healthy respect for their firm, whatever they may think. We went to King's Cross to meet Leeds off the train. I love doing this. I've done it many a time over the years and we're well known for having the bottle to do it. It's a mug's game now, what with all the cameras and the Old Bill, It's a fucking certain nicking but for a while it was fucking magic.

We went into Leeds and the pub they were drinking in before the game. I went straight in the door and it was off straight away. Somehow, the pub caught fire. It was going fucking mad and we didn't have great numbers. It was a crazy move and the pub also got gassed to fuck, which brought them out on the streets. A few got clumped, but just as we were making the move I saw about fucking 200 Leeds coming out of a side road. They were in a pub behind the one we gassed and heard the commotion. It was a brilliant move and we were all elated, but we could also have come unstuck big time if we'd been caught by those numbers. It's a game you win or lose, it's that simple.

I knew that Leeds would be fucking mad when they faced us again next year. We tried it again, searching King's Cross where they usually drink. The Duke of York was empty, the Flying Scotsman, empty apart from a few old tarts going through their routine. Fuck this, where are they? They were obviously not going to fall for it again. I decided to go back to the Lane in case they got there first and went on the rampage with the manor unprotected. We plotted up in the Bull and waited, scouts at the station. What were they playing at? I knew they would not come through. Some of the bods started to get the hump. I exploded on a few that if they couldn't stop moaning they could fuck off to the ground.

There were fewer of us now, about forty or fifty. They were taking the piss. It was 2.50pm. It was obvious the Old Bill were holding them back but that's no excuse. With what they had, they should have fucking come to us straight away. Fuck this. I decided to move further up the High Road before the Old Bill got us as well. I wasn't going to let this fucking firm go, no way. No fucking way. We plotted up in an old black boys' pub called the Ship, where they played dominoes and all that stuff. More importantly, the Tottenham Old Bill would never expect us. 'T, they're fucking coming,' shouted one of the boys. I came out on to the street, which was at the side of the pub, and the sight that greeted me was well worth the wait. They must have had at least 300 or 400 marching past just in front of me. I take it as a compliment when a team brings a firm like that to us, as long as they use it. I had to think quick; no point in going straight at the front, there's too many. They kept coming; it was like a fucking train. I remember thinking that they all seemed to look the same, short and squat. I wanted the middle, right smack in the fucking middle. That would teach them for turning up late. Come on. We exploded out of the doorway and I picked up a traffic cone on the way. 'Come on, Leeds cunts.' We made a beeline straight into them. This was fucking great. I swung the traffic cone like a sword, smacking anyone in sight. There were so many of them that you couldn't miss. I dropped the cone and used my fists; I managed to catch one clean. All around me, the boys were causing mayhem.

Then Leeds started to realise we're only a few handed and regroup. As you can imagine, they were embarrassed and well pissed off. Tottenham Old Bill were on us now and going mental with night-sticks. I was stuck under a horse's head while another was rearing up on its hindquarters, stamping down on anything in front of it just inches from me. We moved back to the pub, battling with the Old Bill all the way. They managed to get us pinned in the doorway. Leeds now tried to take the initiative and started getting brave, coming behind the Old Bill. 'Where were you at midday, you mouthy cunt?' I shouted at one of them. I slipped under the horse's head;

I threw a punch at him and he backed away. A few of the others managed to do the same but a crack across the back of the head from a mug sitting on a ten-foot horse soon brought me to my senses.

I looked back in the pub and we tried storming another door. It was over. Old Bill were everywhere. Leeds were going mad outside, out of frustration and embarrassment. As I expected, the windows soon came in. I swear that through it all the old boys never stopped playing fucking dominoes. Before I left, I had a chat and a laugh with a few locals and got a few drinks in to apologise for the commotion. One of them told me he couldn't give a fuck and actually enjoyed watching me fight with the Babylon police horse.

I'm glad he did. Fuck with the dominoes at your peril. I escaped a nicking that day by the skin of my teeth, only because the Old Bill had to contain the Leeds firm on the High Road. Considering the numbers we had, it was a brave and clever little move that afternoon and I'm going to claim a result on that one. What do you reckon?

LEEDS AT HOME, 1992

There was a time for a season or two where our favourite trick was ambushing vehicles: coaches, minibuses, cars, anything that went up the North Circular. We completely turned our backs for a while on the traditional route down to the tube, as the Old Bill were all over it. I fucking loved it, catching a little firm who had maybe given it large earlier, caught like rabbits in headlights with nowhere to go. For a time, some of the scenes were like something from the Wild West as staves, pavement blocks and anything else was hurled at the buses and coaches. But don't think we were intent on just smashing things up because we definitely weren't. That's the sort of muggy move I leave to Chelsea. It just draws attention to yourself. It only happened in extreme cases, if it was a particularly nasty little firm who wouldn't play ball, and by that I mean getting off the coach and having it man to man.

One such time was when we had Leeds at home. We had run after the firm all afternoon when we spotted a minibus full of them. I went up to the back doors and managed to get them open. (This story is also mentioned in the Aberdeen chapter later.) The Leeds bods dragged me inside: 'You're coming back to Leeds, you Cockney cunt.' I managed to throw a few right hands and fought my way out of the door a couple of hundred yards up the road. Fuck, that was close. The boys thought it was fucking hilarious, as you can imagine.

We headed up to the Globe, right on the corner of the North Circular to chill for a while and lick my wounds. I got talking to a geezer at the bar who said he was a singer. I thought he might have been talking bollocks, but we had a lot in common: like hating that little cunt Brian Harvey from East 17. He said he was in a band that was just shooting a video for their single in Walthamstow and were going on tour to America. He's good, I thought. Then came the killer blow: would I like to be in the video and do some security work in the States for them. 'Yeah, of course, mate, whatever, I'll be there.' We exchanged numbers. It had been a laugh but I was convinced he was a fucking nutter. I threw the number away. The following week I was at home watching *Top of the Pops* and the announcer said, 'And this week's number one is a new entry – East 17 with "The House Of Love".' There, giving it large, is my old mate from the Globe, Tony Mortimer, lead singer and the talented one from the band. Ah, bollocks. I switched over.

Leeds away, 1999
I was just off another ban for this game, so I couldn't be there. I wanted to put it in though, so I interviewed an old mate, Graham, who was there. This is his account.

What was the build-up to the game like?
Graham: We ran two coaches up there and arrived at 11.00am. It was too early and there was Old Bill everywhere. We tried to get in the Peacock but were turned away by the doormen. By then, the Old Bill turned up in force, including the Tottenham Old Bill. They didn't know what to do with us so they took us to Beeston and put us in a working men's club. When we eventually came out, Leeds were on both sides of the road. We kept steaming into them and they ran everywhere. There were less of them waiting at the ground and they were hanging back and didn't really want to know. After the game, as we came out, Leeds were all down behind the goal and everywhere waiting for us, so we got together. I saw a few faces, I won't mention any names, but people I wanted to be with. There was about thirty of us and I got hold of them and stood with them.

There were thousands of Leeds all over the place. We knew we had to stick together and we held each other's coats so that no one could move. Leeds came from everywhere and everyone just kept steaming into them, straight into them. The Old Bill came in and they were getting it as well as Leeds. We carried on walking and some Spurs went into the coach park. Some Leeds followed them in and got done. Most of us carried on walking as the first coach had parked near Wakefield, so we stayed together all the way back to the coaches. Still, Leeds were coming from every direction, but Spurs just kept going into them and we got back to the coaches with virtually no casualties. It was like going back to the 1970s, and I must admit Leeds were well up for it. But Spurs stood their ground and I thought did really well. A lot of Spurs who weren't with us were getting picked off, but the main people stuck together and did what we had to do.

Do you rate Leeds as a firm?

Graham: Sort of. They're very similar to Chelsea in my opinion. You know the old saying 'The Chelsea of the North' is true. They were known for mainly doing smaller clubs and smashing property. To be honest, I've never rated either of them that much, although having said that Leeds do pull the numbers. But we've gone there many times and really taken the piss. One year, we climbed over the fences and had them on the pitch and ran them into the south stand. They wanted revenge the next year but came unstuck again and someone from Leeds died from his injuries. A year later, we went back up there, and there was untold waiting for us, thousands, and we still never had that much trouble. But you still have to rate them up there amongst the Top Ten, along with us, Man United, West Ham, obviously, and Millwall

Where do you stand on the West Ham debate? I think today we have the edge over them, but I hear they were a thorn in our side in the 1970s and 1980s.

Graham: In the late 1960s and early 1970s, Spurs always held their own at West Ham. We went in with a few of the old boys, Ronny Parish, Johnny Hopkins, and would go in the North Bank, and because Ronny was local we were never taken out. But things changed. Early on, West Ham suffered us and we suffered them. There was a bit of an alliance between us, and Spurs used to go in the North Bank for a good few years from 1969 to 1971. But by 1972 things were changing and suddenly West Ham wanted to know. They didn't have it all their own way, but nine times out of ten it was psychological and they did really take the piss in the early 1970s. That was the old Mile End Mob, before their Under Sevens and all that. But then Spurs became a good firm and by about 1976 we really got it together. Unfortunately, we didn't play West Ham in the league for a good few years as they were in a lower division.

We had them in the Youth Cup one night, and they came down in force but still got done in. After that, we played them in the League Cup. We did them as they came in the Paxton Road turnstiles. We held our own for a good few years, so not everything they say did happen. In the 1980s, they thought they took the piss, but not like they do in the books. It was all psychological. We always seemed to play them on Boxing Day, when our firm was scattered all over the place. They were good but not as good as they make out. To be truthful, they were the best mob that ever came to us at any time.

Chelsea we took the piss out of home and away, regardless of what they say. West Ham was a different story; again it was all in the mind, we should have done it better and I believe we had the people there to do better. In the League Cup, we did do better. In the early 1980s, they were there and we did fucking do them. In fact, we took the piss at West Ham that night, and a few nights after that we held our own a lot more than they admit. In the 1990s, I'd say we were the gamer firm, and in the 2000s we've taken the piss out of them.

CHAPTER 14

POMPEY 6.57

'The fighting value of the cockney soldier has been recognised from the time of the Duke of Wellington to the present day.'

THE HISTORY OF RECORDS OF THE
QUEEN VICTORIA'S RIFLES

EVERYONE at Spurs knows I have a soft spot for Pompey as I have family down there. You can find my little girl and me on the seafront in Southsea at various times during the summer. It's a good place to get away from the stress and madness of London, plus I know their top boys and get on well with them.

My first encounter with the 6.57 was in the summer of 1984. I was just a kid really, just starting out on my epic journey with Spurs. I went down for two purposes: to visit family and to watch Spurs. But it got a little bit livelier than I thought and I ended up having a row near the ground with a couple of Pompey. The Old Bill came flying in. 'What's your game, you Cockney cunt?' they asked me. 'I'm Pompey,' I told them and reeled off my aunt's address in Southsea. With that, I got the 'If I ever see you again' routine and fucked off out of it. All this time, the copper's radio was going mental, so something was obviously going off big time. I had a feeling in the pit of my stomach that it was the place I was on my way to, and that if it was I had obviously missed the boat. I was right.

Spurs were in the now infamous Travellers' Rest, about one mile from Portsmouth and Southsea train station, tucked away in a housing estate. It was a good place to meet, no Old Bill, nothing. Obviously, the Old Bill were not as clued up as they are now and this was pre-season, in the middle of summer. We had a good little firm in a pub in the middle of Pompey, but just because we had thrown the Old Bill it didn't mean we had thrown the 6.57. Being on a housing estate, the word would go round like wild fire that the Yids were firmed up in town. In no mood to disappoint, Pompey targeted the Travellers' Rest at least 150-handed. A few of the boys and me got outside to have it. There are some heroic tales from that day, which is a miracle as the pub doors were being targeted with a deadly hail of missiles, keeping the boys penned in. The local Old Bill turned up and Pompey fucked off.

I remember walking past a bingo hall on the corner where the police had Spurs ringed on the steps. I was fucking gutted and had eye contact with a few boys who told me to keep walking, as it was senseless to get nicked as well. That incident was later shown on the national news, where they displayed a load of the weapons left by Spurs on the steps of the bingo hall before they were carted off.

Fair play to Portsmouth, they can claim a little respect that day and I remember walking all the way back to Southsea fucking fuming. When you're that age, you take things personally (I still do now) and I swore that the 6.57 would pay for it the first chance we had. Little did we know that revenge was going to be sweet as we were to play them twice in the old League Cup that coming season.

POMPEY IN THE LEAGUE CUP, 1984/85 SEASON
I was working abroad for these games but this is a truthful account of what happened from someone who was in the thick of it:

The first leg at Fratton Park was a non-event as the Old Bill were on top of things and just escorted us straight from the station down to the away end. Pompey were trying to have a go but the Old Bill were having none of it. The game ended in a draw and on my way home revenge was in the air and all we could think about was payback for the Travellers' Rest. We would soon have our chance in the second leg. We would show them then who the governors were in London. They did have some good results against Millwall and Chelsea but now they had to come to us and we would be waiting.

We had some people at the station. I knew they should get in about 5.00pm and they didn't disappoint and arrived bang on time, 300-handed. They marched up the Seven Sisters Road but we were already having it around the ground with some that had come up in minibuses and cars. The 6.57 then arrived and it carried on, even as they were going through the turnstiles. Nothing happened during the game as it was impossible to get at them due to segregation and police control, which is still the same today with the Tottenham Old Bill looking after the away fans like gold dust, and the cunts who run the club, and treating us like shit. After the game, the walk from the ground to the tube on a dark Tuesday night was not one for the faint-hearted. The ground emptied lightning fast. Pompey were ambushed down every road and street that ran adjacent to Seven Sisters. Pompey were backing off and backing off; they just couldn't contain the numbers we had. They were even being punched and kicked, and thrown down the steps of the tube station. We totally dominated the events that night.

To be fair, the Pompey faces I know held their hands up to this one saying they just could not match our numbers or the organised ambushes we laid on. Credit to them for holding their hands up, which is more than Chelsea or West Ham would do.

Funnily enough, we played them in 1991 in the FA Cup, the same year we went on to beat Forest in the final, the same final when a certain Geordie smashed his knee to pieces, which would have devastating effects on his career and his personal life. Ironically, it was the old miracle man himself who ripped Pompey apart with two quality goals. I think Gazza single-handedly carried us to Wembley that year and for that I will always be grateful. Before that injury, he was the best player in the world, no doubt about it, and it's such a shame to see the state of him now. The poor fucker has been bled dry. Anyway, I wasn't going to miss this one. If you can't get the adrenalin flowing for Pompey away in the FA Cup, you shouldn't bother at all.

Heartbreakingly, I was serving another banning order at the time so I wouldn't be able to go to the game or the coming Cup final itself. My firm was starting to reach its peak now and was really causing havoc with other firms. You can imagine how much we wanted this one. Even though I was banned, nothing was going to stop me being in Pompey. The banning orders were not as draconian then as they are now, so I could actually enter Pompey. I just couldn't go to the game.

I called the meet on for Owens in Southsea, just around the corner from my aunt's place, something she wasn't too happy about when she popped out for a pint of milk to see 150 bods in her local. She still hasn't forgiven me for that. I went down the night before and took in the pleasure at Nero's and Joanna's. I was actually going out with a gorgeous girl who lived just outside Pompey, but back then I didn't give a fuck about women: it was easy come and easy go. All I cared about was the firm and making us number one in the country. Looking back, I cannot believe some of the gorgeous birds I let go, but it's definitely a case of what goes around comes around on that front, that's for sure.

When I walked into Owens, I really thought we might be able to do something. Then I heard the dread word 'Squinty'. He was our police spotter at the time. He would go on to give evidence in the Chelsea trial and I think he actually got promoted on the back of putting me away for three years, the fucker. He was plotted up in the café opposite, which is now called Soprano's. It was really game over, as it wasn't long before the cavalry arrived.

During the game, when Gazza scored his superb second goal, the delirious Spurs hordes came on to the pitch. This provoked a response from the 6.57 and they got on to the pitch as well. But they couldn't live with the sheer numbers we had there that day. We had the whole away end and one section of the south stand, literally thousands. We had a little bit of fun after the game, nothing major, but we did have a naughty little firm out that day. I remember getting off at Fareham or Havant on the way back and we caused a bit of havoc in a boozer there before being fucked off back to London by the Old Bill. This was around the time of the second so-called Summer of Love. I had long, shoulder-length hair that was forming into natural dreads, Stone Islanded up to the bollocks. I was such a vain fucker, still am, I suppose. Everyone was getting loved up and we were all heavily involved in the scene. But my real buzz was violence and the rest of the firm was on the same wavelength. Destroying other firms was our buzz. There's a good insight into this scene in the excellent book *Rolling with the 6.57* by Rob Sylvester, Pompey's face and someone I class as a good friend. The book made me laugh to hear of their exploits at the Downan Tavern. Being a South-London boy, I spent most of my time trying to find ever-more exotic places in order to avoid that shit-hole. It also surprised me to read how far back the 6.57 go with a couple of our older faces on the club scene, people they

Above: Southampton vs Spurs. Just after Spurs tried to get at Southampton (scummers).

Below: Spurs vs Middlesbrough.

Above: Me and Nick in the garden at the Gilpin.

Below: Me and Big Pat in the garden at the Bootlaces.

Seeing in the New Year 2005/2006 with some close friends at Club Aquarium in Old Street.

Above: The Spurs Yoof enjoying a summer's evening in the garden.

Below: France 1998. Even though I was out there I haven't a clue who the bods are. Picture sent to me from Ernie of the 6.57 Crew. The flag is blinding!

Above: Me and Bill after a good night out. Here's your picture as promised, bruv.

Below: Our scrap with West Ham makes the East London Gazette, Thursday 18 April, 2002.

Freddie Foreman and me outside his son's pub in central London in the summer of 2004. Freddie's name speaks for itself but on a personal note he is somebody I respect and think the world of.

SOCCER YOBS CAGED

SOCCER hooligans secretly filmed during an armed clash before a Chelsea v Spurs match have been jailed for their loutish behaviour.

The six men were among a 50-strong mob seen pitching a violent fight with rivals in a crowded street near the Chelsea ground.

Knightsbridge Crown Court heard how men, women and children were sent fleeing in terror as bottles rained down on them last March 20.

Judge Munro-Davies described the behaviour of the six as "outrageous and dangerous".

Referring to the battle, he said: "The public were at risk of being involved, and at risk of serious physical injury. It was a miracle that no one was hurt. This was a pre-arranged rumble and you men came to the pub with the sole object in mind of fighting."

The fight between Chelsea and Tottenham thugs outside the Three Kings pub in North End Road, Fulham, had been arranged weeks earlier.

Violence erupted three and a half hours before kick-off when a mob of 50 armed Chelsea fans were lured to a pub packed with Spurs fans.

Spurs fans were filmed throwing "bottles, bricks and flares" as they clashed with their rivals in the road.

Frightened pedestrians ran into shops and were forced to cower on the floor as flying bottles shattered windows.

A collection of weapons including CS gas, a kitchen knife, pickaxe handle and a bottle containing ammonia was found scattered at the scene by police.

The Spurs fans claimed they had acted in self-defence.

Judge Munro-Davies said Trevor Tanner, 27, a civil engineer, of ▮▮▮▮▮▮▮▮▮ ▮▮▮▮▮▮▮▮, had been a ring leader. He was sentenced to three years in prison.

▮▮▮▮▮▮▮, of ▮▮▮▮ Muswell Hill, and ▮▮▮▮, 24, of ▮▮▮▮ Bounds Green, were both jailed for 15 months.

▮▮▮▮, 29, a labourer, of ▮▮▮▮ Road, Barnhurst, Kent, was sentenced to two years in prison. He was filmed hurling a glass bottle.

▮▮▮▮, 28, a carpet fitter, of ▮▮▮▮ Luton, Beds, was jailed for nine months.

▮▮▮▮, 24, of ▮▮▮▮▮▮▮▮, Hornchurch, Essex, was jailed for two years.

All the defendants denied violent disorder.

Soccer fans on trial over riot

From IAN HEPBURN and NEIL SYSON in Stockholm

FIVE English soccer fans were paraded before a Stockholm court yesterday — accused of kicking, battering and bottling innocent people in an orgy of violence.

Millions of TV viewers were sickened by the scenes after England crashed out of the European Championship on Wednesday.

Among those accused was father-of-three Andrew Porter, 26 — caught on film repeatedly kicking a man in the head.

Porter, a cleaner at Luton Airport, was arrested at the England supporters' campsite after being identified by his distinctive checked shirt, moustache and earrings.

He told the court: "I never hit or kicked anybody. I was so drunk I was not capable of doing any battering.

Heavily-tattooed Paul Jones, 30, of Harrogate, North Yorks, was charged with bottling a restaurant doorman who refused to let him in. Jones, a driver, denied the charge but the prosecution claimed several witnesses saw him running away.

Accounts clerk Andrew Talman, 21, from Hampshire, was accused of attempting to hit a PC and lashing out at a cameraman.

Talman claims video film showing him battering a man with his fists is a case of mistaken identity. He faces a minimum year in jail if convicted.

Peter Colquhoun, 21, whose address was given only at the north of England, was accused of deception.

A police video showed him selling a match ticket to a Swedish fan then refusing to hand it over and making off with the cash.

Colquhoun, whose girlfriend was said to be expecting a child, said he ran away because of the "excitable atmosphere."

All four were remanded in custody.

Civil engineer Trevor Tanner, 26, was accused of assault but freed on a technicality.

Pony-tailed Tanner, from South London, sobbed he could lose his job and said his gran was dying.

Above and right: From *The Sun*, 1992.

Below: Me and Kieron enjoying another drink, summer 2005.

Above: Me and Lee on Waterloo Bridge with the unbeatable London skyline behind us.

Below: Me enjoying the scenery in south east London.

talk about with high regard today. But at the time I wasn't interested in making friends or money; it was pure violence and respect I craved. It's not something I condone; it's just the truth. We all knew the rules.

That was probably the last time we actually had it with them properly. So far in the Premiership, there hasn't been much confrontation with us, apart from when me and my little firm fronted Pompey at Waterloo station but they didn't have their firm together and wouldn't come out of the station. Behind the scenes that day, there was mayhem going on as Millwall were playing Stoke City and were firmed up about five minutes away. I give them their due, though: two of their geezers spotted me in the ring right outside Southwark tube station. I knew both of them. Tragically, one of them is no longer with us, another victim of London life, cut short in his prime. They were well shocked to see me and the boys on their manor but they didn't make a drama out of it and went about their business with Stoke City. We had a proper little firm of all the right people but we were also taking a big risk, as we had no business being in Waterloo. Some of us were on bans, and some, like me, had them coming. We moved on to the Crown in Blackfriars, but someone spotted the Old Bill near by so we all ducked out and headed for the nearest tube and followed Pompey to Liverpool Street. My thinking was that we could get it on the way. We dived into the nearest boozer outside Liverpool Street, as I knew Pompey would be drinking there. There were a few bods in there and a couple who could have been bods. If we were really nasty cunts, we could have given them a slap but that's not our style and in any case we wanted the

163

firm. Someone did say Pompey were in the White Hart and giving it the big 'un. I'm not sure how true that was but it really pissed me off. We were just about to make our way there when the Old Bill swooped in from nowhere with the cameras on full blast. Here we go: names, addresses; as if they didn't already know. They were seriously pissed off that we were there. The Old Bill were all around Pompey at the White Hart anyway, so it would have been a no-go.

There was no doubt there would have been a few of their boys in that boozer but because they are so well supported you get half of the town mixing in with them. We did make a few calls but I'm not into that shit and will only ask once. They didn't want to play and I'm not into attacking Joe Public, so I didn't even bother going over to Spurs. Instead, we plotted up in the West End. At the end of the game, we thought we would have one last attempt on them at Waterloo. As we came out of the boozer, we were spotted by two Old Bill, who followed us to the underground. I was having none of it, so I hailed a black cab and went on ahead of the boys. I was there so early I decided to put up in a local boozer tucked away in a housing estate where a pal of mine was drinking. Next thing, my mate rang: it was going off. I ran out of the boozer to be confronted with Old Bill flying everywhere, with a few of the boys pinned up against the wall being searched. I got the 'fuck off lively' look so I went back to the boozer. The boys had come out of Southwark tube and had bumped into a little firm of young Millwall. These Millwall gave it the big one to the wrong people at the wrong time and after a brief bit of bravado they got run silly, with a couple of them getting a bit of a slap (I bet Pompey will have a chuckle about that). Now, I live in South-East London so I stayed where I was – and who walked in the boozer? Only the little Millwall firm that had just got it. They sat in the corner with the right fucking hump, which I can't blame them for. My pal who I was with was invaluable to me that day. I won't name him because he isn't Spurs and he's threatened to throttle me if I did but, seriously, he stood by my side and was even prepared to go for it with me if they gave it. They didn't, so I decided to make a move as it was a piss-take outstaying my welcome like that. With that, Millwall Old Bill surrounded the boozer and I was fucking locked in with them. If I was spotted by their Old Bill, it wouldn't be good. My game pal came to the rescue and as it was a right local gaff I was taken upstairs where I had to crawl across a balcony with the Old Bill below me. I then had to jump into a tower block balcony, then down the stairs and away. It was like *The Great Escape*.

So now Pompey can read this and have a laugh at the grief they caused me that day. To cut a long story short: me and the boys rate Pompey. I go to Pompey regularly because of family connections and have met all their top boys and I've got a lot of time for them. They still talk about the bits of aggro between us with honest accounts. They're a top little firm and the one you're most likely to have a row with south of London. We've showed up at Portsmouth in the Premiership recently, but due to banning orders, CCTV and the like it's hard to get it on with them there. I'm sure they'll oblige us, though.

CHAPTER 15

THE LION'S DEN?
SPURS AND MILLWALL

MILLWALL AWAY, THE OLD FIRST DIVISION, 1989 – YOUNG, DUMB AND FULL OF COME

This meant a lot to me personally as it was a local derby. It was a chance to pit my wits against my fellow South Londoners; a chance to put our young, emerging firm on the map against the best firm in the land. In a recent article in *Terrace Legends*, I put Chelsea down as one of my Top Five firms. This of course raised eyebrows, but it was only meant as a piss-take, a bit of South-London humour, if you like. I don't mind admitting that Millwall piss all over Chelsea in my opinion. I just didn't want to give them any more credit. Anyway, that's off my chest.

Me and Peckham picked out the boozer weeks beforehand, the Gibraltar, just off the Elephant & Castle on the Waterloo ring road. I actually used to drink in there quite a lot as I was going to South Bank University at the time (fuck knows what I was doing there). I also knew the manor like the back of my hand. I lived locally and had spent, or misspent, my youth in many a bar around Bermondsey: Joanna's Piano bar and Samsons, and my all-time favourite, the Vic in Pages Walk, run by two old friends of mine, Michael and Pat. They were fantastic nights, and even though the boys in there were all Millwall they were as good as gold. They must have got their bar staff from a model agency, because they had some of the loveliest girls I have ever seen behind the drum. Michael and Pat run a good pub, so hello to the both of you. I'll call in again soon if I'm welcome.

At the time, the Old Kent Road was at its peak, with the Frog and Nightgown, the Gin Palace and the Thomas A Becket, just around the corner from the old Den. It was Millwall's boozer at the time, but sadly a lot of these famous old landmarks have been closed down and turned into Seventh Day Adventist churches and takeaways. Anyway, we settled on the Gibraltar. We were going to meet in Charlie Chaplins, but I thought that would be too obvious and too open. A lot of teams have used it over the years and Millwall had it properly sussed. I was determined to show the rest of the country and the rest of London in particular what a naughty little firm we now had, and the only way to get around the media's obsession with West Ham, Millwall and Chelsea was direct action.

The Gibraltar only has one door and an excellent view of the Elephant & Castle and the main roads. We pulled a good firm of 150–200 and made our way around the back of the Old Kent Road through the Aylesbury Estate, the largest housing estate in Europe back then. I actually feel sorry for the people stuck living in that place, but that's another issue. We stuck to the back streets for nearly three-quarters of the Old Kent Road until we eventually popped up near the Henry Cooper and Cockneys pubs. It was game on and I knew Millwall would not disappoint. I knew they would be lying in wait. Sure enough, they came flying out of Asylum Road. They were split in two and copped the full force of the firm. We backed them and backed them before finally charging back halfway down the road. In between, there was some vicious hand-to-hand combat. Millwall had come at us from a cul-de-sac, where there were a couple of boozers. One was the Carlton Tavern (another old haunt of mine). Half of them ran back that way and the other half went straight ahead, all the way back to the Asylum Tavern. I was having a personal battle with a geezer who, like myself, had long blond hair. I chased him straight back to the boozer where he cut me straight across the hand with a Stanley knife. It was time to fuck off lively and get back to the boys, and when I looked round the Old Bill were now between me and my own people. Some Millwall regrouped and were on the estate to the right, giving it large. So I was now fucking trapped between Millwall and the Old Bill, not a good situation. I had to get back to the firm, so I made a charge for it. I got spotted by the Old Bill and one of them threw his helmet at me and another tried to bring me down with a piece of wood. All the boys were clapping and cheering. It must have looked quite funny.

I wrapped up my hand and tried to get back into it. It was off again across the road and on a traffic island. Spurs now had a good 200 outside the Canterbury Arms.

Millwall made a stand, and fair play to the boys at the front they wouldn't budge. But we were too powerful that day and the boys that did stand got served. The Old Bill were going radio by now. They had underestimated us big time. If it had been West Ham or Chelsea doing it that day, it would have made national headlines. I felt fucking frustrated for the boys on one hand, but on the other hand that day's events gave our powerful young firm free rein to carry on causing havoc with other firms. We all went into the ground absolutely elated. We'd had a good result off the pitch. And, for once, we had a good result on the pitch as well

MILLWALL AWAY, THE OLD DEN, 1990

We were greedy now and wanted more. We tried a bit of psychological warfare and ignored the old adage that you never go back to the same place twice. We went back to the Gibraltar again – but so did the Old Bill, and Millwall. I hold my hands up to that. It was a mistake to go back to the Gibraltar, but we'd had so much fun the previous year it was hard to resist. If it had come off, no one would have complained.

The Old Bill were all over us and it was game over. We were escorted all the way to the game with an extra showdown of Millwall's finest. The Old Bill were out in serious force and there was no way to get at each other after the game. A serious storm broke out across South-East London, with howling winds and torrential rain, which if it had happened earlier would surely have caused the kick-off to be delayed. After the game, we put the word around that we were going back to the Gibraltar, which obviously meant that we would have to walk the length of the Old Kent Road again. A lot of people swerved it for whatever reason and took the nearest train. In fairness, it was chaotic and the weather was atrocious, but there we were, thirty-handed, bowling down the road with a couple of spotters for company. This time, Millwall were on the other side of the road giving it the big one. We also had a lot of youngsters with us and I could tell that they smelled blood. We walked all the way back to the Gibraltar without much incident, but Millwall were picking up serious numbers along the route. It was fucking pissing down and by the time we got to the boozer we were all soaked to the skin. There was no time to think about that as Millwall were fucking there. I grabbed a pool cue and so did the others, plus anything else we could get our hands on. It was their top firm. About fifty of them put their heads through the doorway; here we fucking go. The blood was pumping and we were up for it, whatever the numbers. The pool sticks were just starting to swing and we were jumping up and down like loons. Next thing, the riot police stormed the pub. The landlord had pressed the panic alarm.

The boozer was closed down for the night and we were escorted on to the Bakerloo Line into Central London. Millwall had a good 200 outside and there was no doubt in my mind that if the Old Bill hadn't turned up we would have got hurt. To be fair to us, we did walk all the way from the ground to the pub – which is a fucking hike, let me tell you – thirty-handed with a lot of youngsters. That deserves some credit even though we couldn't do anything about the firm that surrounded the boozer that evening.

MILLWALL AWAY, PRE-SEASON FRIENDLY, 4 AUGUST 2001

I couldn't fucking believe it when this one was announced in the press. They have to be having a laugh! I had my suspicions that the Old Bill would use the game just to nick us again. But none of us could resist this one. This was our chance to really establish ourselves as untouchable. The prospect of destroying all before us against that old stager and famous hoolie name, Millwall... let me tell you, it doesn't get any better than that. I sorted out a fantastic meeting place, with the help of a mate, Phil, who lives right on top of the gaff. It was the Gregorian pub, right on Jamaica Road, a two-minute walk from the new Bermondsey tube station. How's that for planning? Right in the heart of their manor. Not many firms meet in Bermondsey, I can tell you. I'm actually really fond of the manor and I used to spend many a great night down there and it's no secret that I live on that side of the river. So being a bit local I wasn't interested in smashing up the manor itself – I leave that to the wankers – but I was totally committed to smashing their firm to pieces and dispelling the myth that surrounds them. So, the Greg it was, a naughty boozer in itself. I called it on for 11.00am, otherwise it could get sticky. I'm really pleased to say that everyone responded, even though it was in the middle of the holiday season. Because everyone was all over the place, and I wasn't actually in Tottenham itself, I have to thank Phil and H for pulling in the same direction, North side.

It was the night before the game and I was getting funny phone calls telling me that I would need an army with me in the morning, and that I was gonna get this and that. Sad fuckers. In the end, I even told them where we were meeting, I had that much confidence in my people. And I was justified: the morning of the game, at 11.05am exactly, the boys came out of Bermondsey station. A fucking brilliant turnout, with no one under twenty-five. I looked around me. This firm was going nowhere, and Tottenham Old Bill said as much to me outside the pub as they strapped on their riot gear. They were fucking here, the sneaky cunts, behind us and in the road and the churchyard next to the pub. Half of us stood facing the road; the other half chased them through the churchyard. This was a promising start. The Old Bill were all over it though. We were itching to make a move and an hour later we did. We marched up Jamaica Road, nothing stopping us. Some of the boys were trying to break away. I stood in the middle of the central reservation, screaming at everyone to stay tight. We went through a couple of estates. They were on the corner. Sonny, game as fuck, jumped the barrier. They were all around us but we couldn't do anything about it. The Old Bill went into us; we went into them. It was going off big time with them: punches, kicks, everything being thrown at them. The difference was that the Old Bill were head-to-toe in riot gear, with metal batons, and they were really dishing it out, the bastards. If we had inflicted the injuries that I saw with my own eyes and received myself, we would have all got a ten. Still, we went into them all the way to the ground, desperately trying to break through to get to Millwall's firm. We tried storming their boozer, but we were again driven back. Where the fuck were the famous

Bushwhackers? Come on, boys, meet us halfway at least. We were on the rampage in their manor and they knew we were taking the piss, outside the ground. We were all shoved into the ground, banning orders or not. There was fuck all we could do now until after the game.

During the game, missiles and verbals were exchanged by both sides, then five minutes before the end they opened the gates, silly cunts. I went charging out, straight round to the home end to confront them head on. 'Come on, you cunts.' I lashed out at one. I then got smashed across the thigh with a metal baton. If my legs weren't so muscular, they would surely have been broken.

'You dirty fucker,' I snarled at the copper. I pulled myself together and got away. At least I hadn't been nicked. By this time, Spurs had broken loose and were off and running back through the underpass into an estate. I was pissing myself laughing, looking at the Old Bill in their *Star Wars* gear trying to keep up. I saw a Millwall bod standing in an alleyway, so broke off and clumped him in the face. During the game, we'd been getting reports that Millwall were hitting anyone in a Spurs shirt – women, kids, Joe Public – because of what we were doing. If that's true, then shame on you. You've lost it. This time, we were determined to smash them and their boozers but we were rounded up five-deep by the riot squad, with vans, dogs and horses, right outside Surrey Quays. The cunts were throwing bricks out from the park, right into us. If we'd got to them, we would have killed them. They knew that and so did the Old Bill. And what did the Old Bill do to them? Fuck all. They even had Chelsea with them that day and they still fucked up.

There was one mouthy fucker in the park and if I see him again I won't be responsible for my actions.

We were escorted into Surrey Quays tube, where we had another go at them on the corner. We also fronted the boozer by the tube and a couple got it bad outside then ran back in. All in all, we had caused mayhem at Millwall, no question. I was fucking elated, even though I could hardly walk. We went back to East London, near the Blind Beggar, for a well-deserved celebration. I was so proud of the boys but my leg was getting the better of me. Plus, Spurs Old Bill told me that if they saw me again that night I'd be nicked. It was time to go home. Later that night, the boys went back to Millwall and annihilated one of their pubs and everyone inside and outside it. What an end to an unbelievable day. No question who the governors are now, surely.

CHAPTER 16

ON BORO'D TIME

BORO AWAY, 1992

We had to go up there. It was a matter of respect. A couple of weeks earlier, they had come down to us with a tidy little firm. I was standing by the Spurs shop, and as they charged towards me a fucking bus stop got flattened. It was quite funny when I look back. The Old Bill were with them and watching me like a hawk. I stood my ground and hoped for the best. But by this time the Old Bill were restoring order and it was game over unless we wanted to be nicked. I was fucking furious and swore that we were going back up there.

This was about the time Boro were starting to make a name for themselves and when our conflict with them started in earnest. We set off at about midday, which I was mad about, as I really wanted to leave earlier. We were about fifty-handed, but a good fifty. I had no qualms about taking this firm up there but I think the boys had a few reservations. As the coach pulled up, it was purple with the word 'Londoners' written down the side. Not very subtle, I know. I got it from a firm in Peckham just down the road from me, which I thought would be funny. Then someone told me that Chelsea had been up there the week before and their coach had been annihilated and it was unmarked. Oh well, fuck 'em. As you have probably gathered, going by coach is not really my style. I fucking hate it, but if we were to take a firm up there we had no choice. The last train back from there was something silly like 7.30pm, so the coach it was. The driver was from Leeds and he was shitting himself. I had been a little economical about our exact plans and destination, hence meeting up at the Embankment.

It was a long, tedious journey, which we broke up by stopping as often as possible. The driver by this time was a fucking wreck and to stop all-out mutiny we had a whip-round for him and he settled back down. 'Welcome to Middlesbrough' the sign said, some five fucking hours later. I stopped the coach driver and he thought we were going for a piss. Instead, we got off, crossed the dual carriageway and fucked off into Middlesbrough. The look on his face was priceless. And, as he drove an empty coach into the Boro car park, the Old Bill of Tottenham and Boro asked him where the fuck everyone was. When they saw my name on his sheet, they went fucking ballistic and nicked the poor fucker.

We came towards a big boozer surrounded by parkland; it was hard to tell if it was full or not. It looked like a nice pub, the sort of place you would find in the country. Except of course it wasn't. (I have to say Boro is a lot nicer than I had heard or thought. It seemed quite green with little terraced houses everywhere. Maybe it was just the posh part of town. It always makes me laugh the way everyone slags off each other's manors, especially Londoners where most of us live in fucking ghettos anyway.) We grabbed what we could outside the pub. There were still no signs of life so we ran through the main door – and it really was empty, which was very strange. A geezer at the bar shot out of the door as we moved in, not that anyone would have touched him. That's outside the rules. I knew he would raise the alarm though. That much was obvious. I made sure everyone was tooled up and alert for what lay ahead. Still, they didn't come. Strange. I didn't like being penned in the boozer so we got the fuck out of there.

We headed off in the direction of the ground. It was still calm up ahead and there was a boozer coming up. It looked packed. I saw a Spurs spotter on my right with a camera and a big smile. Fuck him, here we go. I wasn't holding back now. I jumped into the doorway and pushed my way past two bouncers. 'Come on, you fuckers, we're here.' A sea of startled faces looked at me and before they could react I was in the beer garden doing the same routine. It clearly wasn't their main firm. You always get a few bods scattered in different pubs near the ground and this was one of them. I threw a glass as they came for me. One of the doormen grabbed me and I threw a right hand, which didn't hit home. Back on the street, the Old Bill were going ballistic. Obviously, Boro now knew we were on the manor as well. We were running a gauntlet now. Boro were at the bottom of the road round to the left, Spurs Old Bill to our right. I'll never forgot one of the spotters shouting to me as we charged down the road that Boro's main firm were a good 200-handed just around the corner, and that if we took our naughty forty in that direction we would get battered. Well, that's a silly thing to say to someone who has come 400 miles to have a row, obviously a direct challenge. What do we do? Yes, you've guessed it. We headed straight for them. We tried to get at them but the Old Bill were on to it big time. A few of the boys broke through, and they did have a good firm, but we were on their manor on a Tuesday night and taking it to them.

As I was making my way into the ground, one of their boys came up to me, shook my hand and said he had not seen a gamer firm up there in years. Enough said. This was the first of many an encounters with Boro and my firm throughout the 1990s and beyond.

BORO HOME AND AWAY, 2002/03 SEASON

Boro at home is turning increasingly into a naughty grudge match. I'm still not totally convinced about them. Don't get me wrong, they are fucking game, there's no doubt about that. They just seem to have come from nowhere. I know up North they have been putting themselves about for many years, and the way that certain people go on about them in certain books you would think that they're the best thing since sliced bread. London and the rest of England is a different proposition though.

I'm not going to go on too much about Boro at home as it's covered in minute detail in the police statements for my banning order. Fair play to Boro, it was a good move to come down by train and then get taxis in. I was very impressed with that and it was a good move to meet in the Ship, although maybe the boys left behind when they went to the game will disagree, as they were left very isolated there. They definitely made a fatal error by splitting up.

During the game, Spurs attacked the Ship and the bods inside who put up a good display eventually got smashed. If they're honest with themselves, they'd say that if it wasn't for the Old Bill arriving swiftly they would have got done bad. After the game, Boro came out and for the first couple of hundred yards it went off big time. Boro were well up for it and as usual the Old Bill concentrated on our boys and a few Boro got quite seriously hurt for their trouble, but they're a game old firm, full of big old boys. The Old Bill were well on top by now and Boro got an escort all the way to their train, no black cabs this time. I bet the Boro boys got the shock of their lives when they saw the black-cab fares when they got to us. As Londoners, we're used to being ripped off at every turn by various parasites that live in our great city, but black-cab drivers should wear a fucking mask when they go to work. Forget being a brain surgeon, doctor, lawyer or even working in the City. All you've got to do is travel around the capital for a few years on a little moped with a clipboard on the front looking like a complete cunt, memorising every street in London (which I know by the way) and Bob's your uncle. You now have your passport to untold riches. That's why if you go to any pony golf club in the London suburbs, which I don't, you'll find ignorant, thick cunts standing at the bar with more money in their back pockets than the banker next to them. I've got a good few pals of mine who are black cabbies, believe it or not, so there are obviously some exceptions to the rule – but not many. Don't even start me on mini-cab drivers. They really are scum.

BORO AWAY – LAST GAME OF THE SEASON

First of all, I have to apologise to a few of the boys for this one. I called it on then didn't make the train. My old friends H and T were understanding but I was fucking seriously pissed off with myself. Instead of staying in the night before, I stupidly went to a friend's boozer in Mayfair. I only intended to stay until 10.00pm, 11.00pm at the latest. Some fucking chance. I looked at my watch and it was 2.00am. I knew I had fucked it up as the train was at 7.00am. I eventually rolled in at 6.00am, which was proper messy. If I'd been twenty-one, I'd have made the train no problem. But I wasn't and I'd have probably killed myself trying. Going somewhere like Boro away, you have to be on the ball. In fairness to myself, it's a very rare occurrence for me and I have literally spilled blood for Spurs all over this country, so I think I'm entitled to miss the odd train.

In any case, we took a top firm up there so I knew the boys would be more than OK without me. I think we were a good 150–200-strong that day. People got off at Doncaster as Boro had asked them to, saying it was too on top of the Old Bill there. After marching around the town centre, it was pretty obvious that Boro were not coming.

I've since found out that Boro did say to get off there,

but if they did or didn't it still sounds like a bit of a fuck-up to me. The boys got straight back on the train and made their way to Boro. Once in Middlesbrough, they were met with an Old Bill army. Game over. Much to everyone's annoyance, they were put in a boozer, which the local constabulary had turned into a fortress. Boro wanted it now of course and pleaded with Spurs to try and get out. The next thing, the boozer was going up in flames and everybody was on the pavement, the fire brigade was on its way and the Old Bill were going radio. At least Boro can't say that they didn't make the effort. Must have been an electrical fault.

Spurs were put in the ground sharpish. I think both firms tried to get at each other on the way, but it was a no-go. As usual, the wankers on the pitch were letting us down big style. At half-time, the boys had had enough. They booted over an exit gate and by all accounts had a very naughty row with the riot police, which inevitably ended up with some nasty gashes on heads handed out. My old mate Snowy in particular was on the receiving end of a particularly brutal police attack that day, and to add insult to injury they even nicked him, but he's as game as fuck and I love him to death.

Amazingly, some of the boys actually fought their way right around to the bowl outside the ground but were eventually beaten back. I have it on good authority that Boro were very impressed with the firm we brought up there that day, and knew that we couldn't have done any more to get at them and even said so in their book. I know one thing for sure: if Millwall or Chelsea had pulled a stunt like that, the press would have been wetting themselves to report it. Still, we've always known the truth and now a lot of other people do as well.

As I said earlier, I missed the boat and got some light-hearted banter for it. No doubt there will be some people who will read more into it, but I couldn't give a fuck about people like that. Fair enough, I called it and I should have been there but it's not like you can wake up at midday and jump on the tube for 400 miles. It's like going to another fucking country – as I found out when coming back from Newcastle after the FA Cup quarter-final (see Chapter 19). I think the boys did fine without me and I know that we have Boro's respect for that showing. I would be interested to know how many the Mancs or Chelsea took there.

BORO AWAY AGAIN, 7 MAY 2005 – TOTAL SHUTDOWN

I was sick that I was going to miss Boro away but because of my ban I had no choice. Once again, we took a good 150-plus up there, arriving in the North-East before midday. The Middlesbrough police had been making threats all week after what the boys did up there the previous season. There was even a little header in the national papers during the week with a threat from Teesside's finest telling us not to come for trouble.

Spurs met in a village just outside Boro. I thought it was a good move, a good meet and if it had come off then we could have taken liberties up there again. But it wasn't to be, as the Old Bill thought it would be a good place to meet as well (grasses). Basically, it was an escort to and from the ground with Boro taken out of the equation altogether – and Teesside Old Bill hell-bent on revenge. The Old Bill were fucking well out of order that day. Police brutality just about describes it. And a lot of people had their personal effects 'confiscated'. It's called stealing where I come from.

Tempers flared and Spurs had it with the Old Bill all the way to the ground and back again, which inevitably resulted in some silly nickings. It's a long way to go back up there to court. It just goes to show how powerful the Spurs firm is now because the police presence at our games is phenomenal. It's just gone crazy since we had it at Millwall away in a so-called pre-season friendly in 2001. As one of my pals summed it up at Boro – it wasn't as if we murdered anyone, but the way we were treated you would think we had. Ironically, I flew up to Aberdeen that weekend while a few of them came down for the Boro game. If Boro keep on giving it the big one with us, one day we're going to meet without Old Bill and I promise you it will not be a pretty sight. You have been warned.

CHAPTER 17

SCOTLAND'S FINEST: THE ABERDEEN SOCCER CASUALS

WHAT a weekend I had with the Aberdeen Soccer Casuals. First of all, thanks for all the hospitality, boys, particularly to Steps and Monkey. I went up on the 8.00pm flight out of Heathrow to be met by Aberdeen's finest and taken straight to the Windmill, their boozer right in the heart of Aberdeen. It was handshakes all round until a big fat joker, a tosser of a Millwall fan, can you believe it, started creating. After five minutes of this, I totally lost it and smashed a glass on the table and lunged at him. I had to be dragged out of the door or I would have killed him. If I see him in London, I'll tie him up and throw him in the river. All the boys were embarrassed about it but it was nothing to do with them or their hospitality. I just have a short fuse and you get pricks everywhere. I was taken around the corner to a nice little bar to cool down. I sat next to a geezer whose face was covered in tattoos, like a Maori warrior. There are so many freaks in London that it didn't bother me in the slightest. I got chatting to him until I discovered that he was the local lunatic. When he got up to leave, he shattered a glass against the wall. I couldn't fucking believe it. They convinced me that it was not directed at me but at the wall. Still, I jumped to my feet and was just about to launch a bottle at the back of his head when I was begged to leave it. So I left that pub and was on to my third venue in less than half an hour. Welcome to Aberdeen. As I was being escorted to a waiting motor, we saw the tattooed man being bundled away by the local Old Bill. I just turned to my host and we all burst out laughing at the crazy start to the evening. Again, I hold and harbour no grudges whatsoever towards the boys up there, as they looked after me like gold dust.

I was driven out of the city centre and into a little village called Ellen where I was royally looked after by Steps and Gary, who had a hotel. This was also the formal resting place of one of our old friends, Moog, who tragically died young in 2004, so it was a bit of a pilgrimage as well. The hotel where I stayed had a nightclub, so it was happy days – bags in the room then straight into the club. It was a typical small-town club but I loved it. The people were great and I could not have asked for more. The locals loved my South-London accent and it was good fun being a novelty. I felt like George Best: every time I turned round, a drink was shoved in my hand. If I hear anyone saying the Jocks are tight, then I will argue the toss all day as I have rarely come across such generous people. That just dispels another stereotypical myth about them. I intended to pace myself as I had another night to go, but best-laid plans and all that. I knew I would suffer for this in the morning, but the adrenalin was still flowing from earlier so there was no way I was sleeping. It got very messy and I finally ended up in bed at 5.30am.

We were on the road again at midday, but I thought I was going to die. It was really surreal as I sat next to Steps on the local bus into Aberdeen and we went along the picturesque coastline towards the granite city. I was told that Pittodrie was coming up on the left and just at that moment I caught a glimpse of their main stand at the end of a row of houses. It reminded me a bit of the layout in Pompey. We were going to watch the Celtic–Aberdeen match in the Pitt, next to the ground. The Pittodrie was their pub. I was supposed to go into Glasgow to watch the game but was surprised to learn that they only gave Aberdeen 1,200 tickets in a 65,000-capacity stadium. It's that old Man United trick: stick the visiting supporters up in the gods, out of sight, giving the impression on TV that the ground is only full of home support. In Celtic's case, that's fucking true. It's bollocks though and surely against the spirit of the game. It also denies thousands of Aberdeen's fanatical fans the chance to go and support their team in numbers. It's not as if Celtic don't have enough advantages as it is. It's bollocks and it sums up everything that is wrong with Scottish football. It's a shame as well, as I could have gone to the game: thankfully, English law cannot touch me in Scotland. I was feeling rough as a dog so I decided to try kill or cure and had a pint of Tennants. Luckily, it was cure. It was a great afternoon – and just like watching Spurs, as Aberdeen lost 3–1. I really felt for the boys. We went into town after so I could see Aberdeen properly. I had to eat, so me and Monkey went for a kebab. I have to say it was the best one I've tasted. Probably the beef round there. It's beautiful. After that, it was bar, bar, bar, bar, with a nice little clubby bar in a shopping centre which was right up my street. Then it got proper messy, as we ended up in a little dance club where everyone was off their head. It was 3.00am and I was just about on my last legs. I hadn't slept in about forty-eight hours. Don't the SAS give out medals for that sort of thing? If I'm ever kidnapped and they try that old sleep-deprivation trick on me, they'd be fucked with the training I've had.

The next morning, I knew I just had to get home as my body, especially my liver, couldn't take any more punishment. I got to the airport and paid another £150 to get home. A lot of money, but I didn't trust myself to stay for another day. My plane arrived back at Heathrow just one hour after take-off. Not bad, seeing as the train takes seven hours. As one of the boys up there told me, Aberdeen is actually closer to Norway than London. I staggered off the plane, zombie-like, following all the other lemmings until I found myself staring at the luggage carousel before I realised I already had my bag with me. I couldn't face the tube so I jumped in a black cab. Sod's law, the cabbie didn't stop rabbiting all the way home. Of course, he had to be a fucking Chelsea fan, didn't he? When he realised who I was, he suddenly started saying what a great team Spurs were in the 1960s and how he loved all the London teams. I just sat there like a nodding dog. In fairness, although he wanted £70 to take me home, we settled for £50. I think I slept for a week after that.

Interview with Mr M of the Aberdeen Soccer Casuals (ASC): Spurs v West Ham at home [my comments are in brackets]

We arrived in London on a Friday night. We had a quiet Friday night with a few Spurs boys we know. Our original plan was to meet up at King's Cross together, seventy-handed and we were going to go straight over to where West Ham were meeting. But we were told not to by one of our Spurs pals, so we went back to the Bank in Tottenham. A few of the Spurs boys were like, 'What the fuck's this?', as there were so many of us.

[I remember sticking my head in the Bank at half-time. I couldn't stay as I had my little girl that evening. I must admit I was taken by surprise at first to find such a firm in our boozer, but once I realised who it was and saw some familiar faces everything was cool. I actually took it as a mark of respect that the ASC had brought so many down to be with us. If other people did not like it, tough.]

West Ham came out of the station. Apparently, they'd been fighting with Indians in Brick Lane or something like that.

[West Ham got themselves involved in a naughty row in Brick Lane with some local Indians or Pakistanis. By all accounts, they nearly came right unstuck. I had to laugh when I heard.]

We came out of the Bank, about twenty-five Tottenham and sixty of the ASC. We tried to front them in the middle of the main road but the Old Bill just went mental. I was at the front; S was at the front giving it large. I actually got into their escort and went up the road with them. They were like, 'You Jock cunt, you here with Tottenham? You Hibs cunts.'

'Fuck off,' I said, 'I'm Aberdeen.'

'Ah,' said the West Ham bod, 'the slags of Scotland and the slags of England, you make a perfect couple.'

With that, I burst out laughing. Across the road, the Spurs boys were shouting, 'M, you OK?' Then it started to go off, with small scuffles breaking out. The police came flying in again. West Ham were safe, making a big noise behind the police lines. Spurs challenged them on the corner of the Spurs shop. West Ham could have easily got through the police lines at the corner. West Ham were escorted into the ground and most of the Spurs boys went in as well. So we went back to the Bank. There was about seventy of us and twenty Spurs. We were planning on going to the boxing at the York Hall in Bethnal Green that evening, where a Spurs boy was fighting. Someone came in with the tickets and we all started to get agitated. We couldn't sit there all day with this mob doing nothing, so I asked what boozer West Ham would go to for the boxing. Someone said the Salmon and Bull. I suggested we go there now. West Ham were in the game and we could surprise them when they came out of the tube. We went to the Salmon and Bull and got settled. A couple of Spurs faces walked in and seeing how many Spurs were there started going mental and demanding more there now. We didn't mind as we were here for Spurs and thought we had enough. Soon though, more and more Spurs started to arrive until we had a good 150.

West Ham were coming, you could see them coming through the park. They had got off at another station opposite the park. We were getting psyched up. Come on, this is it. We started to come out the doors when the Old Bill swooped on the boozer from everywhere. They were really heavy, riot sticks and shields, the full works. We don't get the Old Bill behaving like that in Aberdeen. They tried to storm the boozer but the whole mob turned on them to try and get out to West Ham. It went mental. The windows went out, followed by bar stools, tables, chairs, fire extinguishers and even the radiators off the walls. The police were actually throwing it back in at us, we couldn't believe this. [Welcome to London.] When it all calmed down, a few of the Spurs boys still tried to sneak out but it wasn't happening. The Old Bill cordoned the place off and we were all put on buses to the police station. It was just photograph, name and address, then out, which we were well pleased with. Up in Aberdeen, we would have been in all weekend.

We wanted to go back over to West Ham later that night but the Old Bill were all over it so we went back to our hotel in Piccadilly and went on the piss instead. The doormen at the bar asked if we were the

Aberdeen boys who had been fighting with Spurs against West Ham all day at the Salmon and Bull. I just said 'Aye' and started to laugh. It had been a good day. A week later, we sent a postcard down to the Salmon and Bull saying: 'Great pub, sorry about the damage. Aberdeen Casuals.'

[I was absolutely gutted I had to miss that day, but all my proper people knew why and anybody involved in a custody battle will know exactly where I'm coming from. If they don't, fuck 'em. I know for a fact that quite a few of our boys were actually mixing it with West Ham out on the street while separated from the main firm in the boozer. There were all sorts of recriminations after that. Certain people could have done better, but the fact is you can only do and deal with the numbers in front of you, which was the whole West Ham firm. As usual, the Old Bill had split us on purpose but I take my hat off to the unsung heroes who were having their own private little battles out on the street. I wouldn't normally make a statement like this as I wasn't there but I'm absolutely convinced that if we had got to them in that park with our full firm we would have annihilated them. It makes me shiver now, how close it was, but the fact is going back to their manor seriously fucked them off, as I know the way their minds work. It was also splashed all over the papers, to add insult to injury. For the first time, I can now see quite clearly the catalyst for their raid on the Bank. That day obviously hurt them a lot more than a lot of people realised.

Another story about that afternoon was told to me by one of the ASC boys when I was in the Pittodrie and it made me piss myself laughing. He's a big fella, let's call him Frank. Anyway, when the Old Bill stormed the boozer, old Frank had a bit of marching powder on him, which he obviously did not want to declare. In his panic, he swallowed the whole fucking lot. On the bus, as he was being carted off to the cop shop, cuffed up like the others, he started sweating and shaking. Eventually, the Old Bill asked if he was OK and he said he was a bit hot and not feeling too well. They got a bit worried and undid his cuffs. The copper dealing with him asked if he had come down for the Spurs v West Ham game, which he denied. He showed the copper his ticket for the boxing and with that his mobile rang – pumping out an old Spurs anthem. Fucking brilliant. You couldn't make it up. There he is buzzing off his head saying he's down for the boxing, with a Spurs song playing on his mobile and a perplexed copper looking on.]

[I ask Mr M what was the best row he was involved in with Spurs.]

My best row with Spurs was against Leeds at King's Cross in the Duke of York. I went over to the bar first to have a look. This was one of the first times I'd come down with the Spurs boys. I remember you; there you were standing across the road from the pub with a couple of Spurs faces. Everyone was saying Leeds had got hundreds, but at that time Leeds had about sixty or seventy in the bar and Tottenham had about the same. I walked back to King's Cross through the car park to meet back up with the Spurs firm. I told them there were only about seventy of them and that we should do it now or forget it, as we were expecting the main train in from Leeds any minute. I remember you just standing in the doorway opposite staring at the pub. [You can't take me anywhere.] So we went back again and I put my head in the door first. This time I was well clocked and the Leeds boys were like, 'What the fuck do you want, you Jock cunt?'

'Outside', I said. 'Come on now, outside.'

Then the next thing I remember is turning round and seeing you fly past me and that was it. It just kicked off again. I remember when Leeds actually did come out of the pub and it kicked off big style.

[Leeds actually did have another pub full, tucked away behind that pub. So what started out as having it with even numbers escalated into fighting 150–200 of them. It did get a bit hairy. Fair play to Leeds, though. They had brought a good firm with them.]

I didn't realise that they had another boozer full around the corner so you can imagine how I felt when I said they were only sixty- or seventy-handed. I remember thinking, Oh shit, where the fuck did they come from? We were now having it true, toe-to-toe in the middle of King's Cross and Leeds just kept on coming around the corner and we were stuck out in the middle of the road. The few Old Bill that were there just fucked off. They definitely had a good 200-plus that day.

[I remember having it at the top of the stairs by the underground with traffic cones and shopping trolleys being thrown at us, it was fucking radio, but then thankfully the Old Bill turned up en masse, as I'm not sure how much longer we could have held out. You have to remember we were only fifty or sixty. We had also been split up and were more than holding our own against their top bods. Fair play to Leeds. I do respect their firm when they turn out, and they always seem to against us. But, remember, this wasn't Tottenham. This was miles from Tottenham. This was like Leeds coming to meet us in Wakefield or somewhere. Moves like that is what we were famous for at the time. Especially around King's Cross and Euston.]

That same night we went in the opposite direction. Instead of going down to Seven Sisters, we went towards Edmonton. I think it was a pub called the Globe. We caught a minibus full of Leeds in traffic and it was brutal. I remember a bod getting pulled out of the back door, but we didn't do anything that they wouldn't do to us.

[You're right. That stretch of road towards the North Circular always gave us rich pickings. Most teams copped it there. The one that sticks out was Burnley in the FA Cup, when we attacked a bus like Mohicans charging out of the estate tower blocks. I remember a pylon going through one window and out the other side. Going back to the Leeds one, I actually got dragged into the back of the van and they were all for taking me back up the M1 for dinner. I was having none of it, even if there was a spare seat. In another famous incident, we were drinking at the top of the road again and coaches kept flying past. It was Stoke, who had been playing at Brentford or somewhere. A coach stopped at the lights and we stormed it. I managed to get the door open. Right, you cunts. Get off. Yids are here. They were just staring at me in amazement like I'm from outer space. After a brief scuffle, we jumped back off and sent them on their way in their newly air-conditioned vehicle.]

I actually forgot to mention that the pub with Leeds at King's Cross, the Duke of York, was gassed and flared as well and it actually caught fire. The fire brigade came and so did the Old Bill. Leeds actually started attacking the fire brigade and the Old Bill and I stood outside watching it. They were going crazy, they were obviously a pissed-off mob. I remember clearly watching them attacking the fire brigade with stools, chairs, bottles and glasses. I remember thinking, What the fuck are they doing? I was wearing a loud Armani denim jacket, so I stood out like a sore thumb. They spotted me and were shouting, 'That's the cunt who came in the bar.' That's when I came back round to the taxi rank to join you. I remember thinking, I wish these cunts would leave me alone. It was a perfect hit, though, until they were joined by the other mob. Obviously, we didn't know they were there but they were going loopy, they had the whole street sealed off. They were a very angry mob. I remember when I went in the bar, Leeds were right at the back by the pool table. I was laughing and so were the bouncers, believe it or not. They didn't know what the fuck was going on, it was funny as fuck. If they'd caught any Spurs on their own, they'd have probably killed them. Most of the other times that we have been to Spurs, to be honest, there's never been a mob that came and took it to you or arranged it and stuck to it.

[How would you describe the relationship between Spurs and Aberdeen?]

It all started in the early 1980s, when the Aberdeen boys came down to London to buy clothes. They wouldn't go to Chelsea games because it was all a load of bollocks. Spurs were just a football mob. It didn't matter what clothes you wore or what you liked or even what colour you were, the same with Aberdeen. It was about 1988, a few boys moved down to London for work and started drinking in Tottenham and watching Spurs play. There was no baggage, you were just a football firm and that time it was just Aberdeen coming to Spurs. We got to know your boys well but you were the same kind of mob as us, you enjoyed socialising together and so on. It just snowballed from there, with you coming up to us and having a good time and vice versa. As far as I'm concerned, Aberdeen–Spurs is the only real relationship between a Scottish and an English club.

We have the strongest mob connections, not for fake loyalist connections like Oldham, Stockport or Chelsea. Look at Rangers and Birmingham City.

Rangers are like, 'You can come up, but don't bring any blacks with you.' If you're friends with a mob, you're friends with a mob, that's it. It doesn't matter if we haven't seen each other for over a year, as soon as we meet up it's like yesterday.

THE ORIGINAL ASC–SPURS CONNECTION: AN INTERVIEW WITH STEPS OF ASC

Tell me about when you first started to come down to Spurs.

Steps: It was 1989. I've always been a Spurs fan and I used to come along to all the games with a couple of Spurs faces and got involved like that. Way back then, Spurs didn't have the massive mob we have today. There was probably only a handful, a hardcore of about forty. One particular time that sticks in my memory was the FA Cup final at Wembley against Forest. You hijacked the turntables in the Bull and the whole place was going crazy to the tune of 'We won the Cup'.

What was the best row you had with Spurs?

Steps: I would say in 1992, against Man United. We were no more than twenty-handed, drinking in what used to be Sam's Bar. Not all of us got in because of security on the door. One man came up to me and asked who I was. I told him we were Tottenham/Aberdeen. Then another one went, 'Who the fuck are you?', so I said 'Aberdeen. Outside, you cunts.' Then we just went for it big style. The boys outside were going mad trying to get in. They tried to come through the window. It spilled out on to the street and Man United got run straight back in, getting battered as they went. The Old Bill turned up and me and T were nicked. Later that night, someone went back and gave the geezer from Sam's Bar a slap.

Why do you think Spurs and Aberdeen have such a special relationship?

Steps: I think it's because I've always been a Spurs fan. I don't know if I should say this but I was actually a Tottenham fan before I was Aberdeen, as my dad was a Spurs fan during the war. Then, working in London and going to the games I bumped into yourself and the other boys and it was all over, We won the Cup!

Would you say that Spurs and Aberdeen have the best firms in their respective countries?

Steps: The most active firms, definitely.

INTERVIEW WITH D OF ASC

What's the best firm you've seen of Spurs and Aberdeen together?

D: I would say West Ham at Bethnal Green. We had a good sixty or seventy. It's just a shame we didn't make it to the boxing, as that would have gone off mad. I was a bit disappointed in that. Another naughty one was Chelsea at Victoria.

Would you say honestly who came on top, because you'll never get a straight answer from Chelsea?

D: Spurs came well on top, no doubt about it. There were a lot of mouthy cunts there. It was funny hearing the Rangers boys mouthing off with Chelsea. Could have been better but Spurs definitely came on top. Another good little row was when we bumped into a firm of Wolves at Spurs, about twenty of us just down by the British Queen. That was good fun.

Thanks for all your time and your comments, boys. I know this chapter will have been well anticipated all over the country for different reasons: curiosity, jealousy, you name it. People often ask me why Spurs and Aberdeen are so close. It wasn't until I started this book that I realised how many times some of the ASC boys had been by my side over the years in some naughty situations. When you are doing it, you don't take in everyone around you. Obviously, I'm not going to give it away too much because that's between ourselves and Aberdeen. There are some things that are best left to the imagination.

Nobody will ever understand properly apart from ourselves. All this chapter proves is that there is a strong bond between two powerful firms. It's nothing like the pathetic attempts of other English teams paying lip service to the Glasgow teams for fuck knows what.

Also, I want to give Aberdeen's Under Fives (their youth firm) a mention. I was introduced to a few of them and they were all really nice, polite bods. I remember they were all sitting at another table while there was mayhem going on all around. Some piss-head was coming close to getting it. I was screaming at the idiot I brought up there and all the time they just sat there not interfering. Then one of the boys asked if it was OK if they came over to meet me. I said of course, and they put a lot of older bods to shame with their behaviour. I told them they would be welcome at Spurs any time, and by all accounts they're game as fuck.

CHAPTER 18

AN INVITE TO THE PALACE

DURING this book, I have made various references to my close pals at the palace – Crystal Palace that is, not Buckingham, just in case you were wondering!

You're probably wondering why, if I get on so well with them, I haven't done a proper chapter on them. Good question. The truth is, they are my close pals and I've grown up with them and you just don't think to interview close pals, do you? In any case, this book is not an A–Z. The trend is for that bollocks, and the reason other teams have big chapters in this book is because we have a history with them. We don't with Palace, apart from a few skirmishes with both youth firms – which I for one don't want any more. There are plenty of other youth firms to have a pop at that we have a real history with, like the scum teams Chelsea and the Gooners, as well as Millwall.

Contrary to popular belief, Palace have always had a

hardcore of forty to fifty bods of my age, with a lot of them being pals of mine. You don't hear a lot about them as they don't have the numbers or resources to compete with a lot of big firms, but as individuals they can stand up and be counted. As Brighton found out recently in their clash on a dark, wet Tuesday evening. One of the boys described it as a throwback to the 1970s with it going off inside and outside the ground, with a pub full of Brighton and all through the game. They smashed them. Luton came unstuck down there recently as well, when they gamely, or unwisely, put their heads in Palace's boozer and got chased back down the road. It was a bit of a surreal and uncomfortable moment for me when I heard about it, and bods from both sides know why.

We've had some of Palace's faces with us at some of our biggest battles over the years, such as the Ilfield Tavern, something a lot of people forget when they're forging new alliances all over the place. I would have loved some of the action against Brighton, but I wouldn't give the Old Bill the satisfaction, so take note of that!

With my connections, I could obviously have done a massive chapter about Palace, but this is not about that. This is more of a personal message, which I said I would do for people who I have a lot of time and respect for. So here's to you, boys! You know who you are!

I even put them forward for a chapter in a recent book that a pal of mine was doing. They need to start going places like Millwall away, in a proper firm, as I know at home they can hold their own against them. But I'm not telling them anything they don't know, and with their support, which averages 25,000, I believe they are more than capable. In fact, I'll make a prediction that over the next few years, with their young bods coming through and the rest of them there to guide them, I think they will be one to keep an eye on!

CHAPTER 19

GEORDIE NATION, HERE I COME

NEWCASTLE V SPURS, FA CUP QUARTER-FINAL, MARCH 2005

I can remember sitting at home writing this book and praying that we would get a home draw. I know that after following Spurs for many years our best hope of actually reaching the semis – our only hope – was to get a home draw. Of course, with us it never works like that. Neil Webb, the ex-Forest and Man United midfielder, was doing the draw. Not a bad player in his day, but he now looks like he's spent his retirement challenging Mickey Quinn to a pie-eating contest. So, as his fat fingers went into the goldfish bowl I went a bit Mulder and Scully. I knew it wasn't going to go our way. Sure enough, it came out that Newcastle would host either Spurs or Nottingham Forest. If only I had the bottle to put my money on my instincts, I would make a fortune.

Now all I needed to know was on what day it was going to fall. Because of the disagreements with my ex, I was on an emotional curfew for most weekend games. I had lost precious time, time I will never get back. That is unforgivable. Unless the game fell on a Sunday, I wouldn't be able to go – and I wanted to go more than anything. This would effectively be my swansong, as my banning order was due to take effect from 1 April. The only person on this planet who was going to stop me now would be my little girl. I'm not ashamed to say that I will always put her first.

Over the next few days, I had an anxious wait as it was being decided which TV channel wanted to show which game. Unbelievably, BBC1 wanted Southampton and Mancs – a joke fixture – and Blackburn v Leicester, as in 'who gives a shit?' The good news for me was that these would both be Saturday games. This left the parasites from Sky TV to pick up Newcastle v Spurs for the Sunday game on behalf of all the fat couch potatoes. Geordie nation, here I come.

I was on the phone in seconds trying to drum up support, and I have to say I was quite disappointed with the action. OK, it was on a Sunday and, yes, it was a long way, but this was the quarter-final of the fucking FA Cup, against Newcastle in their manor. It was a big one. Granted, if you are generally skint or have personal problems, then fair enough, but, if it's about grabbing another day's money or keeping some whinging bitch indoors happy, well fuck that. You can't buy opportunities, and you can't buy dreams, or ideas or respect.

I know that a lot of the slippery buggers were hoping

we would get through, and have a nice weekend in Cardiff. Well, fuck that as well. I think Cardiff's a shit-hole anyway, and well overrated. Also, with Spurs you have to grab the moment. Semi-final? Don't make me laugh. But come the day it was good to see a lot of the top boys there, among an incredible support of 7,500 souls. It was even better to see some old friends up there, people who over the last fifteen years have had some incredible highs and lows with me. People like Mr S, who I have a lot of respect and affection for. You know who I mean, don't you, Swainey? And Robert, who I go back years with, ditto. Both of them stuck with me up there and I salute you. Oh, and not forgetting my sidekick who drove me up there in style along with his boy.

In fact, I wanted to hire a 150mph Saab, but I think the thought of me wanting to drive (I haven't passed my test) curtailed that. But we still went up there in luxury in a spanking new turbo Freelander, which was just the job for the mountainous (not) terrain of Newcastle and Sunderland. Actually, it was flatter than South London. My pal was also a good and loyal friend who stayed by my side throughout the trip, and how we managed to drive back from Sunderland on Monday afternoon is one of life's great mysteries. Either I'm getting old or he's not human. As I said earlier, for once the footballing gods had been kind to me and given me the chance to go out fighting. Literally.

We left at 4.00am. Once you get over the initial nightmare of getting up that early, it's actually worth it. It was something else to cruise through the deserted streets of South and North London, and then hear the growl of the turbo kicking in as we flew unopposed up the M1 in our off-road warrior. I promised myself some sleep on the way up as I hadn't had any the night before. I was like a little kid on Christmas Eve. But I enjoyed the journey so much that I only dropped off for about twenty minutes just outside Sunderland, and I managed to squeeze in a nifty bit of reverse parking at a service station, much to the horror of my passengers. I can drive, honest, it's everyone else that's shit. All joking apart, I have been fucking robbed twice in my test and even pals of mine who have passed tell me I can drive better than them. So, the moral of the story is: don't take your test in South London, as the examiners are all Old Bill and sexually frustrated wankers. It's all a big fucking con when you have little nineteen- and twenty-year-old toerags driving around at breakneck speed presenting a danger to everyone, especially children, in London's streets. And they give these little pricks licences. It fucking stinks and it's wrong. Mind you, I did chase one examiner back into his office when he told me I had failed, which was worth it.

We cruised into Sunderland, where the hotel was, and also where my pal had some friends who had a boozer with a club. Happy days. We were so early that we couldn't even check into the hotel, which I was a little pissed off about. I'd been dreaming of a nice shower and a change of clothes after being on the road for the best part of five hours. There was nothing for it but to head straight for the boozer and a pint of Nelson.

It was a lovely bright, sunny spring day but still fucking cold. I have to say that the Sunderland boys up there, and the Seaburn Casuals, treated us with great hospitality. But they do fucking despise Newcastle, so we were on to a winner from the start. I couldn't believe how close Newcastle and Sunderland actually are, so there was time for a few beers and a proper Northern roast dinner – which was the bollocks, I have to say. I ended up getting changed in the khazi in the end, which wasn't what I had in mind. Anyway, time was marching on and I knew the boys were over by the Quayside and I wanted to get over there. We drove back to the hotel, called a cab at reception, dropped our bags and went to the bar next door to await the car. The boozer was a strange gaff. It was like one of those Henry's chain pubs stuck next to a Travel Lodge in a car park. Still it was quite busy and did the trick.

Earlier in the morning, we had also taken in a game of pub football, which the geezer we were with sponsored. It was quite a surreal setting. There we were, hundreds of miles from home in a place called Seaburn watching an amateur game with the North Sea as a backdrop. I was pleasantly surprised I have to say. Not with the football, although I do think they were quite good (after watching Spurs they would be). After ten minutes, I was bored, so we moved on to a little boozer, right on the seafront. I tell you, that place is definitely going to get another visit, not least because of the gorgeous barmaid. Before you ask, no, I'm not telling you the name of the boozer.

The cab arrived and we made short work of the fifteen-minute drive to Newcastle. It was nearly 2.30pm and it was a 4.00pm kick-off. I was anxious to get there and my phone was ringing off the hook. I had visions of a big traffic snarl-up, like in London. But it wasn't traffic that beat us, just sealed-off roads due to the extensive regeneration of the Quayside. I can understand where the people of Sunderland are coming from when they see the amount of money being pumped into their media-grabbing neighbours while they are basically left to rot.

Fuck this. Let's get out of here. I knew the boys were close by and ducked into a bar to pay a quick visit to my brief. I proper gave it to him, which was hilarious until he reminded me I would be on a ban in a few weeks' time and had to behave myself. With that done, I fucked off lively to get to the rest of the boys. I clocked a little firm snaking around the corner on the opposite side of the road, about sixty- to seventy-handed. My senses tingled, then I relaxed. It was my own people. 'Are you fucking mad?' they said. 'You'll get nicked. You're too close to the ground.' They thought I was already on a ban, bless them. I realised that there were more still in the boozer, probably waiting for me. We got going and were a good hundred-strong. Good people, a nice mixture of old and new. We marched the march, as I had done thousands of times over the years in different town centres all over the country. This was different, though, one I had been to before, so this could be my final chance. I was fucking buzzing, something that didn't go unnoticed as one of the younger marchers mentioned to one of my pals: 'Has T taken a pill or something?' I had to laugh when I was told later, the cheeky fucker. If I had – which I had not – it must have been a dud one. I thought the idea was to get you loved up.

Newcastle's ground is a vast sight that explodes in between all the surrounding shops like a monster. Where the fuck they ever got planning permission for it, I'll never know. You hear all the bollocks on the TV, and read it in the newspaper, about St James' Park being the Geordies' place of worship and all that, but I have to say that where it is situated the fucking thing obviously takes priority over anything else up there. 'Come on, let's fucking do this,' I shouted. I was hyped up; someone said they were slapping anything that moved by the Spurs end.

We were now in the car park below their monster of a stand. Fuck this. I wasn't going in yet. Up the hill, perched right outside their end, was a shitty boozer standing on the corner on its own. It was called the Strawberry. Alarm bells rang in my head: it's their fucking boozer, let's do it, come on. I was well up for it. I was all for charging up the main stairs and straight into it. Instead, we sensibly went up the stairs, just to the side of it, which were not unlike the stairs to Wembley, so we're not talking about a few steps here. This was our chance for immortality in the North-East. I'd be fucked if I was going to stand and argue the toss.

I was up the stairs and at the side of the boozer. Where the fuck was everyone? There were about twenty or thirty of them, if that. I walked around to the front of the boozer and there was a penguin on the door. Before he knew it, I was on top of him. I even did a really cheeky move and snapped off a picture of him and the boozer as I was fronting it. 'Come on, Geordies. Yids are here, let's fucking have ya.' I don't know who was more stunned, them or us that we were fronting their main pub with these numbers. I was floating and really proud of the boys with me. We moved back to the side of the pub on top of the stairs and waited. I wanted these pricks badly. I lashed out at one, but we had to move. They weren't playing ball and the Old Bill were on us. But we had stirred up a hornets' nest and the fuckers were everywhere. It was brilliant, with people going into each another all the way to our end. I was buzzing like I hadn't in a long time. I was going to miss this, the whole plethora of pleasure. I was right under our stand now, and it was like an underground circus with everyone mixed in. A little firm of Geordies came running through. 'Come on then, you mouthy cunt,' I spat through gritted teeth. The hood of my Eco tracksuit was nearly pulled off. 'Fuck off, you cunt, don't rip it.' It was Old Bill, Spurs Old Bill. I was so hyped, I let them have it: 'You are fucking out of order, trying to ban me from London.' They just stared at me like I had come from another planet. They knew that in a few weeks the banning order would do their job for them. In the meantime, I was living on the edge, but even I knew not to push my luck too far so I went in.

I climbed up the gigantic stand. It was never ending. The view from the top was well worth it though. I have to say it is one of the most impressive stadiums I have ever been to. If they built up the other stand to your left it would piss on Old Trafford, and the atmosphere is electric. I didn't want to sit down so I just stood on the main causeway. I stood there like a king surveying his kingdom until I was told to sit down by the Old Bill. Fuck it. I went down to the bar and it had just shut, although I bumped into some old friends who I hadn't seen for years.

I was really pissed off because I had lost my camera and I was going to take a few pictures of the stadium for this book. Luckily, one of the boys had a camera on him and took a few funny snaps under the stands. The Geordie Old Bill were frothing in the background and really wanted to do something, but we weren't doing anything wrong.

We lost as usual. All the usual bollocks. A disallowed goal. Once again, they didn't have the bottle out on the pitch. Fuck them. They were not going to spoil my day. I'd seen them do it too many times and they certainly didn't deserve 7,500 fans up there – and 5,000 the week before at Forest, on a Wednesday night in the snow.

The game was over and we made our move down the stairs from the gods. It had just turned dusky. I put my hood up and I must have looked like one of those street robbers who infest our inner cities, and prey on the weak and elderly. These are the people I despise with a passion. If some of these little parasites were forced to come to football, and have it with different football firms toe-to-toe, I know how long they would last.

So, my hood was up on my £200 tracksuit, I'd lost my camera, and wanted it bad. I was feeling lawless. We poured out on to the road, just beyond the car park. My eyes were like lasers looking for friend and foe. I could feel all the shit my ex and the Old Bill had given me. I was going to come out with some like-minded individuals. We were about twenty-handed, with a few youths with us. I was focused on the little firm who were just about to come straight into us from the left. The little stocky Burberry pricks went straight for one of the youths; I came straight up on his blind side and unleashed a savage right hand. He went down, but credit to him he got back up and grabbed my leg to try and throw me off-balance.

'Come on, you Geordie cunt,' I screamed dementedly. Thankfully, his pals were not as game and after a couple more rights he was away. I was frothing. Then, as if by magic, a safety mechanism kicked into my brain. I knew I had to get the fuck away, and so did the boys.

A couple of weeks away from a banning order, I would be fucked if I was nicked now. It's really hard to keep a sense of perspective when you're in the middle of the fight club. It's an exclusive club. It's by invitation only and the head doorman is your own brain. I had to focus on somehow getting back to Sunderland in one piece and not being nicked. Both would be great. So there I was, hood up, shifting through Newcastle thinking that because my hood was up no one could see me when I probably stuck out like a Sunderland fan. I saw a big park in front of me, Victoria Park, I think. This will do. I should be able to get lost in there, except it was slightly smaller and more open than I thought. Do you ever get that feeling that someone is behind you? Well, I did and I was right. I approached some stairs but decided to sit down and take in the lovely scenery (it was a nice park). I was sitting there for what must have been seconds when two shadows loomed up behind me. 'You Cockney bastard, what are you doing in our city?' Old Bill, fuck it. Have they seen my earlier performance or have they just decided to keep an eye on me?

'What the fuck's up?' I snapped back.

'You know what the fuck's up,' Bad Cop replied. 'We don't want you in our city.' Blah, blah, blah. And then the magic words: 'If I see you so much as fucking spit, I'll fucking nick you right now.'

I breathed a sigh of relief. 'I don't want to be in your fucking city either, I'm just trying to find a fucking way out of the fucking place.'

With that, Bad Cop drew his cosh. Here we go. Still, I'd rather take a bit of a clump or have a stand-up row with the pair of them than get nicked. I leaned back on my foot in anticipation of gloved hands gripping either arm as Bad Cop radioed my details through and checked for warrants. He then contacted the Football Intelligence Unit, which told them to escort me out of the city, all the way to the station. Bad Cop and myself were having a pop at each other now, and Not-So-Bad Cop was trying to keep the peace. Then Bad Cop upped the stakes by deciding to play an amusing game of Get Out of Our City in Ten Minutes. Always up for a light-hearted challenge, I took him up on it. The reward: my liberty, if I do it in time. If I don't, it's a trip to the nick.

I shifted towards the train station. There was a queue of motors snaking around the hill and towards the Tyne Bridge and freedom. Then, like a gift from Heaven, a taxi stopped in front of me. 'Can you take me to Sunderland, mate? I'll pay you extra.'

'That's OK, bonny lad. Jump in.'

I couldn't believe it. In London, they would probably run you over. Cheers, mate, you probably saved my arse. Actually, he was a good fella and even stopped to pick up my pals from the station on the way through. We headed to Sunderland like conquering heroes arriving back at the boozer, eager to drink in the moment. My hand was fucked but I didn't care. Fingers, bones and heads don't mix and mine had been broken four times. Once more wasn't going to make a difference and soon the Jack Daniels and Coke anaesthetised the pain away.

For a little while, everything was good in our corner of the North-East. The boys up there were as good as gold with us, so cheers and respect for that. Obviously, they loved what me and the boys had done, but they were good people besides that. Despite the best efforts of certain people to keep me away from this fixture, all I can say is 'Fuck you'. And to the boys who missed this one or ducked out of it for whatever reason, it's your loss.

I even ended up talking to a Kat Slater look-alike towards the end of the evening. Just like her TV counterpart, she was as mad as a bag of nails. On a serious note, the objectives had been achieved. It was well overdue that we went to Newcastle and gave it to them. I'm biased, but I believe that on our day we have the best firm in the country. You cannot make statements like that unless you can back it up. Taking 7,500 up there on a Sunday afternoon does that; going for their main pub before kick-off does that; having it toe-to-toe in the shadow of their main stand does that. We cannot expect everyone to be in London. We have been systematically robbed of our identity in Tottenham by the Old Bill's hatred for our form and the more so for their hatred for me. The banning order they were about to put me on was criminal in itself, and I swear that if I find one loophole in it I will fight it. I will leave the last word to the Geordie cab driver that told me that the Chelsea scum took pathetic support up there. Enough said.

CHAPTER 20

OLDHAM

SPURS VS OLDHAM –
SATURDAY 18 SEPTEMBER 1993
Like a lot of these little Northern towns, Oldham like to put it about on the England scene, and good luck to them if that's their thing, but I had it on very good information that they were coming down

They plotted up in the Holloway right next door to the Tube, drinking with among others, Gooners and Chelsea. I wasn't impressed with this, as you can imagine, what's the fucking point of coming all the way to London, three hours on the train and going for a drink next to the Gooners ground when they were fucking playing us? We're quite used to it with a lot of teams. If it were me, I honestly wouldn't bother going at all if I had no intention of going anywhere near the home team crowd.

We were standing outside the British Queen, shooting

the breeze as you do, and if I'm honest at that moment I couldn't have given a fuck whether Oldham came or not. We had enough on our plate in the next few weeks anyway, as you would imagine by now.

So a motor reversed towards the boozer, stopping just short, a couple of bods in the back and one in front. A couple of the boys confronted the motorist to find out what was going on. Turned out that they're only Oldham, with a few bods with them, a few Gooners probably. Can you believe it? They only tried to call it on when they're not even in the manor. I'm all for fucking them off, but the boys are all really wound up now and well up for it.

We had a good 60 or 70 and jumped on the overground at Seven Sisters. No Old Bill, fucking great. All we had to do was get down on the Tube network and we would make it. We were soon at Holloway Road Tube. The boozer was right next-door, perfect, but then we realised we had to go up in a lift. I looked at the emergency staircase spiralling all the way up to ground level, I looked at the boys, we had to go for it and we did. I always remember leading the boys up the staircase, and turning round to my pals and putting my finger to my mouth to tell the boys be quiet like you do to a little kid, and of course they all started doing it back to me which made us all laugh.

As we got to the top adrenaline and natural instincts took over and you could hear a pin drop. We were like coiled snakes waiting to pounce out of the station and Oldham, Gooners and Chelsea were going to get the shock of their fucking lives.

I said, 'On the count of three we fucking storm it.' I

hardly got the three out of my mouth when the boys exploded out of the station with me. We were on top of the pub in seconds, I was in the doorway, M was beside me, 'Come on you cunts!'

We crammed in the doorway. punching and kicking anything that moved. I could see the fear in their eyes. They knew that if we got inside en masse, they were fucking dead. Bottles, tables, chairs were being thrown to keep us out. I looked up and someone was caving the windows in with a shovel. The rest of the boys were trying to storm a locked door to the right. The faces inside were showing sheer terror.

Smash! A bottle and then another just missed my head by inches. Looking up, I shouted there was someone from the boozer, the dirty fucker was chucking crates of empty bottles down on us from one of the flats above. I stepped back and, to my left, a few of the boys screamed at me to come round the side of the pub. I sprinted around where a little firm of Gooners had broken free and were going to try and sneak off. Half of us went straight into them, probably got Oldham with them, but what a fucking muggy turn out.

While the other boys kept on smashing the pub and Oldham to pieces the Gooners stood for a few seconds, bouncing up and down, chucked all the tools at us and then turned and had it on their toes with one or two getting the helping boot and fist on the way.

OLDHAM VS SPURS, 1993 SEASON
I had already written this chapter when I heard about some mug from Oldham who slagged us off big time in

Cass Pennant's *Top Boys*. Though in itself that's nothing new, as every fucker, especially Chelsea, likes to come out with some bullshit or other, but this I do take personally as evidently this prick has said that Oldham battered Spurs outside the pub in Holloway. It would be laughable if we weren't so fucking pissed off about it. I must confess I haven't actually read the book and I don't intend to but my phone rang off the hook when it came out, and all our firm are fucking fuming about it.

The only thing that annoys me is I gave Oldham some credit in my chapter, and I don't know if it's the Chelsea or Gooner connection in their ranks that influenced this piece. If it is, you've been taken for a complete mug along with your firm. If it isn't and you've just decided to write a load of bollocks because you hate us, then shame on you and it's because of mugs like you that I've had to write this book to get our story across.

If you want to get personal, why were you and your little firm drinking in Holloway when you were playing Tottenham?

Fact: we came to you.

Fact: the firm we had would have battered anyone, least of all fucking Oldham.

It's like saying West Ham got turned over by Leyton Orient, it's complete and utter bollocks and deep down you know that. I would take a bet that a lot of your boys are pissed off about it as well. I was fucking there, I saw the shock and fear in your eyes when we stormed the Holloway, and again when you made a little show around the back of the pub only to get run back inside.

So why come out with all this rubbish?

If you get done, you get done, there's no shame in it, it's happened to us at one time or another. The truth is, Oldham, Chelsea, Gooners and whoever else was fucking with them got absolutely terrorised by some naughty people. That's it, end of story.

To finish on a happier note, I was reminded recently by my pal that I was drinking with him at the time that everyone was making a move over there and apparently I was adamant that I was having none of it and I left, he thought for the toilet, when another one of our pals asked him what he was doing.

'Nothing,' he said, 'Me and T are having none of it, we're in court on Monday.'

'Well, how come T's running up the station stairs then?'

'Fuck it, fuck it, fuck it, I can't fucking believe him!' So much for court. With that, he put down his beer and came out to join me. The moral of this tale is to tell the truth, as you never know when someone who was actually there has a book deal.

CHAPTER 21

CARDIFF

**SPURS VS BLACKBURN, WORTHINGTON CUP
FINAL, MILLENNIUM STADIUM, SUNDAY 24
FEBRUARY 2001**
We don't get too many Cup Finals, I know that, so we
make the most of it even if it is against a poxy team like
Blackburn. No disrespect to them, but it's hardly the final
you want. It was a no-win situation. We were expected to
hammer them and in true Tottenham tradition we were
once again beaten by a shit team.

So there we were: Cardiff, Millennium Stadium, Cup
Final. I woke to the sound of what I thought was a hoover
but in reality was actually the noise of nasal passages
being cleared. See, that's the great thing about sharing a
room with J, we get a room together in a top hotel and I
never see him for the rest of the weekend, cushty, I love
Jim though, even if he is a bit of a fruit loop.

It was pissing down with rain: lovely, lovely start. We eventually made it, got out of the cab at the Hilton Hotel where I'd arranged to meet someone about a ticket. The place was heaving, a lot of the boys were at the bar enjoying themselves, everyone was spread all over the city centre. Cardiff was absolutely heaving, we made our way around to the Prince of Wales, which was fucking ridiculous; you just couldn't even see the bar. It was also full of shirts, acting like pricks, singing and dancing and throwing beer.

We made our way upstairs where it wasn't too crazy, next to the bridge running right over the boozer from where I could see everything. It was a monster of a boozer and in a normal Saturday situation you would find Cardiff in there. It was so fucking packed and big, we had to communicate by mobile, I kid you not.

Now me, H, Paul and Del were pals with some of Cardiff's boys and it wasn't long before I got caught. or rather one of my pals did, saying they wanted to come and see me for a beer. Well. it would be rude not to, wouldn't it? A few of the boys gave me inquisitive looks but I had no hesitation in inviting Mark and his pals to join us.

I've been searching for Blackburn all morning and the Cardiff boys confirmed what I thought, that they didn't want to know. Still, it was early doors. The result of the game could change all that and, besides I never take anyone or any firm for granted. The rest of the Cardiff boys were enjoying the banter and it turned out Mark generally loves Spurs and has watched them on his own numerous times, which I can vouch for when we first met at a Spurs vs Newcastle game just before the final. I thought he was a spy who had been sent down to find out what our strength was before the anticipated battle with Cardiff City.

Anyway Cardiff didn't really turn out that weekend out of respect and because the Old Bill were all over them and us. It was awkward with a section of their firm wanting to get close to us but have no doubt, if both firms met head on, it would have gone. Mark even had a ticket for the Spurs end, which I thought was a nice touch. I missed the kick off while we stayed in the Prince of Wales getting on with the Cardiff boys. I asked for a tour of the city, which could take us past where Blackburn would be. Mark tried his best but we couldn't find anything to spark off. I remember Cardiff Old Bill looking very concerned when they saw me walking with them. I could see the massive stands of the Millennium Stadium towering over the narrow streets of Cardiff like an all-seeing, all-knowing monster.

There was a few moody things going on in town that I wasn't happy about, like little firms of locals picking off individuals the night before because we were all firmed up in Swansea. With that many bodies on the street it wasn't worth falling out over and, unfortunately, you cannot look after everyone.

We had only been in the ground five minutes when Spurs took one of their famous early leads. The whole place went fucking mental and to my right the Cardiff boys were going equally mental, which was really good to see. The rest of the game was a pile of shit and we lost as usual. I was fucking steaming. Blackburn had half the end so they must have had some geezers, we thought. If they did I was fucking going to find them, make no mistake about that.

I said to one of the Cardiff boys, 'Take me to the Blackburn end.'

'Are you sure, T?'

'Yeah, I'm fucking sure, get me right outside their end when the cunts are coming out.'

There followed the slow exodus of Spurs fans who had once more had their dreams and their hopes shattered for another year by an overpaid, under-achieving bunch of mercenary cunts. I was going to do something about it.

We made our way around the crowd coming towards us, big fat Northerners jumping up and down, sweaty bodies in elation and who could blame them? If we didn't have such a shit team we would be doing exactly the same thing and, just as I was in this forgiving mood, right in front of me this fat bloke started shouting, to no-one in particular how Spurs were fuck all.

Well, I agreed with him, the team that day was fucking shit, no argument there but the cheeky prick started to spout off about the firm too. I couldn't believe it. We had already been in Wales waiting and ready for a day-and-a-half, the cheeky fucker. Now I'm not suggesting this geezer was a top boy or anything like that. He was late-20s, early-40s and old enough to know better. He was surrounded by thousands of his own people while on the other hand I was on my own with a handful of Cardiff, deep in enemy territory. Still I was too wound-up to care. It would have to be in and out. I went up behind fatty and let him know exactly where the Spurs firm was – right in his face. Bang! it was a picture. The Cardiff boys couldn't believe it.

'Get me out of here,' I said to Mark and he duly obliged.

The adrenalin was pumping as we made our way through the narrow back streets of Cardiff, laughing on our way. I asked the boys to show me the sights and we called into a few of Cardiff's haunts. I remember going into the Rat and Parrot in the town centre where I was introduced to some local prick who happened to support Chelsea. I had to walk away from him, as I didn't want to spoil the boy's hospitality. There was a little mob of Blackburn in there and the doormen didn't want us to bring the Old Bill down so we moved on and any case I now wanted to get back to my own people.

I had arranged to meet a local man Bernie, who was nothing to do with football, who happened to work with people I was connected with in London. He was a very well-respected man in Wales and indeed London, so it raised a few eyebrows among the Cardiff boys when I said who I was meeting. We had arranged to meet in a pub right near Cardiff's railway station and it also happened to be the pub where my firm were.

I spotted Bernie straight away even though I had never actually met him before. There was a photo of him and his boys from the valleys hanging in my friends' pub in London alongside the likes of Freddie Foreman, Dave Courtney, and the now late-and-not-forgotten Tony Lambriano who. with all his faults, was an absolute gentleman. I for one did not realise how much I would miss him.

Me and Bernie shook hands warmly and went inside. A few of the doormen were getting funny around the boys, so I spoke to them and asked them to move on as I didn't want any drama in the pub, but I also understood the boys were fuming after such a pathetic result.

I was driven down into Cwmbran. Bernie was treated like a king in his home time and in turn so was I. We were also joined later on in the evening by Louis who owns the Aquarium nightclub in London. So you can imagine the evening started to get messy. After finishing off in a local nightclub it was all back to Bernie's where I think I talked him and his wife to sleep.

The next morning, needless to say, I felt like the living dead. All I wanted was to get back to London but for some reason, which I'm still fucked off about today, I went back to Lou's Hotel with a promise of what I thought was a lift home. Instead after hours of fucking about I was cramped in the back of some shitty motor, eventually got to the outskirts of London where they all lived and were obviously going no further, only to have to get a cab home, which probably cost me more than the fucking train fare would. Bernie told me to go by train. Would I listen? Would I fuck. My aversion to using public transport cost me a nightmare journey home; I eventually got home another day and a half after the game to be greeted with a stony face and an ear-bashing.

CHAPTER 22

CLUBLAND

SPURS have always had a big input in the club scene, with the likes of the legendary 2001 Ibiza warehouse raves at Kings Cross and the one and only Labyrinth. Also, there is the legendary Wag Club and a few other little gaffs. Most of the guys that were doing it then are pals of mine now and good luck to them. I wish I was a pound behind them.

The buzz you can get can be compared to the real buzz we all craved at the time. Everyone knows I have always been a frustrated promoter. I would enjoy other clubs, but I was too interested in kicking arse and putting the Spurs firm back where they belong – on top – so I had no time to devote to promoting during that lucrative era. The money wasn't my god and never has been you cannot buy an idea or the respect from your peers. My time in clubland would have to wait a while.

We would have a routine on a Saturday night. If we had played away, we would get back into London for about 9 or 10 O'clock. We'd have a few beers on the Embankment, in my beloved *Tattershall Castle*, which is moored on the river. Then it would be on to the Gardening Club, the place to be at the time. We were snobs really, but I liked to find exclusive venues, playing our music instead of the warehouse and pit bull scene. After kicking the fuck out of Southampton away or Chelsea, we surrounded by beautiful happy people and this was our ritual for months.

Then we would go on to an all-day club called Crazy Larry's, over in Chelsea, believe it or not. We also loved the Dark Side of the Moon over at the Deptford Empire. When Nancy Noise was burning up the floor and played the anthem, the light show projected the moon onto the floor, so we would be off our faces, literally, dancing on the moon.

As time went by and the Firm grew more powerful I decided to have a little dabble at promoting. My first venture was with an old pal of mine, Roger. He introduced me to John Paul, a French DJ, who also ran Vinyl Junkies, in Soho. The venue was TKO in Shoreditch. One of the two biggest mistakes I made was relying on the firm to pack it out, as apart from my close-knit 50 or so, most people stayed away, probably expecting trouble or some bollocks like that. I was pissed off with that. John Paul played a blinding set, so I just entered into the spirit of it, with everyone else and got trolleyed.

After that I drove down to see my pal Nobby, who tragically isn't with us anymore, or rather my pal drove all the way to Leicester jail. I remember feeling like absolute shit on that visit, especially when the electronic door shut behind me as I had only just got out. Those days were absolute mayhem and I am amazed I survived them.

I decided after this experience that I would have to move up a gear, as all it had turned out to be was a glorified piss-up for my pals with a top DJ. And the guy that owned the place was pissed off as everyone seemed to be out of it and there wasn't money he expected coming over the bar.

I started to put on some nights in an old mate's pub, Charlie Breaker, in the back streets of Peckham. Although not one of the most salubrious areas of London I really liked the place and had some great nights down there. It was actually set up like a club and many a face had been through its doors. Charlie had had a few high profile reggae artists staying with him when they came over to play. We had some good nights and packed the place out.

Then I met Louis, who owns the Aquarium in Old Street, central London, EC1. I persuaded Louis to let me have the place and it was a good night. Not packed but not bad either. A lot of people were wary of the football connections so I left it awhile before trying it from a completely different angle. This time I would go into partnership with someone who had his own crowd in effort to shake of the stigma with football. Les was a real character and we clicked straight away and who he didn't know and what he didn't know wasn't worth talking about.

Eventually I got tired of all the bollocks that went with the club scene as, more than anything, it was having a major effect on my private life. All I was doing was trying to get a club night off the ground and I know my ex thought I was having the time of my life and up to all sorts with birds hanging off my arm, which was all bollocks. The fact was I didn't want to be surrounded by a lot of these people any more then she did, but that definitely put a big nail in the coffin of our already problematic relationship. You've got to be single or have the total backing of your partner to make a success on the club scene, that's a fact. I'm sure there's many a club owner or promoter out there reading this that will back me up on this.

So we had our night at the Aquarium and everyone had a good time. All the boys came and supported me along with a few of palaces top boys who I've grown up with and come and support me wherever I am. It was a good atmosphere and I brought a lot of people to the party.

It was to be a short-lived promotion with my new partner, as he had a lot on at the time and I wasn't convinced his heart was in it. So we parted friends and, to be fair to him, it was a crazy time for me as well, what with the arrival of my little one, trying to do the house up and hold a relationship down. It was too big a task.

The only thing that comes close to the buzz of football is a top club night surrounded by your pals, playing fantastic tunes to a sexy crowd. It can get naughty and can turn as quickly as it can at football but mostly it's cool. Only a few times has the football scene really spilled over to the club scene. One time during one of my nights, a couple of bods got a bit mouthy with me and then suicidally declared they were Chelsea. How they got out says a lot about the club night I ran. It was touch and go though.

Just after I had split with my ex, I was minding my own business in the VIP lounge of a club when a bod strolls up.

'You're Trevor Tanner.'

'Yes.'

'I'm West Ham, you fucking...' I clumped him before he could get the sentence out and he was carried out feet first. Fuck knows who he was but that can happen anywhere.

There were a few boozers, three to be exact, that I know one time or another meant a lot to all the boys. To start with there was the Bull. The name says it all. This was a famous old football boozer that meant so much to all of us. It was our stronghold, our fortress if you like, from the late 80s to the mid-90s. It was the place to be in Tottenham, I loved the place and you could find me in there most weekends. Obviously a boozer is as good as the landlord allows it to be. It was run for years fantastically by two spurs faces, Tony and Terry; I salute the pair of you. You really know how to run a boozer. We were always made to feel welcome and a drink would be offered as soon as we got through the door. Something I've always appreciated. They have exactly the right idea. You buy someone a drink and they don't mind putting a fortune over the bar. Something, which is sadly missing in todays soulless, shitholes.

You could be in a pub in London, spending more than £3 a pint and not get offered so much as a diet coke by some faceless wanker working his ticket. Tony and Terry were also our pals and over the years they put up with a load of crap from me and the boys. Like Chelsea attacking the boozer twice and numerous other incidents, too many to count and they were proper men though and never took anything personally.

Those were fantastic days. We were youthed up and on top of our game and having fun at the same time. As we had some great nights there. Blissful days.

There was a little DJ booth in the middle with a top sound system and in the evenings it would transform into a pre-club boozer, attracting some lovely young ladies. More often that not, they blew the clubs out and partyed with us in to the small hours. Lots of different firms tried to take it but never succeeded apart from smashing a few windows. It was definitely the prize to have in football and any bod from another team who were lucky enough to get an invite couldn't believe the atmosphere in there.

As usual the Old Bill were going to spoil the party. They hated the fucking place and would have a camera pointing at the front door hidden across the road in the North London Tec College and we would all wave to the camera. This cold war went on for a while until eventually the boys had enough of all this bollocks and moved on. I can't blame them. Alex and Liz then took over. Alex was a jock and at first I was sceptical at how he would be received, but I should not have worried as he made a real effort and soon became a firm favourite with the boys. Although for me it was never going to be the same. We still had some fantastic years with Alex and Liz but the Old Bill were beginning to tighten their grip on us and on the pub in general.

I chatted up a stunning barmaid and offered to drive her home, the only problem being I didn't have a car and didn't drive. I persuaded Mark my pal to lend me his car and stupidly he agreed, even with my other pal Terry shaking his head vigorously behind his back. I went around the one-way system in first gear and wrapped the motor around the first lamp post. The bird jumped out screaming and ran away whilst I walked back in to the boozer without a car or girlfriend.

I came out with the immortal line, 'You never gonna believe this...' Mark sank to his knees . I brought Mark a drink, as it was the least I could do and after he calmed down he actually found the funny side of it, believe it or not.

Then he came up with the classic line, 'Don't worry about it, T, it's not my fucking car anyway, it's my bird's.' After that episode and to this day, unfairly I think, if the words car and me are mentioned in the same sentence people shit themselves and run a mile.

The Old Bill continued in their quest to run down any landlord that we got on with was. Alex moved on and the Bull was no more. Then it was reopened as a tacky Irish-themed pub, much loved by plastic paddies everywhere.

THE PLEASURE ROOMS

The Pleasure Rooms was another favourite with the boys. It also doubled up as the Labyrinth during the evening and was run by our pal Joe, who was also Spurs. It was an incredible place. It was set in an old workman's club half way up the High Road. Once you went through the narrow doors, you would never believe the size of the place. It was enormous, with three different areas playing different tunes. The first bar was a regular bar and a shrine to Spurs. The back bar was where all the action was and you could find Samantha Jessop (Page 3 model) doing a turn. She actually travelled down from Newcastle every other week. I suppose when you think about it a couple of hundred hungry young bods salivating at your every turn tips well. She was fucking gorgeous though, I'll give her that. It is just business to them pure and simple. It's tragic watching geezers trying to chat them up, thinking that they actually give a fuck.

Joe got Chaz and Dave down there one afternoon and there was nearly a fucking riot. They went down such a storm. It was surreal place to have as our boozer. Tragedy struck, which was nothing to do with the owners or football-related, but it gave the Old Bill all the ammunition they wanted and another one of our watering holes was shut down.

The only place left standing was the Coolbury Club, which was situated just next door but one to the Old Bank between the Bootlaces and the Bricklayers Arms. It was also a club at night and everyone knows I love the place. It rates in my affections along with the Bull in its peak. Man United got caught right outside on a bus; they got smashed to pieces with the Mancs cowering on the top deck while the doors on the bottom were totally ripped off. If we had got to them we would have killed them.

Another time after an end of season game against Sunderland in 2000, there was literally a riot outside the club with the police driving their horses into the doorway to beat us back and how that was never reported by the papers is anyone's guess. If it had been Millwall it would have been front page news.

Sadly, the pub has been left empty for the last few years, much to the delight of the Old Bill who hated walking into the place. It's now forced us to drink in fucking shitholes that aren't worth a mention. When are the Old Bill gonna realise that, unless they shut the ground down, we're not going anywhere? It's that simple.

Two pubs outside Tottenham that meant a lot to me and the boys are the Vic in Bermondsey and our beloved *Tattershall Castle* right in the heart of London. It's a boat with a restaurant and club permanently moored right opposite the London Eye with Big Ben to the right and the rest of the river snaking up to East London to your left. You can never get bored of a view like that. As the writer Samuel Johnson said, 'When a man is tired of London, he is tired of life.' I think that's very true. The *Tattershall Castle* has only recently had a five million pound refit but I loved it the way it was.

I had my birthday on there last year and that's something that needs getting straight. I woke up on 29 August last year feeling like shit. I had come down with some kind of virus, I felt really bad and if I hadn't invited a few people I would have cancelled it. I arranged to have a private bar for the night, which was kindly given to me by the management and much appreciated. August is a time when a lot of people are on holiday etc and it also fell on a Saturday. So you wouldn't have all the workers around and at the end of the day they guaranteed a full bar which has got to be good business all round, hasn't it?

Like I said, I was feeling worse as the day progressed but I didn't want to let anyone down, including the boat who had supplied the venue. It proved to be misguided. First there were only a few people there, but we had Birmingham at home that day and obviously a lot of the boys came through later to give me their good wishes. There was about 20 girls there and old school friends so it wasn't just a football turn out, far from it. Maybe a hundred turned up through the night. Not in one go, everything was cool. There was no trouble whatsoever. You had pals of mine from Palace and Pompey mixing with all the boys.

I felt worse as the night went on and at about 1am I had to leave my own party, which wasn't good, but the bollocks that was going on after the party was unbelievable. Spurs Old Bill paid a visit, threatening all sorts (allegedly) if they let me on there again. I told the governor to tell them to go fuck themselves, as this was nothing to do with them and I had done nothing wrong which in fairness he eventually did, but then Chelsea supposedly had a go at the door.

But then Chelsea were supposed to have had a go at the door, something I find hard to believe with the wankers. I say one thing to a certain member of security on there, you know who you are. I don't control the whole of London, I cannot be responsible for what goes on when I'm not there, so I do not need all this fucking hassle. It's our city and we're not going anywhere. That off my chest, the boat will always have a special place in our hearts. I said for my co-defendants to keep each other going while inside, how when we were out we would be on the boat in the summer having a cold one. That seemed like a distant memory, as we were driven over Lambeth Bridge in a sweatbox on our way to jail with the boat glistening on the water.

Finally, another little venue, the Vic in Bermondsey, which is close to my heart, and a few of the boys over the years, they have all been there with me at one time or another, Terry, Clive, Carl, the Aberdeen boys, Martin. It was run by two brothers, Michael and Pat and one was mad Millwall, the other West Ham, believe it or not. Mike is the tallest man in the world, but an absolute gent with it. They both had the right idea about running a pub and would always stand around. It was sheer class and even though it was obviously a Millwall boozer I had no grief in there whatsoever as I only lived a few miles away. It had a great little sound system in there, it reminded me of a smaller version of the Bull, and the two brothers had the same respect and way of running the pub as Tony and Terry.

Friday night was the night when the Old Kent Road was at its heyday. It was on the circuit along with Joanna's and the Gym Palace, both closed now. The world turned upside down when it burnt down with the Tanners Arms, the Grange and the Blue Anchor, all staunch Millwall pubs at the time. Nine times out of ten I would just plot in the Vic as it also had the best looking barmaids in London. I swear they must have recruited them from a model agency but it's also an excellent business ploy. Nice girls to look at, good atmosphere, good music, open until 2am – where else do you need to go?

My old mate Terry used to come over there the most and he loved the place, but he's like a robot and bang on 11.30pm he would leave to get the last northbound Tube back to Barnet. We still laugh about that today. Although he was the sensible one, by then I would have the flavour and end up out on it all night, which used to annoy Tel no end.

I even took some of the Aberdeen boys down there once, then we went to Caesar's opposite, where I stressed to them to behave themselves, and then I lost my phone, and because it was insured on the way home I popped into the Old Bill station to make a claim. I thought I spotted some toerag with it and started wrestling through the doors with this geezer to the astonishment of the Aberdeen fellas who I told to behave all night. It's such a naughty manor down there that the Old Bill just fucked me off out of it, leaving behind some poor bastard clutching his mobile phone.

Yes, they were great times, and the Vic was a nice change from Tottenham and the West End for us. I kept saying I would pop in there again soon and if I'm welcome I will. They ran a good pub so I will see you again soon. Take care boys and thanks for the gesture when I went away, something I've never forgotten.

CHAPTER 23

BANNED!

BANNING ORDERS AND GUANTANAMO BAY – IS THERE A DIFFERENCE?
Banning orders are those clever devices that the football authorities have come up with to keep people like me away from games. Over the years, the terms of banning orders have become more and more draconian, as you'll see. Here is a brief history of the banning orders that I have been put under in my time. I know it sounds strange to compare banning orders with the treatment handed out to those accused of acts of terrorism, but I consider them to be wholly inappropriate responses to the issue of football violence and a severe infringement of my civil liberties. My banning order states that I shall:

... be subject to a football banning order and must report initially to Lewisham Police Station at 43

Lewisham High Street, Lewisham, within a five-day period, beginning with the date of making the disorder (Belmarsh Country). Subsequently you must endure the duration of the order, not to enter any premises for the purpose of attending any football matches in England and Wales that are regulated for the purposes of the Football Spectators Act, 1989, and when required to do so under section 1936 of that Act report to that or any other main Police Station in England or Wales.

What is more, I must also, 'Subject to an exemption surrender [my] passport at the time or between the times specified in a notice'. As you see my banning orders becoming harsher and harsher as I go through the court system, I'll leave you to judge whether they are 'fair' or not. I know what I think.

At the end of 2003, I was handed a banning order from Tottenham Old Bill. Happy Christmas, boys! It came right out of the blue. And there was me thinking that we lived in a free country, not Stalin's Russia or Nazi Germany. Sometimes I think we really do live in a police state. I can't believe that scum like rapists, nonces and muggers are allowed to walk the streets while the police target all the wrong people.

They tried to put me on one of the severest bans ever handed out. They wanted to ban me from a two-mile radius of Tottenham's ground but also, get this, from an area stretching from the River Thames to the A406 – this basically covers the whole of Central London – for a five-year period. On top of that, I have to hand in my passport whenever England play and sign on at Lewisham Police Station. Now, here's a quick geography lesson: Lewisham nick is bang in the middle of Millwall country. As one of the complaints laid against me was from my actions at Millwall v Spurs, I'll let you draw your own conclusions as to why they've done that.

Pathetic, isn't it? They make out that there's a shortage of police, but anyone who has been to Spurs v Arsenal or Spurs v Chelsea will know what I'm talking about. I think that they must have a special underground factory where they press a button, punch in 'Spurs v Chelsea', and thousands of robocops come up from their bunker in full stormtrooper outfits. As soon as the game's over, they all disappear underground again. That is the only explanation I can think of for their lack of appearance on our streets from day to day. So don't be fooled by all the propaganda that the Old Bill spout about football taking them away from policing crime. If the cowardly fuckers were to get out of their warm cars and stations, and actually walked the streets, they might make things better for our children and the vulnerable. Everyone on the street knows that this is true, so stop protecting buildings like Parliament and Buckingham Palace that already have enough protection, and look after those who need it instead.

It seems that the police have been putting a case together on me for many years. A lot of the boys have been picked off before me so I would be lying if I said I didn't expect it. I think Tottenham Old Bill have had their pound of flesh from me, and so have the club. I've been stabbed, cut, served three years in jail, lost numerous jobs, caused my family a lot of heartache and I think I deserve a break. The Old Bill have got to understand that these people are my friends as well, people I have grown up with. Some of them go back nearly twenty years with me. No amount of banning orders or jail sentences will make me totally turn my back on that. It's not possible and it's not right and the Old Bill can go and fuck themselves if they think I'm going to. I will not be told who to associate with by the likes of them. I will fight for my basic human right to share a drink with whoever I choose, whatever they do to me.

By the time this book comes out, I shall probably be on a banning order. At present, I am fighting the order on specific issues, such as the ridiculous ban from Central London, which is pathetic as I live only twelve minutes' journey by train from the heart of London. What they are proposing, effectively, is that if I want to travel into London to take my daughter for example to Hamleys, or go to the theatre or visit friends, which we often do, I could be arrested. Well, not even the Police Commissioner himself is going to spoil my daughter's days with me without a fight. Incidentally, it is the Met that is pushing for the West End ban. Tottenham police are laughing, saying it's nothing to do with them. How pathetic is that? I suppose the Commissioner woke up one morning and thought, Fuck all the street robbers and assaulting lunatics plaguing London's streets, I must ban Trevor Tanner from London. Yes, that's what I'll do today. Fuck him. I shall be fighting this part of the order in particular, as it is totally ridiculous. Of course, just to make life even more difficult, you cannot get legal aid for an adjournment on these orders. This has almost certainly forced a lot of people given these orders to give in straight away, as they cannot afford the cost of fighting them. We're not talking peanuts here, and on that point I would like to thank Ola, who not only represented me on this case but has always been there for me while I fight the greatest battle of my life – the struggle for custody of my daughter. I will never forget his advice and guidance. Cheers, brother.

Obviously, if you're reading this, you are clearly a fan of great literature. So here's some more fine words for you. This is another extract from that great work of art, my banning order:

The above main person must not go within a two-mile radius of any regulated football match after a time, four hours preceding the advertised kick-off and before a time four hours after they advertise their actual kick-off time.

In relation to Condition 1 above, the radius only is reduced to a one-mile radius of any regulated football match being played at Crystal Palace Football Club, Selhurst Park Stadium, Holmesdale Road, South Norwood, London, South East, 266P6U.

The above named person must not enter within the London area as defined by the borders of the A406 (North Circular Road) and the River Thames when Tottenham Hotspur Football Club play a regulated football match in London on a match day for the twenty-four-hour period of that day.

The above named person must not enter any town

or city where Tottenham Hotspur Football Club play a regulated football match on a match day for the twenty-four-hour period of that day.

Nothing very democratic about that order, I think you would agree. It's probably one of the most draconian orders handed out. I don't know of another one as harsh, that's for sure. As far as I know, the bods from Guantanamo Bay – who obviously deep down hate this country, whereas I love it – have been subjected to the same sort of restrictions that they are trying to impose on me. This is absolutely outrageous: no trial, just 'take that' because of your history. Am I a terrorist? Am I affecting national security? It's fucking bollocks, and that's the reason why I am fighting it. What good would it do for the increasingly sinister and paranoid police? I really do not know. What chance have you got when Scotland Yard and the Commissioner of Police himself, no less, sanctions a ban from Central London and the surrounding areas? If I have to go into Central London for work, as most people do, what am I supposed to say to a future employer? 'Sorry, mate, but come midnight on a Saturday or Sunday, or a Tuesday or Wednesday, I cannot come to work as I'm not allowed in London.' Yeah, right. Don't call us, we'll call you. Are the Old Bill going to pay me for loss of earnings? No. I will never accept that part of the ban and they can go and shove it.

THE OFFICIAL VERSION

After a lot of thought, I decided to include in this book a breakdown of all the police reports that have been used against me in court as evidence. You will have read my accounts of these incidents earlier in the book, so it's worth seeing how the authorities portray them. It's probably something we'll have to agree to disagree on. The reports are from the various intelligence officers that have followed me all over England for years. They give a fascinating insight into how clued up and well organised the football Old Bill are. And obviously how badly they wanted me off the scene. I am going to give details of the video evidence rather than the actual written statements – there's enough of that to fill a book on its own. I'll show the statements as they were presented, with my comments in brackets.

20 MARCH 1993 – ATTACK ON THE THREE KINGS PUBLIC HOUSE (SEE CHAPTER 4)

This is the one I got my three years for, so you can check what the police say here against what I wrote back in Chapter 4.

THE THREE KINGS PUBLIC HOUSE, VIOLENT DISORDER, 1993, SPURS V CHELSEA

Clip 1 – Video from police observation post; Trevor Tanner with long, dark brown hair in a ponytail, wearing a green anorak, with eye holes in the hood and on the left arm cuff. [Anorak, my arse! It was a £600 CP Company Limited edition coat.] Outside the Three Kings public house, North End Road. Known THFC hooligans can be seen behind Tanner in the doorway of the pub. Tanner throws a bottle of liquid at unknown target to the left of the camera view. As more THFC hooligans exit the pub missiles are landing in front of the pub. The camera concentrates on Tanner as he reaches into his left lower anorak with his right hand to pull out what appears to be a short wooden stave, whilst holding what appears to be a Stanley knife in his left hand. Tanner appears to shout, 'Come on!' and then the THFC hooligans charge out of the pub, throwing missiles as they go. Tanner disappears off screen to the left. [To have it with the scum.] Other THFC hooligans can be seen brandishing wooden staves.

Tanner then appears back within the group before charging off down the middle of the road and off screen [Chelsea are on their toes!] with his stave in hand whilst other THFC hooligans also run off down the road in the same direction. A police protective carrier then arrives on the scene and the THFC hooligans begin running back towards and into the pub. [The Old Bill filmed it all going off until they had enough on video evidence to come through our doors.]

CHELSEA AT HOME, 3 APRIL 2004
(CHAPTER 4)

THFC played Chelsea in the Premiership. A bit of rivalry exists between the two hooligan groups. [That's one way of putting it!] THFC hooligans met initially at the Cockerel public house and, following open abuse from the management of the public house directed towards police intelligence officers, and the finding inside of the THFC football hooligan on breach of a banning order, the public house was closed by Public Order, s.179 of the Licensing Act, 1964. As police were dealing with the male in breach of his banning order, Trevor Tanner was seen to go into the public house, but the premises were closed down soon afterwards. [Let's recap: the pub was shut because someone swore at the Old Bill; or because of a breach of a banning order; or because of me. The systematic culling of our boozers has got to stop.]

THFC hooligans regroup north of the stadium in the Gillespie public house and Trevor Tanner was again present. [Maybe you would rather we just stood on street corners.] The match itself was quiet [only because the scum never showed, as usual], and following the game the THFC group finally formed up at the Elmshurst public house, Lordship Lane, N17, and was monitored by police intelligence offices. A police van soon arrived at the premises and soon afterwards a brick was thrown from the rear of the beer garden at this vehicle and for the next thirty-five to forty minutes four bricks were thrown from the rear of the pub garden at this vehicle. The premises were subsequently entered by police [full-on riot squad] and three THFC hooligans were arrested with the premises being cleared of the rest of the THFC group.

Trevor Tanner was inside the premises when entered by police and his behaviour was such that he was handcuffed while police searched him. However, he was not arrested and left the premises once he had been dealt with by police.

Again, by no coincidence was Trevor Tanner found

at a venue where disorder was occurring. He chose to socialise at a venue where THFC hooligans were present and disorder was likely.

MAN UNITED AWAY, 20 MARCH 2004, PART 1 (CHAPTER 5)

Clip 1 – (Video Film PC 44477YAR Totty) Group of THFC hooligans being monitored by the police as they walk towards the Manchester United Football Club, Old Trafford Stadium. Trevor Tanner can be seen with short-cropped hair [Correct. Not a crime, is it?] wearing a beige knee-length coat [Maharishi raincoat], white top [Adidas trackie top], blue jeans and white trainers [Stan Smith]. The shouted words 'Come on!' can be heard.

Clip 2 – THFC hooligans running across the road, the words 'Come on!' can be heard. PC Totty narrates to the camera. Trevor Tanner can be heard shouting repeatedly 'Come on!' [Myself, T and a few others broke away and fronted their boozer, which was rammo. If they had taken the bait it would have gone radio.]

Clip 3 – THFC hooligans walking down the road, some spilled into the roadway itself. PC Totty can be heard to shout, 'Go on, lads, run right by me, go on!' Another voice, believed to be that of a known hooligan, shouts back, 'You'll get it as well!' The camera pans left and Trevor Tanner can be seen in the centre of the road among the THFC group.

Clip 4 – THFC hooligan group walking off to MUFC stadium.

Clip 5 – Large group of THFC hooligans exiting MUFC stadium. THFC hooligan group becomes more defiant as they continue to walk away from stadium. Mounted police can be heard shouting at the group to keep moving. [That's one way of putting it.] Trevor Tanner can be seen furthest from the camera, near to where the mounted police are advancing. The THFC hooligan group then turn right away from the main group of dispersing supporters. Repeated shouts of abuse can be heard and the group starts acting in a disorderly manner, while police attempt to control situation. [!] PC Totty can be heard shouting at the group [he's always shouting] to bring their attention to him video filming them. Trevor Tanner can be seen to the rear of the THFC hooligan group as they become involved in an attempt to confront rival supporters and acting in a disorderly manner, while police attempt to control situation.

A small group of THFC hooligans hang back, loitering and repeatedly turning round to look back in direction of rivals. Manchester United supporters are being moved on by police in distance. Police presence then have to rapidly change attention to the other THFC supporter stragglers, including known football hooligans who are again attempting to seek confrontation. These males are again moved off by police. The main THFC group can be seen even further in the distance.

Clip 6 – Concerted attempts at confrontation by THFC hooligan group, which is barely contained by police, with mounted police shepherding the main

THFC group away. [Spurs taking it to the Mancs big time on their own manor.] Manchester United hooligan suspects then approach from opposite side of dual carriageway, with police in middle of road preventing the two hooligans [Just] from engaging in outright violence. [Spoilsports.] Trevor Tanner can be seen at the front of the THFC group during the confrontation. Trevor Tanner can be seen at the front of the group just behind a mounted police officer taking pictures of PC Totty with a mobile phone camera.

MAN UNITED AWAY, 20 MARCH 2004, PART 2 (CHAPTER 5)

[The following is taken from the statement provided by PC Totty, the intelligence officer assigned to us. It gives a tiny glimmer of the respect even plod had for us at the time.]

At about 11.15am I was deployed at Manchester Piccadilly Railway Station, monitoring trains as they arrived from London. A train duly arrived and a THFC hooligan group, numbering about forty persons, disembark from it. This group pass through the concourse of the station and then into Manchester City Centre. Police followed the group, which subsequently settled in a pub on Deansgate in the City Centre, called the Moon Under Water.

At about 12.30pm Trevor Tanner arrived at this venue and went inside. At about 1.30pm the THFC group left the pub and tried to head in the direction of two other pubs, The Sawyer Arms and The Pig and Porcupine, where I was aware part of the THFC hooligan group were resident. The THFC hooligan group was not allowed to do this and was forced to go in the opposite direction by police. [We should have broken through the Old Bill then. It would have been helpful if the Mancs had at least made a fucking effort.] Trevor Tanner was again part of that group at that time and was followed through Manchester City Centre, where he and his associates boarded a tram that took them to the vicinity of Old Trafford Football Stadium, the home ground of MUFC. [A fucking nightmare journey. London Underground, all is forgiven.] The group alighted at Salford Quays Metro Station and walked to the ground. On route to the stadium the group approached a pub called Sam Platts, which is a well-known members-only pub, used by Manchester United fans. Trevor Tanner turns to face the camera. He is a white male, with stocky build [Fucking cheek! Tall and lean I would have said], short, cropped hair and can be seen wearing a long, beige-coloured raincoat, a white tracksuit top, dark trousers and jeans. The camera pans left and the group can be seen crossing the road to the opposite footway. Sam Platts public house is positioned to the right of the group, moving to the right side of the road was a good strategic move by the group. It afforded them a better angle to view the premises and allowed them more time to respond to Manchester United supporters or hooligans coming out of the venue to confront them. As we moved closer to the pub the mood of the THFC group changed as they began focusing on the pub and grouped tighter together. On the commentary on the tape I can be heard mentioning Trevor Tanner, who appeared to be trying to organise the group by shouting 'Come on!' Although there were some police officers present my opinion was that there was insufficient resources to prevent disorder, should either the THFC group storm the pub, or the Manchester United hooligans come out of the pub to confront them. [Why the fuck didn't they? We were on their manor fifty-handed, taking the piss and fronting their boozer.]

I ran to the footway outside Sam Platts public house to get between the pub and the THFC group. If disorder did occur I was well placed to secure video evidence. Concerned that disorder was about to break out, I highlighted my presence to the group, who had witnessed me filming them for most of the day, by shouting: 'Go on, lads, run right past me! Go on!' This did indeed get their attention, as was desired, and the hooligans shouted back: 'You'll get it as well!'

Calls of 'Yids' can be heard and numerous males can be seen looking past the camera at Sam Platts. He is clearly assessing the chance of a fight. A police van crosses from left to right and stops between the THFC group and the venue. [We then make our merry way to the stadium, where I bump into a few old friends working with the Manc ground security.]

[This part of the account is from after the game.] Police statements continued, the command team had given a direction that the THFC hooligans should be made to go to the right alongside Sir Matt Busby Way, towards Trafford Park, rather than left towards Chester Road. Members of the THFC hooligan group come out together from the stadium. I am heard telling them that they had to go left and not be allowed to go to their right. Trevor Tanner is one of the lead hooligans and on video I can be heard speaking to him. The group moves off in the preferred direction and they are followed in the initial stages. The group is intermixed with bona fide supporters who are leaving the stadium. However, as the group nears Trafford Park Road the crowd was thinned somewhat and the THFC group is more apparent. Mounted police are on the scene at this stage and position themselves near to the group. They can be heard shouting, 'Keep moving!' Trevor Tanner can again be seen amongst the group being moved on. Shortly afterwards, they can be heard shouting to one of the THFC group to keep out of trouble.

The group, not one compact unit but spread out, reached the junction with Trafford Park Road and must turn right along this road. The THFC group is not contained, however, and several hooligans have evaded escort and are crossing from left to right in front of the camera. Numerous other males are looking in the direction of the police escort, with their back to the camera and it appears to me that most of the men are actually Manchester United supporters, but amongst the Manchester United supporters are mixed a number of other THFC hooligan stragglers.

The camera pans left then moves forward to the THFC group, as it was my assessment that disorder was imminent. With the THFC group not under effective control I felt that to position the camera overtly near to them could help to prevent disorder.

As the camera moves forward the chant 'Yids, Yids, Yids!' can be heard. As the camera reaches the THFC group Trevor Tanner can be seen walking backwards, looking in the direction of the Manchester United hooligans, positioned behind the camera. I can be heard pointing out to the THFC hooligans that they are all on camera. Mounted police try to move the THFC group on, but instead the THFC hooligans can be seen fanning out across the road, from right to left, attempting to get at Manchester United supporters behind the camera. The camera then rotates 180 degrees and hundreds of supporters, mostly Manchester United, can be seen spread out across the road. [Tell me about it!] On the right, some sort of incident is occurring and foot-duty and mounted police are drawn to it. It is unclear exactly what has happened [No it's not] but it becomes apparent THFC hooligans are intermingled with Manchester United supporters. I could be heard pointing out to local police officers the THFC hooligans known to me. These hooligans are allowed through the police cordon in the direction of their THFC associates. As we are running after the THFC hooligans I had to remove my helmet to prevent it falling off. My peaked duty helmet remained in my left hand and the camera remained in my right. My personal protective equipment, baton and CS incapacitant remained holstered. [Good job as well!] To my left, not caught on camera, were Manchester United supporters. I cannot recollect the precise numbers. [A lot.] Several THFC hooligans can be seen running from left to right and some of them can be seen jumping over metal central reservations that divide the two carriageways, heading for the Manchester United supporters out of camera shot. I witness, not caught on camera, a male throw a missile [It wasn't me] with his right hand towards the THFC group. [It definitely wasn't me!] I then filmed the male and recorded verbally what I had seen.

The camera pans right and the main THFC hooligan group can be seen. We have succeeded in getting to the front of the group, who had spread out across the road and come forward, threateningly, some shouting: 'Yids, yids, yids.' Most of the police resources are on the wrong side of the group, not positioned to keep them back from the Manchester United hooligans who are approaching from behind me. Trevor Tanner is still part of the THFC group. A white male with a dark, hooded top can be seen, beckoning with his right hand, shouting 'Get up here!' in a Mancunian accent.

The camera moves back in the direction of the main THFC group and at this stage I felt that serious disorder was imminent. [It would have if you weren't such a spoilsport!] I was becoming increasingly concerned for my own personal safety and all of my defensive equipment remained holstered. Police officers using cameras often become targets in disorder situations as criminals realise that video footage secured against them normally carries significant weight in a court of law. [Tell me about it] The video footage now moves to the floor and myself in the middle of several THFC hooligans. It was unclear if they were trying to attack me or to get past me to get to their opponents. [That's more like it!] I swung out at shoulder-height to try to create some space, trying to stop them coming forward and protect myself. My helmet was still in my left hand and I connected with a male to my left. I am unsure if it hit him on the side of the head or the shoulder. The male was white with dark hair, about twenty-five years old, wearing a dark coat. He shouted something at me [Probably: 'That fucking hurt!'] and then moved back... the camera comes up and the hooligans can be seen moving backwards. 'Switch it off, Totty' can be heard shouted twice. [Fair enough.]

This only served to highlight my concern that I was a possible target to attack. However, I continued filming as I felt this was a key aspect in preventing the THFC group becoming involved in all-out disorder. [Can't have been that fucking worried, eh?] Mounted and foot-police can then be seen shepherding the THFC group backwards and I can be heard shouting to PC Wilmot to shoulder me. The camera pans 180 degrees in the direction of a group of males approaching on a footway. This group is not known to me and I assume that they are Manchester United hooligans. [Nope!]

Mounted and foot-duty police officers deploy down the footway to move the Manchester United hooligans backwards. The camera spins to view the THFC group again and police officers start moving the THFC hooligans down one side of the dual carriageway towards Manchester City Centre. This road is Chester Road. PC Wilmot and I move to the right to take up position on the central reservation. Mounted police officers are trying to control the THFC group but they are obstructed by them. The camera moves left to view some THFC stragglers and then continues to rotate round to view the opposite side of the dual carriageway. Tens of Manchester United hooligans can be seen stalking the THFC group. The camera focuses on a white male with short hair. He can be seen shouting towards the THFC group: 'Is this all you've got?' [It was enough to take the piss on your manor, wasn't it?] My view is that he is trying to bait the THFC group and provoke them into confrontation. [No flies on you, are there?]

The camera swings round to the THFC group and they have indeed come forward, still positioned near the central reservation. PC Wilmot and I were effectively in the middle of the two groups. Several of the THFC group had come forward and I was genuinely concerned that with police outnumbered serious disorder between the two groups would commence and that we would be attacked.

The video footage becomes blurred, as to protect myself and prevent disorder I swing out with my left hand, with my helmet still in it. A known THFC hooligan had flanked me and I connected with his upper body on the side, I cannot be certain exactly where. I can then be heard shouting 'Back off!' The fact that this male is so near to the central reservation barrier with willing opponents nearby is a clear sign to me of his violent intentions. The THFC group continues to look in the direction of the camera across the carriageway. As several people start jogging backwards and forwards, left to right, a mounted police officer intervenes at the barrier to stop the THFC hooligans going over it.

Trevor Tanner can be seen moving back from the central reservation. Although not caught on camera fighting, his advanced position at the central reservation clearly indicates his desire to confront his Manchester United rivals. [Fair enough.] He is again giving leadership by his actions. The camera spins to the Manchester United side of the carriageway where there are now numerous police officers. Summing up... an organised THFC hooligan group travelled to this event. Trevor Tanner was part of this group, prior to the game and during its dispersal from the stadium. Prior to the game as the group approached Sam Platts public house Trevor Tanner was clearly trying to organise the group and during dispersal he actively went in search of disorder. The video evidence secured and my account of the day's events confirm that Trevor Tanner does pose a real threat to supporters and community safety and that pro-active steps should be taken to prevent Trevor Tanner from engaging in any such further behaviour.

ARSENAL AWAY (CHAPTER 6)

[My account of this game doesn't appear in the book, so you'll have to take plod's word with a pinch of salt. Of course, I provide a running commentary in brackets throughout.]

On 25/04/04 THFC played Arsenal at Highbury in the Premiership, kick-off at 4.05pm. At about midday a group of Arsenal hooligans was found loitering outside the Red Lion public house, High Road, N17, about half a mile away from the THFC stadium. [Well spotted, because we never saw them all day. In fact, a good friend of mine said that his firm used to call them the invisible firm. As far as I am concerned, that is spot on. They are a waste of time, worse than Chelsea. The best row I ever had with them was on a tube train and that was only because they had to stand and fight as we were in a tunnel and outnumbered ten to one. On their day, they can pull a herd together but I don't think they have the desire we have.]

The pub had been closed for several months and was newly opened for this fixture under new management. The pub was traditionally known as a visiting supporters' pub, but the new management had decided to market it as a home supporters' pub. The Arsenal hooligans numbering about fifty persons were placed on police transport and moved to the

Park Hotel public house. [I wonder if the police would have moved us on like that. I don't think so!]

About half a mile east of the THFC stadium on N17 the THFC hooligan group were aware of their Arsenal hooligan counterparts meeting at the Red Lion and were immediately aware of their relocation to the Park Lane Hotel. [Might have had something to do with the boozer being surrounded by fifty Old Bill. Probably a bit of a giveaway.] The THFC group had been relatively spread out but now regrouped in large numbers at the Olive Branch public house in Park Lane. As it was along the escort route to the stadium the licensee was spoken to at the Olive Branch and it was agreed that he would stop serving and close. [Here we go again. How stupid can you be? Put 200 bods out on the street. Duh!] Many of them loitered in the street nearby.

At 2.55pm Trevor Tanner was one of those loitering on Park Lane looking in the direction of the Park Lane Hotel. The THFC hooligan group were subsequently forced by the police to disperse towards the stadium to prevent any confrontation between rival supporters. [To prevent a massacre.] Yet again Trevor Tanner had placed himself in a location where disorder was a possibility. At 3.00pm a police escort of the Arsenal hooligans was placed on public transport and taken to the Highbury area. [There were only thirty of them. They were going for the Championship in our manor and they brought thirty! Fucking pathetic.] The escort of the main Arsenal group along Park Lane was a slow one, especially as when the escort reached the stadium hundreds of THFC hooligans and supporters formed up in Park Lane. [It was an unbelievable scene!] A significant use of force by police was necessary to drive them back. The escort reached the visiting supporters' turnstiles without confrontation and the Arsenal supporters began to enter.

Despite a protective police cordon around the visiting supporters' turnstiles, the density and the ferocity of the THFC supporters in Park Lane was unprecedented. Various uses of force by the police were needed to keep THFC hooligans back. [Tell me about it. There were dogs, vans, robocops, helicopters – have I forgotten anything?] The occasional bona fide Arsenal supporter became the victim of attack. [They shouldn't attack innocent fans in hotel bars in Manchester then.] But by and large police prevented any serious escalation.

WOLVES AWAY, 15 MAY 2004 (CHAPTER 9)

Clip 1 – THFC hooligan group arriving and entering Pie Factory public house, Tipton. Trevor Tanner can be seen at the side of the public house, with short, cropped hair wearing a white V-neck T-shirt, green/brown US military-style combat trousers [Maharishi], white trainers [Stan Smiths], a white top with black arm ties around his waist [German tracksuit top] and a yellow metal bracelet on his right wrist. [Hello! It's fucking silver. You definitely need those mincers tested.]

Clip 2 – THFC risk supporters group brought out of

Pie Factory public house and contained in police bubble escort. Tanner can be seen making a V for Victory hand signal to the camera.

Clip 3 – THFC risk supporter group exiting stadium post-match. Trevor Tanner now wearing a white top with black stripes down the arms [Did they think I was going to change clothes?] can be seen at the front of the THFC hooligan group as the camera pans right and the THFC hooligan group walk uphill away from the stadium. THFC hooligan group walking through car park attempting to turn towards public house where Wolverhampton hooligans are present and police prevented this.

Clip 4 – THFC hooligan group turning into ring road, St Patrick's, whilst a Wolverhampton hooligan group appear on opposite side of dual carriageway. Police try and contain THFC hooligan group, who run down in a disorderly manner and once contained attempt to break out. Trevor Tanner can be seen amongst the foremost group of THFC hooligans as police try to stop the advance of THFC hooligan group, who are mainly on the footway. Tanner climbs over the pedestrian barrier to avoid this. Tanner then walks out into the road, he appears to move his arms around in a confrontational manner and repeatedly turns around to see where the rest of the THFC group is and appears to be shouting to rally the THFC hooligan group. [Wolves directly in front, just behind Old Bill.] A West Midlands evidence gatherer then can be seen concentrating his video filming on Tanner and pushing him back once.

Clip 5 – THFC hooligan group mainly in middle of dual carriageway, with police unsuccessfully trying to contain them, have formed a cordon to stop their advance. [Old Bill lost it!] THFC continue to try to advance and engage in a confrontation. Trevor Tanner can be seen to again climb over the pedestrian railings. THFC then halt at a junction near the railway station subway. Trevor Tanner then appears from the left of the screen directly in front of the camera. Tanner paces back and forth, looking past the position of the police cordon, behind the camera position and at one point raises a hand/arm to obscure the view of his face and appears to say something like, 'Fucking cameras!' A police officer then makes him stand on a footway. THFC hooligan group loiters at the junction with Tanner with them.

Ordinary football supporters begin to approach from the rear and join the group. Repeated shouts of 'Right!' can be heard and the THFC hooligans respond by surging forwards towards the police line, shouting, 'Yids! Yids!' Trevor Tanner can be seen at the forefront of this surge. THFC hooligan group then continues to loiter, still interested in a confrontation with the Wolves hooligans further behind the camera position.

Clip 6 – THFC hooligan group running under railway bridge in disorderly charge and then making off to industrial area unpoliced. Trevor Tanner can be seen at the front of the breakaway group heading for the industrial estate and PC Totty can be heard to shout, 'Trevor Tanner at the front is leading!'

Clip 7 – THFC hooligan group continuing to walk towards the industrial estate area.

Clip 8 – THFC hooligan group continuing to walk around the industrial area. [Where the fuck are Wolves? We should have annihilated the boozer in the estate just to teach them a lesson!]

Clip 9 – THFC breakaway hooligan group crossing road, walking in direction of Wolverhampton railway station. Trevor Tanner can be seen at the front of this group.

Clip 10 – THFC hooligan breakaway group approach Wolverhampton Railway Station. Police move THFC hooligan group into station.

MILLWALL AWAY, 4 AUGUST 2001, PRE-SEASON FRIENDLY, PART 1 (CHAPTER 15)

Clip 1 – (Video Film Metropolitan Police Photographer) THFC hooligan group gathered outside Gregorian public house. [Fucking brilliant place to meet, bang on Jamaica Road. Piss-take!]

Clip 2 – THFC hooligan group under police escort to New Den stadium. [150–200 top boys marching through Bermondsey, taking it to Millwall. Where are you?]

Clip 3 – The same.

Clip 4 – THFC hooligan group involved in disorder with police during escort. Trevor Tanner, with short, cropped reddish dyed hair, wearing a white T-shirt can be seen briefly near the front of the THFC group shouting, 'Cunts. You're nothing!' Disorder then occurs and police use force to defend themselves.

Clip 5 – THFC hooligan group leave stadium early to confront Millwall supporters outside. Disorderly behaviour and scuffles with police. [Tottenham taking the piss big style!] Trevor Tanner wearing a white T-shirt [Maharishi], blue denim jeans [Evisu] with a white motif on the back pockets, white trainers [Adidas Stan Smiths], and a yellow metal bracelet or watch on his right wrist [My baby girl's hair band actually. I was also wearing a chunky silver bracelet. Maybe he was colour blind!], can be seen walking purposefully to the forecourt of the group. A police officer behind him can be seen to draw an extended telescopic baton. Both Tanner and this police officer move off camera to the right of the screen. An incident then occurs off camera [Fucking tell me about it!] and Tanner can then be seen to limp away in the opposite direction. [So the fuck would you if your leg had been hit with a metal riot baton!]

MILLWALL AWAY, 4 AUGUST 2001, PRE-SEASON FRIENDLY, PART 2 (CHAPTER 15)
THFC exiting the stadium. PC Totty's statement:
Clip 6 – THFC hooligan group exiting the stadium prior to the end of the match, disorder immediately breaks out as the THFC group attempts to make its way towards the turnstiles of the Millwall supporters' section of the stadium. Tanner continues forwards towards the Millwall section, despite the presence of foot-duty and mounted police. THFC hooligan group running away from stadium. [Go on! We were actually sprinting down the underpass

trying to lose plod, which we very nearly did, so we could get to Millwall's boozer before plod and smash the fuck out of it. If we had broken loose we would have done, without a shadow of a doubt.]

Clip 7 – THFC hooligan group, including Trevor Tanner contained by police. [We had a ring of steel around us, which was impossible to penetrate. It included robocops, five deep at least, with horses and dogs and then vans beyond that. The clever cunts decided to situate us just under the brow of a hill, next to Southwark Park, while on the hill, in the safety of the park, every piece of scum from the local estates was happily allowed to rain us with bricks and bottles. The difference being we did not have fucking steel helmets and body armour.]

Clip 8 – Serious disorder between Millwall and THFC hooligans groups. [Across the road, which was a total head fuck, a few of Spurs who had broken free were ripping down fences to get at Millwall in the park and were met with a barrage of missiles for their trouble. From what I could see Millwall were doing anything they could to stop the boys getting in the park. And, apart from a few of the old faces, they were running up and down the hill with demented looks of sheer shock and horror, trying to hold them together. I don't blame them, as by the looks of the kindergarten boys on the hill throwing missiles, if we had broken free we'd have fucking annihilated them.]

Clip 9 – THFC hooligan group contained by police. [Game over.]

MILLWALL AWAY, 4 AUGUST 2001, PRE-SEASON FRIENDLY, PART 3 (CHAPTER 15)
Witness Statement 496YR John Foreman
[Here's an extra eyewitness account from a different copper, to go with the star witness account from PC Totty. It uniquely authenticates my own account, something I don't believe has been done before, so enjoy.]

Trevor Tanner can be seen for the first time just back from the front of the THFC group and the front of the cordon. He has cropped and dyed hair and is wearing a white T-shirt. He is shouting obscenities [Bollocks!] and the words 'Cunts, you are nothing!' can be heard with this abuse, apparently directed at a small group of Millwall supporters behind the police cordon. The camera then concentrates on a white male, with cropped, dark brown hair, stocky-to-fat build, wearing an open, zip-front tracksuit top, royal-blue crewneck with white top ribs around the body and a Nike tick on the front. The man is picked from behind by the shield of an officer to which he turns and reacts by saying, 'Shut up! What's the matter with you? You start hitting me with things like that, that don't hurt me!' A number of mounted police can then be seen coming into view to the left of the screen to move the THFC group back and down the junction into Silward Street. This incident has a catalytic and catastrophic effect on the mood of the THFC hooligans, who react violently. THFC hooligans at the front of the group surge forward and engage in disorderly and threatening behaviour towards the officers. The THFC officers attempt to defend themselves and their colleagues and maintain the cordon to prevent serious disorder occurring should the group break out and confront the Millwall supporters. [That's the idea!]

I can recall seeing a number of THFC hooligan subjects confronted with police officers carrying shields and wearing protective public order helmets, resorting to kicking out at the THFC officers legs, trying to stamp on their knees, which resulted in me using my baton in defence of these THFC officers being kicked. [Good for you.]

The disorderly group was literally beaten back by the THFC officers [That's true] and whilst they are still contained by police the THFC groups are angry and aggressive towards the police. Overall this incident lasts two minutes. Clearly multiple arrests for threatening behaviour are appropriate but impossible due to the sheer number of persons involved in this conduct and the presence of so few police officers.

[PC Foreman now goes on to describe the events as he saw them as we exited the stadium.]

Disorder immediately breaks out as the THFC group tries to make its way towards the turnstiles of the Millwall supporters' section of the stadium. I can be seen running right to left across the screen carrying a shield and striking with my baton. The foremost THFC hooligan, immediately after this,

Trevor Tanner, can be seen walking left to right across the screen. He is wearing a white T-shirt. [Yeah, we know.] Tanner continues going forward towards the Millwall supporters' section despite the presence of foot-duty and mounted police. A police officer to Tanner's right draws his telescopic baton and opens it and can just be seen bending down and pulling back his right arm to strike with it. [Halle-bloody-luiah, someone actually admits it!] From my position in front of Tanner and this police officer I watched as the police officer struck Tanner with his baton across his right leg. This immediately stopped Tanner's advances.

The THFC group is forced back by the presence of mounted police and police using batons. A police cordon is quickly formed to prevent the THFC hooligans from confronting their Millwall rivals, but this does not contain the group who run off away from the stadium, back towards Silward Street. Trevor Tanner is not seen again on the video footage until 17.08pm, when he is seen with the rest of the THFC hooligan group contained by the TSG in Lower Road, opposite Southwark Road. Video footage continued and showed very serious disorder, including missile throwing between THFC and Millwall hooligans in the vicinity of Hawkstone Road and Southwark Park Road, as Millwall hooligans carry out a concerted attack on the THFC hooligans still contained by police. Trevor Tanner does not feature in any of this disorder as he remains with the rest of the main bulk of the THFC hooligan group still contained by the police, preventing their involvement in the violence. [I think that says it all.]

The THFC hooligan group is very organised that day [Nice one!] as demonstrated well by their meeting at a specific venue [The Gregorian in Jamaica Road] before the game and leaving the Millwall stadium in an organised fashion near to the end of the game. [Top move.] Trevor Tanner is part of the group escorted to the stadium and actively participated in the disorderly behaviour of the group.

BORO HOME AND AWAY, 2002/03 SEASON (CHAPTER 16)

[I was going to write my own account of this one, but Totty has saved me the bother as he has decided to mention it in detail in my banning order statement. I think it is only fair to share it with you, so take it away, Totty. For more on Boro see Chapter 16.]

A good example of home behaviour of the THFC hooligan group occurred at the THFC v Middlesbrough fixture on 28/09/2002. An organised Middlesbrough hooligan group attended this fixture, first going to King's Cross and then travelling on to Tottenham by taxis and by rail. By 11.30am, Middlesbrough hooligans had started meeting in the Ship public house, High Road, N17. By 1.00pm this group numbered about 100 persons. [Not bad.] The THFC hooligan group were aware of the presence of their rivals and initially started to meet in nearby public houses, mainly the Elbow Room and The Plough, both situated on the same road. With the

MFC hooligans heavily policed and unable to leave the Ship the THFC hooligan group relocated to the Victoria public house.

By 1.30pm a THFC hooligan group of approximately seventy persons had formed at this venue. At 2.15pm the Middlesbrough hooligan group were escorted from the Ship public house to the stadium. However, a group of ticketless Middlesbrough supporters were kept at the Ship pub, without a police presence. The route to the stadium for the escorted group meant passing the Victoria pub. The THFC hooligan group made no real effort to confront the Middlesbrough hooligan group [Why bother?] and the latter was escorted to the stadium without incident.

At about 2.40pm police received information of serious disorder at the Ship public house and attended the venue to find two smashed windows, several bar stools on the pavement outside the venue and some type of incapacitant chemical having been discharged inside the pub. [Oh dear! The words 'horse' and 'bolted' spring to mind.] At least two persons inside the premises had suffered glass cuts and most were suffering from the effects of being gassed. None of the Middlesbrough FC hooligans wished to make allegations to the police and were escorted to Bruce Grove Railway Station nearby. [Respect for that at least.]

The only noteworthy incident during the match was the arrest of a Middlesbrough fan for racist behaviour. [No surprise there, mug.] Post-match saw serious disorder as dispersal commenced southwards from the stadium. A group of about 100 Middlesbrough hooligans had re-formed and they became involved in sporadic fighting with their Tottenham counterparts in the first 200 metres of the southbound dispersal route. [A few Boro got seriously hurt.] Police eventually brought the situation under control and bubbled the Boro hooligans and escorted them south to Seven Sisters underground. [All joking apart, I take my hat off to Boro for making the effort and coming down in black cabs – it was a good move and very clever. Not so clever hanging around in the Ship, though, I think you'll agree. That's just pushing your luck too far. You just can't do that at Tottenham, which they obviously know now. I think you'll also agree that they took quite a hiding on the High Road, with a few of their boys paying a visit to the North Middlesex, which I don't envy as I've been there myself a few times. If the Old Bill had not been there I think it would have been a massacre. But respect where it's due: nine out of ten for effort, but must try harder next time.]

TOTTY'S TALES

[You'll be well aware by now that PC Totty is our regular police intelligence officer. The following are his comments on the Spurs firm in general. Let's leave the final word to him.]

It is important to distinguish between the individual who commits a violent act or becomes involved in disorder in a spontaneous manner, and the individual who acts in concert with others in a pre-planned fashion. [Who can he be talking about?] This statement concerns the second aspect, specifically as it applies to the THFC hooligan group and a member of the THFC hooligan group named [You've guessed it] Trevor Tanner. The THFC hooligan group varied last season, 2003–2004. The size of the travelling THFC group has been a maximum 130 persons, this was for the fixture against Wolverhampton Wanderers on 15/05/2004. High-risk away fixtures give a good indication of the current strength, as the group tends to come together and act as a unit. Whereas at home fixtures the THFC group can be somewhat spread out. [Well, it's a long fucking High Road; it would be a bit pointless being all in the same place. But be warned: we'll find you wherever you are, wherever you go]

Each hooligan group varies in size, composition and preferred pattern of behaviour. [Yeah, go on. You would love to split us, wouldn't you. Well, let me tell you, we all come under the one umbrella whether certain individuals like it or not. It's the firm as a whole that counts, which lots of visiting teams will testify to.] THFC hooligans are described as follows: the entire THFC hooligan group is male, with ages ranging from eighteen to about fifty years old. The ethnic appearance of the vast majority of the group is white-skinned European, however significant numbers of hooligans of African/Caribbean appearance are also active within the group. THFC has links to the Jewish community, indeed during the 2002–2003 season the club suspended and successfully requested the movement of the home fixture against West Ham United Football Club from Monday, 16 September 2002, to Sunday, 15 September 2002, as the original date clashed with the date of the Jewish Day of Atonement, Yom Kippur. [That is total bollocks and just goes to show how out of touch the club itself is with what is going on around it. There may be Jews in the boardroom, but no more than in any other club, like Abramovich at Chelsea and Dein at Arsenal. Don't get me wrong: I know some Jewish people and I like them very much and have absolutely no problem with Jewish people whatsoever. But to suggest there are large numbers of them who have the power to change fixtures is total bollocks, certainly as far as our firm goes anyway. And as the police state themselves, the firm is white and Afro/Caribbean, but you can also add in Turks, Greeks, Indians and Italians, to name but a few. It is a truly multi-cultural firm, and we have no more of a Jewish following than Arsenal or Chelsea. I think it is offensive to Jewish people to suggest otherwise.]

The THFC hooligan group has different patterns depending on the fixture concerned and whether THFC are playing at home or away. THFC hooligans do not organise and engage in disorder at every fixture. [Methinks you think we are stupid.] It is only at certain games that they become active: high-risk fixtures where the risk of violence and disorder are assessed as high. At this present time this includes all games against Chelsea Football Club, CFC; Arsenal Football Club, AFC; West Ham United Football Club, WHUFC and Middlesbrough Football Club, MFC. [Can't argue with that.] If THFC are playing at home against one of these clubs then the THFC hooligan group will become territorial and will go to public houses that they consider to be theirs from early on in the day and defend them. In terms of hooligan etiquette, to allow a visiting hooligan group to come and take over a home pub would be a source of great embarrassment. [Don't even think about it!]

The THFC hooligan group will see how any visiting hooligan group acts and respond accordingly; it is not guaranteed that any visiting hooligan group will come. [Nine out of ten don't.] Visiting hooligan groups tend to draw attention to themselves [Because they want an escort], and are usually contained and escorted to the stadium inside a police cordon. Individual THFC hooligans often assess this escort and as it draws nearer to the stadium groups of THFC hooligans will be waiting to seize any opportunity to engage in disorder. These escorts tend to be heavily policed and confrontation is usually prevented.

Following the game, THFC hooligans will again loiter in disorder hotspots, waiting for their counterparts to leave the stadium. The size of the loitering group can vary from a handful to the hundreds. The risk of disorder is higher at this stage of the operation as any visiting hooligans dispersing from the stadium are not under escort, as they were prior to the game. [Bollocks.] If disorder does not break out, THFC hooligan group will stalk their opponents and look for a later opportunity to fight. Sometimes the THFC hooligan group will avoid these disorder hotspots altogether, group in an unusual place and attempt an ambush. [Thank you very much, David Fucking Attenborough!] This type of behaviour conflicts with that of genuine bona fide fans. Genuine fans drinking in public houses can be boisterous and passionate. [And a fucking nuisance.] However, they do not loiter, stalk and pay detailed attention to the movement of the visiting hooligan group. The genuine fan may be aware of the presence of a visiting hooligan group, but will make no attempt to become involved. He will not group with others on the street and act in a manner suggesting an intent in disorder.

If THFC are playing away and the fixture is of interest to them an offensive strategy will be adopted. The hooligan group will often travel to a fixture together and when they arrive in the host area will move about as a large recognisable and organised group. This is a highly provocative course of conduct to the home hooligan group [A proper liberty], especially as the THFC hooligan group will often try to take over a pub that has some sort of affiliation to the home hooligan group or team. [Something we do well.] Following such fixtures the THFC hooligans often leave the stadium together as a mass group, waiting either just outside or inside the exit, until sufficient numbers have come together to allow them to provoke or respond to violence from a sufficient position of strength as they disperse from the stadium.

Two other behavioural characteristics are worthy of note. The first is individual members' willingness to attend the vicinity of the stadium and to seek to engage in disorder, even if they have not got match tickets to the game. [I didn't realise that this was a police state and that gathering with your mates is illegal.] It seems to make no difference to the hooligan whether he watches the match in the stadium or on television in a local pub. This is where football banning orders with preventative geographical conditions are attached to help prevent crime and disorder. A football banning order without conditions does little to alter the violent culture of the THFC hooligan group. Only by preventing hooligans from socialising with violent associates in high-risk areas can communities and bona fide football fans be made to feel safer.

The second issue is Central London, especially areas surrounding transport infrastructures, such as railway stations. These venues continue to be high-risk disorder areas. Members of the THFC hooligan group come from all over the country and often travel through Central London on their way home. Very few THFC hooligans actually live near the stadium or in the London Borough of Haringey. It is as easy for the THFC hooligan group to meet rival counterparts as it is to plan to meet them near to a football stadium. Again football banning orders with a geographical condition can impact on their behaviour significantly.

During the 2004–2005 season Trevor Tanner has continued to attend the THFC fixtures. He was present at the Calgary game on 07/08/2004; the

Newcastle game on 21/08/2004; and the Norwich game on 12/09/2004. He continues to associate with known and suspected football hooligans. [Shall I stop drinking with myself then?] The initial stages of this statement detailed patterns of behaviour exhibited by the THFC group at home and away fixtures. It is important to stress that hooligan behaviour ebbs and flows, and that organised hooligan activity does not occur at every game. Instead, it only happens at the majority of fixtures.

This inactivity is an important factor to note about hooligan behaviour. It is a widely held view within the football policing community [Old Bill to you and me] that certain factors can limit hooligan behaviour on a temporary basis. These factors include imminent international tournaments in which England may be playing and when members of hooligan groups feel they face an increased risk of obtaining a football banning order. During last season both these factors would have been pertinent as members of the THFC hooligan group would have been interested in travelling to the Euro 2004 football tournament in Portugal, and members of the THFC hooligans did obtain football banning orders upon conviction and by complaint during that season. In my view this has limited THFC at home games especially, but the group and Trevor Tanner [I thought you had forgotten me] still pose a threat and have to be rigorously policed. [You better believe it.]

The possible conditions that can now be attached to football banning orders are now invaluable in preventing organised disorder. Domestic football stadiums are relatively safe places now, with outbreaks of disorder, especially in the Premiership, rare occurrences. Disorder tends to focus in and around the vicinity of the stadiums and around transport infrastructures, such as railway stations. Match-day geographical conditions preventing hooligans from coming within a fixed distance of stadiums and certain key railway stations are essential for THFC hooligans. A match-day condition not to come within two miles of any football stadium where a regulated football match is being played for four hours before advertised kick-off time, and not before four hours after the advertised kick-off time, has proved very effective in preventing disorder around key Central London train stations. [In your opinion.]

A match-day condition not to go within one mile of King's Cross or Euston mainline stations, four hours preceding the advertised kick-off time and not less than four hours after the adjusted kick-off time, or to any regulated football matches being played in London would also be affected. [Why not just banish me to Elba, like Napoleon?]

It is true to say that most football hooligans have allegiance to one particular club and their national team. [Well spotted.] However, they do also form relationships with, amongst others, Barnet, Luton Town, Watford and Aberdeen. Although the latter is a Scottish club it could meet Welsh and English clubs in pre-season friendlies and European competitions.

Trevor Tanner's full associations are not known to police, and in my opinion limiting any conditions to only games involving THFC would give him scope to become involved in football-related disorder elsewhere.

Finally [Thank fuck for that!], it is my strongly held view that FBOs, Football Banning Orders, without geographical conditions do little to deter hooligan behaviour. Without preventative geographical conditions there is nothing to stop the THFC hooligans travelling to both home and away fixtures and engaging in disorder in city centres or around the vicinity of football stadiums. [Chance would be a fine thing.]

It is my assessment that the law in relation to football banning orders is intended for persons such as Trevor Tanner. [Thank you!] He has a violent history, continues to put himself in high-risk situations and gives leadership and credibility to the THFC hooligan group.

Domestically, hooligan activity increases the amount of police resources allocated to a football fixture, with a corresponding increase in costs. Successfully combating the hooligan behaviour of the THFC hooligan group will allow police to reduce resources at certain fixtures and allocate them to other crime areas, such as robbery, drug supply and burglary. Football banning orders with conditions as introduced by The Football Disorder Act of 2002 are powerful tools that can have a significant impact on hooligan activity and enhance community safety. [If you say so.]

CHAPTER 24

SPURS ON THE UP?

As I write this, Spurs are still in Europe. I hope we go all the way. I'm not totally convinced about Martin Jol, never have been, but I cannot fault the man when it comes to his European team selection. For the European games, the boys look like a totally different squad from the one that chokes big time away from home at the likes of muggy Bolton or Newcastle. We look like we do on our best nights at home – an invincible team playing at the top of its game in front of fanatical supporters.

If, by some miracle, we actually go on to lift the UEFA Cup, I would be one of the happiest men alive – even if I have missed every fucking game (talk about a wind-up). While all the boys have been having fun abroad at places like Turkey (against Besiktas) and Germany (Bayer Leverkusen), I was signing on at the Old Bill station. It drove me up the wall, what with the boys doing well in

287

Europe and the England Euro 08 qualifiers. I even offered to leave my passport at the nick, which I was told I could do, but they also added that I still had to turn up and sign on anyway, otherwise I'd be nicked. I could rant on about all the nonces, muggers and illegal immigrants running around as free as they like, but, so long as the Old Bill are making sure that people like me are behaving themselves, that's OK!

Let's face it, the government has fucked this country up, simple as that. Most people who live in the capital can't tell now if they're living in London or Iraq. It's like a war zone – and the police do nothing about it. You've got kids shooting each other – and not giving a fuck if anyone gets caught in the crossfire – and all for what? Money? Drugs? Respect? Bullshit. Any mug can shoot a gun, and it's only a matter of time before ordinary people start taking the law into their own hands if the police continue to sit on their arses and do nothing. As for those muggy right-on middle-class idiots who voted in Blair and his cronies, and those pain-in-the-arse campaigning pop stars and parasite celebrities – well, they deserve everything they get. Good riddance to them if they're too scared to walk out their front doors at night. They helped to make this country what it is today and now the rest of us have to suffer. Welcome to Blair's Britain.

The sooner that slag Blair resigns the better. I'd love to see him fall ill and get put in a stinking NHS ward surrounded by fruit loops. See how he gets on. Trust me, I know what I'm talking about. When I was stabbed in the neck, I ended up in a decrepit hospital where all the other patients were a bunch of geriatric lunatics. The porter even tried to drag me off to the gym the next day, which would have done me in completely, considering the state that I was in. What the government's done to the NHS is a disgrace. As far as I can see, the majority of the doctors and nurses do a brilliant job – as they did on me – but it looks like they're fighting a losing battle.

And talking of battles, what about our boys who are out there in the world fighting to protect this country? Look at how they're treated. That's why I'm including the words of a soldier in this book. I want people to know how the men who sign up to defend the citizens of Britain feel about this country.

A SOLDIER'S STORY – NAME AND RANK WITHHELD

I have served with the British Army now for the best part of 10 years. My unit is very well known for its operational capacity and the devastating firepower it can deliver when called upon to do so. The unit nearly always deploys as a spearhead force.

I am immensely proud of the unit I serve with and the things I have experienced on a first-hand basis have been absolutely mind-blowing. I have always said that, if my luck runs out and I get the 'good news', then that's the way it is. I don't want any slagging contest on how British soldiers should never have been sent wherever in the first place. I signed on the dotted line to serve queen and country! Right or wrong, we will do our job and go and fight. The politicians and the MPs can gob on about it as much as they like. For my part, me and my colleagues won't get tangled up in the political correctness of it all.

What I believe in and fight for are the men who serve alongside me on the battlefield. When I look to my left and right, I know that I am surrounded by like-minded men who have the same drive, determination and all-out bollocks of steel to see it through to the bitter end. It's a reassuring feeling like no other in times of uncertainty.

I am sure you are all aware by now of the army-kit disgrace that has received a lot of media attention recently and which dates back to the Iraq war in February 2003. After that story broke, I don't know how anyone could still believe that the army's combat equipment is up to the job. Look at Afghanistan, where the British Army is deployed today. What are the troops riding around in? Tanks? No. More often than not, they're left to patrol in armoured Land Rovers. These wagons were first brought into service in the late 1970s and early 1980s, during the conflicts across the water in Northern Ireland. They did offer the necessary protection from petrol bombs, small blast bombs and pipe bombs, but none of these undoubtedly dangerous devices could be classed as hardcore weapons. Fast forward to the present day, where the big threats are roadside bombs and RPGs. How do you think an ageing Land Rover would fare if hit by one of these? Are these MPs for fucking real? Tell you what: here's my helmet, body armour and assault rifle – go and do my job for 24 hours and then come and tell me that the kit is up to the job. Any takers? Didn't think so. That's what I call on-the-job training. Enough said.

SPURS ON THE UP?

FUN AND GAMES IN EUROPE, 2006/7

As I said earlier, Spurs have been having a bit of a European adventure while I have been in enforced exile. Apart from a few naughty offs abroad, nothing major has really happened to write home about, mainly because no one would come and play with us because of the phenomenal firms we took to every game.

We had Sparta Prague home and away, but nothing major was expected to happen on either one, even when Spurs went out there in their thousands to sample the delights of Prague. Unfortunately, a couple of my good pals got separated from the main firm and bumped into a proper naughty little bunch of Red Star Belgrade boys. Game as they were, my pals were outnumbered. Nevertheless, they went for it. They came out with a few battle wounds, but nothing major was hurt except their pride. It could have been a very bad situation but, thankfully, they are both fine now. It's a tough lesson you have to learn when you go to Europe – never get separated from the main firm.

Next up was Besiktas in Turkey. They are not in the same league as Galatasaray but they still like to mix it up a bit. However, even though our boys went out there firmed up and prepared for the worst, it was all peace and love (well, apart from a bit of internal rucking and a few Galatasaray being told to fuck off in no uncertain terms). We were even treated to the astonishing scene of the Spurs team being applauded off the field at the end of the game by the whole home support. I would love to have seen the Spurs Old Bill's faces.

In the good old days (when I was actually allowed to

watch football), the UEFA Cup was played home and away. Now, the system is all over the fucking place, so when we came up against the Belgian side Brugge there was only one fixture, with them taking us on at White Hart Lane. Now, the Club Brugge firm can be a little tasty, as Chelsea found out the year before when they turned up early and went on a rampage around Shithole Bridge, smacking everyone in sight. Laugh? I nearly pissed myself.

When their boys arrived for the game, the police weren't exactly keeping them under close watch. Maybe the Old Bill didn't take them seriously, or maybe they were secretly hoping that the Brugge firm was going to pull another stroke like they had at Chelsea the previous year, but somehow about 50 of them got away from the escort and decided to go for a little stroll up Seven Sisters Road. Unfortunately for them, they wandered past the wrong boozer. I should think that the boys inside were pretty surprised to see their Belgian counterparts ambling past the pub window, but it didn't take them long to send out a welcoming party to greet them. Let's just say that those Brugge boys will think twice before going walkabout again. By all accounts, they were on their toes so quick it was embarrassing.

The next away game was in Germany, against Bayer Leverkusen, and this was supposed to be the draw of the whole round. If you believed everything you'd heard, the whole of Germany was coming to fight us, skinheads, hooligans, neo-Nazis, the lot. This wasn't just coming from the Krauts themselves, but from a few idiots over here as well. I was always sceptical that this would happen. The Germans are game in their own little way, but nowhere near as much as they think. They are just not in our league, simple as that. Combine that with banning orders and with the Old Bill all over everything, then you get the picture. Spurs did take it to their boozer the night before, as usual, and by all accounts the Germans actually stood their ground for a while, but apart from that it never really came off.

So here we are now, in the knockout stages. As anybody who has followed Spurs over the years knows, to quote a certain Manc knight, it's squeaky-bum time. You just don't know what Spurs team will show up. And can you believe it, who do we draw but the old enemy Feyenoord? Of course, since the draw was made, Feyenoord have been thrown out of the competition, pending an appeal, because the silly cunts played up in France and denied us the chance of going over there and giving them a good hiding.

On top of that, at the beginning of January we drew Cardiff in the FA Cup. Happy fucking New Year to you, too. I must admit, I was sorely tempted just to say fuck it and travel to Cardiff anyway. But I didn't want to give the Old Bill the satisfaction of nicking me. No fucker is going to persuade me to give up my liberty again. If I could have guaranteed that I would have made it to Cardiff unseen, then I would have got myself down there and had a straightener with their firm no problem. I promise you, if I could, I would be on the first train to Chelsea, Feyenoord or any place where their cunts want it with us. I'm fucking dying for it, but my wings have been clipped, simple as that. When I'm back in circulation, there are a few nasty little cunts that'll be in for a surprise. I'll leave it at that. Anyway, as it turned out the Cardiff game ended 0–0 and the bastards had to come up to our place. The real Spurs turned out that night and we battered them 4–0, as you'll see later.

LOOKING BACK IN ANGER

When this book first came out in April 2006, we had a successful book launch at my pal Mickey's club. I must thank Mick for trusting me and giving me the venue, and Dexter and Keely for making the night go with a bang with their superb DJ sets. Most of all, though, I have to thank all the boys who turned up to support the book. At one stage there was a good 150–200 people rocking the place. It's a night I will never forget. Total respect to you all.

But that was one of the few football-related highlights of that year, especially with what happened in the World Cup. It just had to be too good to be true, all those Chelsea players like Terry and Lampard telling the public that we were going to win it, ditto the Scousers and the Mancs. They were all fucking useless at the end of the day, letting the whole country down again. Owen Hargreaves was the only one that came out of it with any dignity. Rooney was useless – unfit, overhyped and a proper sucker for letting the Portuguese wind him up so easily and getting himself sent off when we needed him the most. As for Beckham, I'm just glad he's finished with England: 'We're gonna win the World Cup, we're gonna win the Euros, we're gonna win the world fucking tiddlywinks championships.' Fuck off.

The thing that made my blood boil the most was just

how shit we played – even for us. You had all those England fans out there – half of whom couldn't even afford the trip – while at the same time all those so-called Wags were swanning around and spending money like it was going out of fashion. Wags? Slags more like. (How is it that ugly fuckers like Rooney, Gerrard, Lampard and the rest attract these birds? Has it anything to do with money or status?) So there we have the players and their Wags out every night on the piss and living it up – all with the consent of the FA – while all the other countries are pissing themselves laughing at us. No wonder we went out and bottled it against a shit Portuguese team.

With our boys fucking up on the pitch, the so-called experts were expecting a bloodbath off it. But that never happened either. The Old Bill handed out 3,000 banning orders beforehand, stopping a lot of boys getting out to Germany. But, even with the invasion of families and barmy army-style prats with drums and flags, I knew that the few proper bods who did get through would be too good for the Germans and so it proved. Spurs once again had one of the biggest firms out there, which just goes to show how powerful they are becoming on the England scene, as I stated earlier. For me personally, it was a bit of a nightmare, as I spent the whole World Cup shuttling back and forth to the police station so that they could make sure that I was being a good boy. Add that to my inability to see Spurs in Europe and you can see that the whole year was a nightmare.

Now, fast forward to the end of 2006 and our great British sportsmen were at it again. This time, however, it was our cricketers who let us down, getting battered

Down Under by the Aussies in the Ashes. I don't want to go into too much detail, as this book has fuck all to do with cricket, but as it's against the Aussies, who I fucking hate, it's worth a mention. I don't profess to know a lot about cricket, but I know the basic idea is to hit the ball and catch it when required once every hour, something our useless bunch of cunts doesn't seem to have grasped. You could tell they were fucked before a ball was bowled in anger, and morale was not helped by Trescothick going home and Harmison telling the world he was homesick. Of course, the whole squad had their birds and kids out there, staying in five-star hotels and being waited on hand and foot in the Australian sunshine at Christmas. It must have been so tough for them!

I personally believe that they shouldn't send another team to play the Aussies again until they have learned to play the game properly. The current bunch obviously just use it as a jolly up in the sun. Either that or they shit themselves when they realise what they are up against. As for the Barmy Army – who are these people? Just a bunch of accountants and stockbrokers who can afford to spend three months in Australia. They're not fans. I couldn't believe the sight of them clapping the England team off the field when they had just been humiliated. The players must have been laughing their bollocks off, the mugs. The fans should have kicked their arses all the way back to the dressing room.

Worst of all, as another sporting year ended in disaster for England in the football and the cricket – with tens of thousands of punters well out of pocket – do you think any of the piss-poor players gave a toss? Of course not.

SPURS ON THE UP?

I suppose the one good thing that came out of England's shit World Cup was that it meant we could finally get rid of Sven Goran Eriksson. Unfortunately, we had to wait until he'd made England the most expensively assembled crap squad in history, but at least he's gone. I won't go into the money he has made off with, because that just shows what mugs we are in this country. All I will say is that, when we do finally get a chance to change things for the better, who do we appoint but Steve McClaren. Fucking unbelievable! You only have to look at the ginger tosser to know he's not up to the England job. Every fucker knows that. Still, at least he had the bollocks to get rid of Beckham.

So far, 2007 hasn't been that eventful. Towards the end of 2006, the boys had the usual run-ins with the Chelsea scum. There was one in particular, when they were outnumbered in the West End and still managed to have a result. Because of that, the silly cunts automatically thought that I was there, even though I'm not allowed in London on match days. I ended up with some silly mouthy prick wasting his phone bill, screaming and shouting at me down the line for half an hour. It's nice to be popular, but I'll deal with him another day. In the end, a pal of mine sorted out the embarrassment before it got out of hand, so cheers and respect, Kev. Credit where it's due.

REGRETS, I'VE HAD A FEW
One question I am always asked by people is: Do you regret doing the book? To be totally honest, no. I regret a few of the things I have said about personal matters, but

that's for me to deal with. I did read somewhere that a good book is part confessional and it is very hard not to let emotions get in the way. Again, on a personal level, I have no regrets about anything I wrote about the boys. I never mentioned anyone's name unless they wanted me to – even though deep down a lot of them would have loved it if they are honest.

One thing I did find sad was the negative attitude of some of my so-called pals. I know it's to be expected when you have the bottle to put your head above the parapet, but it's still sad when the criticism comes from within. They should be able to see that I did what I did to put our firm on the map. Just five years ago, we were not recognised in the way that we are now. They might think that it's OK for Chelsea, West Ham and Millwall boys to make films and write books and call us every cunt under the sun, but not me. I proved that I was not going to sit back in silence while those slags spouted shit about us. We all know deep down that they ain't fit to lace our boots, and if other people can't see that, fuck 'em. As a good pal of mine said, 'If they don't like it, tell them to go and write their own fucking book.' On the flip side of the coin, I've had much more positive feedback than negative. And this came from the people that really matter, the people I wrote it for in the first place – the firm.

On a sombre note, we all lost a good friend at the end of November 2005 in a tragic car crash. I would just like to give my man Ginger Richie all the love and respect in the world. He passed away in his prime and it is one of my biggest regrets that I could not make the funeral, for reasons I cannot go into now. I remember Richie as someone who always had a positive and uplifting word for me as I fought my way up. The man was class, simple as. Rest in peace, old friend. Sorry I wasn't there for your big day.

ARSENAL SCUM: CARLING CUP SEMI-FINAL, 2ND LEG, 1 JANUARY 2007

The stakes were high for this one as the prize was the chance of going on the rampage in Cardiff against Chelsea.

Some things never change: Spurs v Scum in the semi-final of the League Cup. Before the game, you had the Dutchman making noises about us having the upper hand (which was bollocks). Even our own players were giving it the big one in the press. But what was this based on? We'd been leading 2–0 in the first leg, only to concede two goals from that mug Baptista, who isn't even wanted by Real Madrid. Second team, my arse. What the fuck is it with Arsene Wenger? Where does he keep getting these players from that no one's ever heard of and that can run like the wind? Is he into people-trafficking?

This one was well and truly fucked up by us in the first leg. Deep down, everyone knew we didn't have a prayer, despite what Keane, Defoe and the rest were all spouting in the papers. My message to them is: You ain't good enough. Simple. To top it all off, our best player Aaron Lennon is mysteriously out of our biggest game of the year an hour before kick-off. No fucking mention of what was wrong with him before or after by that mug Jol. Anyway, what with the little fucker pulling out and Spurs doing their usual running around for 45 minutes like Jol had slipped some Charlie into their Lucozade before finally running out of gas and conceding late goals, the whole thing was a wash-out. Once again, Spurs sent home the fantastic support that they don't deserve with the fucking hump.

Even worse for me personally, they denied us all the chance to go to Cardiff and get it on with Chelsea. Banning order or not, nothing would have stopped me going to Cardiff for that one.

Off the pitch, it was a different matter, as usual, and the boys were representing big time. I was thinking about going over there, but didn't give the Old Bill the satisfaction. Instead, here's the view of one of the boys who was there. Take it away, mate:

Before the game, we met up right on Arsenal's manor, very near to their pubs. Not the best numbers, but top quality none the less. By 3:00 p.m. we were about 60-handed, until the Old Bill showed up and then we thought it was game over. But, after a lot of grief and Section 60s, we lost them and were walking the back streets making our way to Holloway Road, having a little look in every pub on the way, just in case. By this point, we were only about 25-handed, when we reached the Holloway Road and found out they were only round the corner. So, we've gone for it, bowled straight in one of their main pubs and let them know we were there. About 15 or 20 of them, older lumps, weighed up our numbers. Then, one of ours told them to fuck off and within two seconds they were all fighting each other to get out of the door. It was every man for himself and they were even quicker than Brugge. Within minutes, we were surrounded by the Old Bill. I can only speak from personal experience, but I do know of a few other naughty little rows over there that night, with Tottenham getting a result each time with inferior numbers. If that is what success does to your support and to your firm, then I don't want it.

CARDIFF CITY, AWAY, FA CUP THIRD ROUND

I had to sit this one out, which was pure torture. I agonised about going there, but, as I said earlier, I've got too much to lose. I'll let one of the boys tell his story of what happened down there. I know Spurs took a massive firm there and I knew it would be too much for Cardiff to live with. The boys were up there the night before, a good 100-handed, and had some fun and games in the town centre. Funny thing was, the next day I got a call from a good mate of mine who lives there and who knows all the local faces and doormen. He'd been trying to track me down, as some Cardiff City boys had told him that they'd done me outside a pub. Turns out they done my mate, who looks like me. I had to laugh, as I was 200 miles away. He then followed up his call with a text praising the firm for the show they had put on up there the night before. Anyway, I'll let my pal take this one away and give you all the gory details:

For weeks beforehand, the buzz was going round White Hart Lane. To draw Cardiff away when you know you're the best firm in the country is all you can ask for. No one was talking about the football, just the chance to go to Wales and show the taffs what Spurs are about. There was a good firm going up the night before, just to leave their mark before we turned up later on the 8:37 a.m. from Paddington. Getting off the tube, Sunday morning at 8:00 a.m. and walking up into Paddington, I was not sure what to expect. Everyone said they were going, but would they turn up? I soon got my answer – a 300-strong mob of black and white faces, most over 30. There were boys that had battered Chelsea on the pitch in 1975, faces that I recognised from the days when we used to take the North Bank at Highbury every year. Faces from when we were one of the most active casual firms in the 1980s; faces from when we caned Chelsea at the Ifield Tavern in the 1990s, and loads of faces from the last few years when we'd caned Millwall in the testimonial. I recognised people from a mad one up at Man United three years before and from when we smashed Cardiff in the League Cup at White Hart Lane, as well as faces that battered West Ham on their manor three hours after last season's game.

This was 300 of Tottenham's finest on the move. I had been in touch with the Northern Spurs and they had 50 waiting to jump on at Newport. As usual, the Old Bill tried to fuck it all up by cancelling the 8:37 a.m., which would have got us into Cardiff for 11:00 a.m. The only other train after that was the 9:05 a.m., which meant changing at Bath, but we had no choice. We had a quick beer in Bath then got our connection to Cardiff. The 50 Northern Spurs jumped on at Newport. I've known some of these boys for 25 years and trust them with my life, so by 12:30 p.m. there were 350 of us marching out of Cardiff station.

In a perfect world, there would be no Old Bill waiting for us, but it's a shit world and there were hundreds of the fuckers. They took us to a massive pub called the Great Western, where we were met by the 150 Spurs who had come up the night before and those who had travelled up early that morning by car. With the arrival of another train after that, pushing our numbers to 600, this was now our biggest away firm for a long time.

An hour before the game, the Old Bill began to escort us to the ground. We'd already made our minds up that if Cardiff's firm showed we were going to go through the Old Bill and smash them. The chance came when we were 10 minutes away from the ground and 50 of them came out of a side street, chucking bottles and glasses. The roar of 'YIDS! YIDS! YIDS!' went up and the escort was broken. But Cardiff quickly saw what we had and backed off. Still, at least they had a go, unlike all of our so-called rivals in London.

The rest of the journey was quiet. We arrived at the ground just after kick-off. The annoying thing was people watching at home on TV would have seen our firm arriving in the ground at 4:15 p.m., not realising that we had firms bowling around Cardiff from 10:00 a.m. onwards. Most of the game was quiet, apart from the abuse being thrown in both directions.

With about 15 minutes to go, the word went round that there was a good mob of Cardiff outside waiting and a few of our boys got out and had a toe-to-toe row with them. For those of us stuck inside the ground and missing out on the action outside, the roar went up: 'On the pitch!' Suddenly, everyone started to climb over the seats and attempted to get on the pitch, the aim being to get into the Cardiff end where they'd been giving it the big one all game. A 10-minute battle went on with police and stewards as they tried to keep us off the pitch, but I firmly believe that a goal either way would have lead to the final push and we would have been on the pitch. It would have been nice if Cardiff had tried the same thing to pull the Old Bill away from us but, for some reason, they didn't.

The game ended in a 0–0 draw and we were all hoping for the chance to have it outside with them afterwards. But on the walk to the station there was no sign of them. I don't doubt that they were around somewhere, but the sheer weight of police kept both sides well apart. I have to admit, I still rate Cardiff as a top-five firm, but the truth is, boys, you or any other firm would not have lived with the sheer numbers and quality of our firm that day and it goes to prove we are still number one by a long way.

CARDIFF CITY, HOME, FA CUP THIRD ROUND REPLAY

Anticipation lay heavy in the air as we were about to host Cardiff. After the show the boys had put on up there the week before – and considering the history of their last visit to the Lane a couple of years before in the League Cup (documented earlier in this book) – we all expected something would happen. The whole manor was on fire – us and the Old Bill. Not for the first time, the Old Bill from N17 showed that there was no recruitment crisis in their area.

There were coppers swarming everywhere, but in the event it was a wasted effort on their part as Cardiff never showed – apart from mouthing off on their buses, which I have to say fucks me off more than anything else. In fairness to Cardiff, a lot of them had been fucked about at South Mimms service station, where, unbelievably, they had to go to collect their tickets and then they were put on a bus to be escorted to the ground (and they say the Old Bill ain't organised). There were hundreds of Spurs waiting for them on the street if they had turned up, so I don't think it would have been pretty.

For once, Spurs did the business on the pitch, cruising past them 4–0. We drew Fulham in the next round and did them 4–0 as well, so maybe things are looking up.

SEE YOU LATER!

I can safely say that my life's been an incredible rollercoaster ride so far, with some amazing highs and lows. I wouldn't swap any of it for the world. I have a beautiful daughter, who is also my best friend, and I have all my faculties (just about) and some of the best friends a man could have. As anyone with kids will tell you, you spend most of your time worrying about them, me more than most as I know what horrible little cunts there are out there. And by that I don't mean football bods. By and large, they are all good people in one way or another. It's everyone else you have to take a stand against, especially the cowardly little shits that are trying to destroy our country, or what's left of it.

I suppose in a way this is a new chapter in my life. I like to think that I have played my part in putting the Spurs firm where it is now. Most people now regard it as the best around, and that's a big change from when I first started. Maybe some of the backstabbers out there might like to think about that before they open their mouths again. Will I come back after my ban? What do you think? See you all soon!

I would like to thank everyone who has supported me with this book, who have put their words into action and who have contributed to it in a positive way. I want to give a big thanks to my mum, who has supported me all the way, and to my two cousins Kate and Lucy, as well as Terry, Marc, Snowy, Seamus, Craig, Eamon and Billy (Palace), Graham, Rob and the boys in Pompey, H, Tony Mac, Martin, Nashy, Ronnie, Dex, Carl, Kevin Ed, all the Spurs youth and anybody else who has helped me out. If I've left anyone out in one way or another – you know who you are and you have my respect and thanks.

Finally, I dedicate this book to my little princess, Eleanor, who, like a shining light, has kept me sane through the dark times. It's all love.